M000004394

AN INTRODUCTION TO
Sociocultural Anthropology

A N   I N T R O D U C T I O N   T O
Sociocultural Anthropology

Adaptations, Structures, Meanings
S E C O N D   E D I T I O N

David W. Haines

U N I V E R S I T Y   P R E S S   O F   C O L O R A D O
Boulder

© 2017 by University Press of Colorado
First edition published by Pearson Education, Inc.

Published by University Press of Colorado
5589 Arapahoe Avenue, Suite 206C
Boulder, Colorado 80303

All rights reserved
Printed in the United States of America

 The University Press of Colorado is a proud member of
The Association of American University Presses.

The University Press of Colorado is a cooperative publishing enterprise supported, in part, by Adams
State University, Colorado State University, Fort Lewis College, Metropolitan State University of
Denver, Regis University, University of Colorado, University of Northern Colorado, Utah State
University, and Western State Colorado University.

∞ This paper meets the requirements of the ANSI/NISO Z39.48-1992 (Permanence of Paper).

ISBN: 978-1-60732-718-9 (pbk)
ISBN: 978-1-60732-719-6 (ebook)
DOI: 10.5876/9781607327196

Library of Congress Cataloging-in-Publication Data

Names: Haines, David W., author.
Title: An introduction to sociocultural anthropology: adaptations, structures, meanings / David W.
   Haines.
Description: 2nd edition. | Boulder: University Press of Colorado, [2017] | "The first edition of this
   book was previously published by: Pearson Education, Inc."—Title page. | Includes bibliographical
   references and index.
Identifiers: LCCN 2017010446| ISBN 9781607327189 (pbk.) | ISBN 9781607327196 (ebook)
Subjects: LCSH: Ethnology. | Human geography. | Ethnobiology.
Classification: LCC GN316 .H35 2017 | DDC 306—dc23

LC record available at https://lccn.loc.gov/2017010446

Cover illustrations, top to bottom: Terraced rice fields © Saravut Whanset / Shutterstock; Great Wall
of China © Hung Chung Chih / Shutterstock; Arabic callilgraphic design © javarman / Shutterstock.
Photographs on pp. 21, 101, and 199 by David W. Haines.

Contents

Figures

Preface

When I was ten years old and living in Middletown, New York, my parents decided to move to Japan. The morning after arriving, I walked out onto a small street behind the house where we were staying and into a new world. As a man on a motorcycle zipped by, I managed to get out an *ohayo gozaimasu* (good morning). The man had already passed me, but he shifted all the way around in his seat and returned the greeting—without, as I feared, crashing into the wall along the road. Much of anthropology for me is in that moment: the envelopment in a different culture's sights, sounds, and smells; language as the key to crossing into that culture; and the sharp pleasure I feel even now whenever I return to Japan and walk down the narrow, twisting side streets I met some fifty years ago.

When I was twenty-two years old, I was in the highlands of southern Vietnam. I was an interpreter in Vietnamese and a civil affairs specialist for the US Army. I found myself one day in a minority village near where we were working on a gravity-pump water system. A woman motioned me into a house. It was a long house with bamboo matting across sleeping platforms. Smoke to keep away mosquitoes curled up through the matting from smoldering fires on the floor. It was the home of the village chief, who was extremely ill. My efforts to teach myself their language from a Vietnamese text had not progressed very well, but I was fairly sure this was malaria. Back in the provincial capital, I convinced a Vietnamese medical team to move up their periodic visit to the village. It was indeed malaria, and the village chief rapidly recovered. Much of the rest of anthropology for me is in that episode:

the ever-beckoning image of yet another culture and another language as different from the last as the last was from my own; the involvement in practical issues that are sometimes minor and sometimes life threatening; the strange world of power where a young and unimportant outsider like me could mobilize the resources to heal an important and senior tribal member.

When I was forty-five and a senior manager at a state workers' compensation agency, I went into work one weekend. The head of the data-processing department, who reported to me, had just left and I was now the only one who had access to, or even understood, the data systems on which the agency relied for active legal cases and more routine administrative reports. As I gingerly logged in, I felt a sharp pang of concern. Data are very, very real, and when they are lost the effects can be serious and permanent. Somehow I had to figure out this new virtual environment and make sure it was protected and functional by Monday morning. This was a different kind of environment and not one for which I was trained. Yet it was also a familiar challenge: another language and culture within a new virtual world of relational databases.

For me, these experiences are the crux of an anthropological way of thinking. But how do you put that kind of anthropological experience into an academic class and make it relevant to students' lives? One answer is to use a text and perhaps supplement it with a reader. That approach will work well in conveying what anthropology has become as a field of study and the range of insights it has produced. Yet, for many of us, the time (and money) spent on such a text divert attention from the heart of the anthropological experience: a connection between anthropologists and the people and places—real or virtual—that we visit and inhabit. For us, one answer is to use a few book-length ethnographic studies that focus on specific people in specific places, whether far away in different lands or at home in rapidly changing and supposedly fully modernized societies. Another answer is to focus more on actual student field projects, since, for students as well as career anthropologists, the biggest insights usually come from one's own immersion in anthropological inquiry. Yet another option might be to use an excellent body of anthropological film to help visualize human life under different circumstances.

However, extended ethnographic material, field projects, and film have their own limitations. After all, there are some general insights that anthropologists have gained over time that can help illuminate such material. That argues for a text, but the full-length texts—of which there are many good ones—are too time consuming to permit the incorporation of other more detailed ethnographic material. Even the mid-length texts—of which there are also some very good ones—are hefty enough to limit their use. This book is designed specifically to fill this gap. It provides a rough guide to the major insights of sociocultural anthropology that may be especially helpful in courses that aim to include more detailed ethnographic forays, whether through book-length ethnographies, film, or student projects.

Two aspects of the book deserve note. First, I have tried to give equal attention to what I see as the three major strands of anthropological interest. One is overall environmental adaptation and is the focus in part I. Here are the traditional categories of foraging, horticulture, agriculture, pastoralism, and industrialism. Together they provide the broad range of how people live in different and changing environments, and how people increasingly change those environments in the process. Another strand is structural and is the focus of part II. Here are the general anthropological lessons about how people fit together in different frameworks, whether of kinship, politics, economics, or religion. The final strand is more strictly cultural and is the focus in part III, with its emphasis on meaning, its construction, and its expression. Here is more of what life is like as lived by people, not just what people do but what life means to them. In giving equal attention to these three strands, I have also tried to keep the logic of the three separate. The adaptational sections are thus unabashedly materialistic, the structural sections show all the virtues and limitations of systemic analysis, and the sections on meaning steadfastly refuse to reduce ideational issues to materialist ones.

Second, I have taken a broad notion of what anthropology is about and a particularly broad notion of culture as a kind of buffer (material, social, and ideational) between human beings as biological entities and the environments in which they live. To me this is a better way to introduce culture to students than to focus on all the many definitions of it, though I have used Edward Tylor's definition at several points because of its inclusiveness. That inclusiveness is particularly important to me since my own work has been as often in the nonacademic as in the academic world, and as often on the contemporary United States as on places overseas, particularly for me in Asia.

My major debt along the way is to my anthropology students at George Mason University. Those in introductory classes field tested the original version of this text, and students there in upper-division and graduate courses consistently reminded me that both academic and practical work are important, and that anthropology is indeed a good approach to both. Special individual thanks go to Alexander Munoz, for insisting on the importance of Aztec *chinampas*; Bettina Guevara, for insights on American body-piercing; Erika Tsuchiya and Sam Brase, for monitoring my attempts to integrate Japanese-language examples into course material; Tam Tran, for very helpful comments on the Vietnamese kinship examples in the book; Alison Meyers and Golnesa Moshiri, for encouraging my belief that anthropology and information technology are a good fit, even for non-IT types; and sociology students Jennifer Myers and Christine Melcher, for enduring in sequential semesters my newly developed classes on information technology and on interdisciplinary synthesis—the latter based on the premise that anthropology is indeed the discipline from which to integrate material from the sciences, social sciences, and humanities. I also benefited greatly from teaching introductory anthropology twice at George Mason's new campus in South Korea. That experience helped sharpen my notion of what a useful text should be in different national environments as well as for differently trajected students.

Several colleagues also deserve particular thanks. Sheila Barrows and Fred Conway read and commented extensively on the initial manuscript as a whole—the former with a clear editor's eye and the latter with a supportive teacher's one. Karen Rosenblum offered invaluable critique of several of the chapters and strong support for the overall intent of this kind of alternative text. Karl Zhang—colleague and teacher—kept up my spirits as I learned some elementary contemporary and classical Chinese and began to piece together a broader linguistic and historical understanding of East Asia.

For the second edition I must thank Jessica d'Arbonne of the University Press of Colorado for encouraging me to undertake this new edition, in which I have had an opportunity to sharpen the writing and to tilt the approach more toward an anthropology that will fit the future. I have updated in many places and especially expanded the discussion of current economic and political structures, the increasingly flexible ways people are organizing their social universes, and the way human expression both marks the physical world and draws from that world. Those new trajectories were especially encouraged by the keen comments of Anne Lewinson on how this second edition could improve on the first. I had excellent detailed readings of the full manuscript by Aziza Bayou, Rachel Kenderdine, Daniel Klinger, and Andrea Mendoza. Additional reviews from Donna Budoni, Deborah Altamirano, Analiese Richard, and Gerald Waite were also valuable. Additional thanks go to Laura Furney, Sonya Manes, Dan Pratt, and Beth Svinarich for editorial, design, and marketing work.

Many of the revisions in this second edition reflect overall changes in the discipline, but they also reflect my own work over the past decade, especially in the areas of migration and policy. Migration provides the opportunity to see humans as they move beyond their everyday environments, and that gives us a much better opportunity to see what the real range of human adaptation can be—and also what endures across such changes. The world of policy is of increasing interest since the very complexity of the contemporary world requires a more careful consideration of options and mechanisms to construct policy that is thoughtful, fair, and effective. The consideration of the relationship between anthropology and policy provides a renewed opportunity to match anthropology's global reach in understanding with the world's need for a more holistic approach in both understanding and practice.

AN INTRODUCTION TO
Sociocultural Anthropology

1

The Anthropological Vision

Anthropology as an academic discipline has its origins in the late nineteenth-century as an attempt to grasp the full range of the human experience: that *all* aspects of *all* people's experience belong together as an indivisible subject of study. To that broad sense of inclusion was added an emphasis on direct fieldwork as the best way to understand how people live and how they experience their lives. In North American anthropology, that sense of inclusion and the commitment to field research were applied initially to native Americans (whose lifeways anthropologists feared would soon disappear); to the people whose lives and work were reshaping the North American continent (white and black, native born and immigrant); and ultimately to the full range of people throughout the world in both technologically simple and complex societies.

Today, anthropology consists of an extensive body of knowledge accumulated by anthropologists and a set of conceptual approaches that help organize that material. Yet anthropology also remains a very personal quest for understanding. That quest usually hinges on long-term, direct immersion in the cultures being studied. That field experience is structured not so much by formal research methods as by the unique talents and interests of the anthropologist guided by the accumulated experience of other anthropologists: the basic questions they have asked and the ideas about human interaction that they have developed in the field. The quest for anthropological understanding also continues to have a strong link to the professional practice of anthropologists as they seek to improve the human condition by addressing how people interact with their environments, how their social organization can be made more effective and more equitable, and how they can more fully achieve their human potential given the context of increasingly more intrusive global political and economic forces.

This chapter introduces anthropology in two ways. The first is an overview of anthropological theory, method, and practice. The purpose is to provide a general sense of how anthropologists think about issues ("theory"); how they try to gather information about the world ("method"); and the kinds of work they do—and lives they lead—as they do so ("practice"). The second is a review of the early history of anthropology. The purpose there is to indicate the major intellectual decisions that have formed anthropology as it is today. The most important of these are a commitment to inclusiveness (anthropology is about all aspects of all people's lives); a recognition that all people have their own distinct histories; and a determination to understand other societies on their own terms. The chapter concludes with a discussion of the way this book is organized around three sets of questions that have emerged in anthropology: how people relate to their environments ("adaptations"), the basic ways in which human society is organized ("structures"), and how people make sense of their lives ("meanings").

BIOLOGY, CULTURE, AND ENVIRONMENT

Although anthropologists have many different ideas about how the human world works, there is a common framework shared by most anthropologists. That framework (diagrammed in figure 1.1) includes three major domains: *biology*, *culture*, and *environment*.

Human biology is the specific focus for some anthropologists, but all anthropologists recognize and must factor into their analysis what human beings are in physical terms. Often that consideration of human biology is very much in the background. Thus the specific physical characteristics that permit human language receive little comment in most anthropological research, since those characteristics can generally be assumed. On the other hand, the consideration of human biology may be central in other work. For example, the relative effects of biological sex and the socially constructed issues of gender have long been of concern to anthropologists. Much of the work of Margaret Mead, perhaps the most widely known anthropologist of the twentieth century, was concerned with exactly that interaction between biology and culture. Her first research concerned adolescence in Samoa, particularly how smooth the adolescent experience was there compared with the United States. That suggested to her that the traumas of adolescence in most Western societies had both cultural and biological roots.

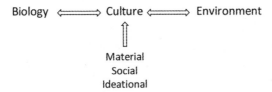

FIGURE 1.1. Biology, culture, and environment

Human beings, however, do not live in a vacuum. They live in physical environments that broaden their options in some cases and constrain them in others. Much of the uniqueness of human beings lies in their ability to adapt to a wide range of environments. Thus it is impossible to understand the meaning of human biology without studying people in the full range of environments in which they live. This helps explain the anthropological emphasis on the details of the physical places in which people live. Many anthropological case studies begin with extensive discussions of the physical environment: the quality of the soil, the rains, the temperature changes, the kinds of vegetation, the animals. Franz Boas, who held the first university position in anthropology in North America, and who will be discussed in more detail later in this chapter, was originally a physicist. His initial aim was to study the physical environment in the arctic but then found that the human beings who lived there were of rather more interest than the environment itself.

Although anthropologists deal with both biology and environment, their greatest concern has been with the third domain in the diagram—culture. Culture, in its broadest sense, is a buffer that exists between human beings as biological entities and the environments in which they live. If the weather changes sharply, human beings have the options of putting on clothes or taking them off, of heating their homes or cooling them. That greatly expands the options that they have. Canadians do not need to migrate south to the United States in winter, though they might like to, and those in the southern parts of the United States do not need to migrate north to Canada in the summer, though some of us do just that.

The buffer that is culture is often very physical and very practical. A simple tool, for example, can sharply change the relationship between human beings and their environment: a stone or bone scraper permits the fashioning of hides into clothes; a piece of chipped stone at the end of a big stick (spear) or smaller stick (arrow) permits better hunting; a plow revolutionizes the cultivation of plants. But culture is not just about tools. It is also about social arrangements. Human beings may not be unique in being social and in having families. Yet the human capacity for social groups is impressive in its variation and in the sheer size of human groups. Those social arrangements also provide a buffer between human beings as biological entities and their environments. Cooperative groups permit the hunting of big game, fishing with large nets, or even whaling. Small groups, such as the nuclear family, permit people to spread out across a large area and be relatively self-sufficient. Large groups with hundreds, thousands, or millions of members permit massive mobilization of people for large-scale action, whether in peace or war.

Culture is not only about tools and social relationships. It is also about ideas, beliefs, and values. This is the way the word "culture" is usually used in everyday life. At its broadest, this aspect of culture can be understood as referring to the overall vision that people have of themselves, of the world, and of how they should orient themselves to that world and to the other human beings in it. It is what makes them who they are and sets the parameters for what they can accomplish. On a more specific level, culture can refer to ideas that might help people work together (such as a belief in the nobility of sacrifice and service) or that might help people survive against their adversaries (such as a belief in the justness of war).

Anthropologists are thus interested in human beings as biological entities, as located in specific environments, and as cultural entities. That makes anthropology a very broad discipline. On the positive side, this broad framework helps anthropologists avoid simplistic arguments that some aspect of human behavior is "caused" by biology, or "caused" by the environment, or even "caused" by culture. Instead, anthropologists know they must account for the biological, environmental, *and* cultural aspects of human life. As an example, consider race. Whereas many people might accept the idea of race as a simple description of physical differences among people, anthropologists recognize that "race" is, after all, a word. Understanding race thus requires attention to people's ideas and values—to their culture in the everyday sense. It also requires attention to how supposed racial differences are used in social arrangements. Anthropologists might note, for example, that issues of race in the United States have their origins in a system of slavery that provided cheap labor for difficult work that the original settlers did not want to do themselves. Even though anthropologists know that there are not clear biological differences between so-called races, they readily understand how convenient it is for people who are enslaving or abusing other people to claim that biological differences justify it. One of Franz Boas's achievements, for example, was to show that supposed racial differences between northern and southern European immigrants to North America actually disappeared among their children.[1]

---

[1] For a round of debate on this aspect of Boas's research, see Clarence C. Gravlee, H. Russell Bernard, and William R. Leonard, "Boas's Changes in Bodily Form," *American Anthropologist* 105 (2003): 326–32; Corey S. Sparks and Richard L. Jantz, "Changing Times, Changing Faces," *American Anthropologist* 105 (2003): 337–37; and David Haines, "Anthropology and Policy," in *The International Encyclopedia of Anthropology*, edited by Hilary Callan (Hoboken, NJ: Wiley-Blackwell, 2017).

RESEARCH AND PRACTICE

This anthropological attention to human beings as biological entities, to the environments in which they live, and to their material, social, and ideational culture, affects the way anthropologists go about their work. Anthropological theory greatly affects anthropological methods. If anthropologists are to study biology and environment and culture, they know they will have to locate themselves in a specific place. If they do not, how can they possibly begin to understand the interactions of biology, culture, and environment? So the first methodological rule is "go there." Since the environment is such an important factor in human life, then the period of time spent in that place will need to be at least a year to grasp the annual cycle. Almost all human environments have sharp seasonal changes of temperature and precipitation; those seasons greatly affect the food people are able to obtain, the shelter they will need, and usually their most important ritual events and celebrations. So the second methodological rule is "and stay there for at least a year." Finally, since much of culture is ideational and hinges on language, there is a third methodological rule, which is "and learn the language." Those three rules create the minimum requirements. Many anthropologists prefer to stay longer than a year and to return later to see if what they found was a relatively durable pattern or a more transient one. This standard of fieldwork is daunting. It is extremely time consuming, often disorienting, and sometimes dangerous. It is even more complicated when the people the anthropologist is studying are themselves in motion. Studying migrants, for example, may well require going to the places from which they come, the places to which they go, and the routes by which they navigate between them. Yet the result of that daunting standard is that anthropological fieldwork provides more depth and range of understanding than other research approaches. Thus, the anthropologist often can give the richest portrayal of other cultures: what people do, why they do it, and what they themselves think about it.

The broad anthropological framework of biology, culture, and environment and the demanding method of intensive fieldwork greatly shape the way in which anthropologists go about being anthropologists. Their jobs vary greatly. Of those with PhDs, some go into academic positions: some entirely teaching and some entirely research, though probably most with a combination of the two. Others go into a range of "real" jobs, many of which are continuations of their own anthropological research. For those with MAs, the proportions shift with more in nonacademic jobs. Of both groups, some work in the areas of international development or humanitarian action, often on behalf of people they already know from their fieldwork. Others bring their skills to bear on issues in North America. Some focus on populations of immigrants and refugees. Others focus on ethnic or racial minorities or on other kinds of diversity by gender, sexual orientation, disability, or legal status. Yet others have become involved in technological areas, for example, looking at computers and other IT products as newer members of the ancient lineage of human tools. The human hand holding a smart phone, after all, looks quite a bit like the human hand holding a scraper. Humans are still tool users—and they still have strong emotional attachments to those tools.[2]

In considering the range of work that anthropologists do, there is a tendency to categorize anthropologists as academics (those in full-time university positions); applied anthropologists (usually split between university and research activities); and practitioners (those in "real" jobs). Yet there is often considerable overlap. Even the most academic of the academics are usually involved in research that has quite practical implications. Often the practitioners are working in areas (such as computerization, genetic engineering, and international migration) that have challenging theoretical implications. Although they sometimes disagree, all share a commitment to an overarching vision of a rich and varied humanity that demands respect for the human condition and for help in moving a complicated and globalized world toward a better and fairer future for all people and all cultures.

THE DEVELOPMENT OF ANTHROPOLOGY

TYLOR AND MORGAN: EVOLUTION, ETHNOGRAPHY, AND HOLISM

The basic theoretical orientations, methods, and practice of anthropology can also be illustrated through a review of the early history of anthropology as a specific discipline. A full review is too hefty a subject for this book, but a short review suggests there are three basic pillars on which the discipline is built: evolutionism, historical-particularism, and structural-functionalism. The labels may seem contorted, but they are actually simply descriptive: the *evolutionists* emphasized the importance of evolution in organizing information about different peoples, the *historical-particularists* emphasized the importance of history and of the particular details of how people live, and the *structural-functionalists* emphasized that societies were indeed structured and that the different elements of those societies had practical functions.

The story of anthropology as we know it today began in the latter part of the nineteenth century. The world was changing rapidly. The industrial revolution had given Europe and North America a vastly increased ability to produce new

---

2   For a recent review of anthropological jobs, see Daniel Ginsberg, "Anthropologists in and out of the Academy," *Anthropology News* (November/December 2016): 19.

goods, sometimes goods of better quality, certainly goods of increased quantity, and often goods—such as weapons—of greatly increased destructiveness. This resulted in an enormous power differential between those countries and the rest of the world. That power differential ultimately reduced much of the rest of the world to colonial or near-colonial status. The industrial revolution also resulted in great social dislocations within Europe and North America and a newly urban life of grit, grime, and crime.

Yet the latter part of the nineteenth century was also a time of hope that the human capacity for reason could resolve these social dislocations and create a better material and social world. That belief mirrored the confidence that science had done well in increasing human understanding and promoting great leaps in productive power. The first anthropologists—the evolutionists—were part of that time of change and hope. They had more information about a broader range of people in a world that was being brought more closely together. To their great credit, these first anthropologists recognized the extent of human diversity and accepted that diversity as their focus. They claimed all these different human beings throughout the world as one integrated field of study. Further, they claimed that all aspects of these people's lives were within the scope of this new discipline. Thus anthropology was at its very creation the study of all people (any time, any place) and of all aspects of their lives. As Edward Tylor (1832–1917), the most eminent of the evolutionists, put it, the focus of anthropology was to be culture, for which he offered the following extremely broad definition: "Culture or civilization taken in its wide ethnographic sense is that complex whole which includes knowledge, belief, art, morals, law, custom, and any other capabilities and habits acquired by man as a member of society."[3]

Two of the words he used deserve emphasis because they continue to be central to anthropology today. The first is *ethnographic*. Its literal meaning is the study or description (*~graph*) of a people (*~ethnos*), but it conveys to anthropologists the need to be detailed and thorough in that description. Tylor's use of the phrase *complex whole* is also crucial and is echoed to this day in the anthropological emphasis on *holism*, which means that all the different pieces of what people do add up to a comprehensive whole. We cannot understand the pieces without recognizing the wholeness of human life, but we cannot understand that wholeness without detailed understanding of the pieces.

That broad anthropological vision, however, posed some problems, and still does so today. Even in Tylor's time, there was a wealth of information on different human societies, and it was growing. How could all this information be

---

3   E. B. Tylor, *Primitive Culture* (London: John Murray, 1871).

Phantoms
   ↳Ghosts
     ↳Spirits
       ↳Guardian spirits
        ↳ Deities
         ↳Supreme being

FIGURE 1.2. Tylor's sequence of religious ideas

sorted into a meaningful structure? Here, influenced by the new popularity of evolutionary theory in biology, Tylor and others began to sort the information they found into general stages of development—of social evolution. It is for this that they are called evolutionists. As two examples of the attempts of evolutionists, consider Tylor's own work on religion and the work of Lewis Henry Morgan on technology.[4]

Tylor was interested in religion and attempted to think through from the available information how human beings developed their sense of the supernatural (see figure 1.2). His argument began with the mystery of death. When someone died, the body was still there, but the something that had made them who they were was gone. That the spirit of the person simply disappears instantaneously without a trace would, he reasoned, be unreasonable to most people. Surely at least there was some brief passing phantom of that person. If people had the notion of some temporary continuation of the essence of a person, then they might well develop a more elaborate notion of a spiritual entity that retained the full personality of the dead person for a longer and possibly indefinite period of time—what we would call a ghost. Surely, Tylor further reasoned, if people had the notion of an enduring spirit of a person who died, they might also develop the notion of an independent spirit that had *not* previously been a person. Perhaps the spirit that is the living person, in fact, comes from somewhere else and enters the child at conception or birth, and then leaves the body again at the time of death. From such notions of spirits, Tylor reasoned that notions of guardian spirits, deities, gods, and ultimately a supreme being would develop not out of simple superstition but as a result of logical reasoning. Tylor was thus proposing an evolution

---

4   The discussions that follow are drawn from E. B. Tylor, *Anthropology* (London: MacMillan and Co., 1881); and Lewis Henry Morgan's *Ancient Society* (Tucson: University of Arizona Press, 1985; orig. 1877).

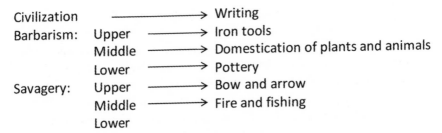

FIGURE 1.3. Morgan's evolutionary stages

of human thought about the supernatural, emphasizing that humans are indeed rational thinkers—at least much of the time. The consideration of that totality of human thought on religion, he implied, gives us a much better way to understand the full human experience of both the seen and the unseen—and to do so without making a priori (before the fact) determinations of what beliefs are correct or incorrect.

Another crucial early anthropologist was Lewis Henry Morgan (1818–81). He was an American who had spent much time with the Iroquois. He developed a framework for understanding societies based on their material culture. His reasoning was that technology had pervasive effects on societies. The items he chose as critical advances were fire, fishing, the bow and arrow, pottery, domestication of plants and animals, iron tools, and writing. Rather than merely note them as important factors, however, Morgan organized them into an evolutionary scheme (see figure 1.3). Those societies that had fire and fishing, but lacked the bow and arrow, were at the middle stage of "savagery." Those who had pottery made it into the "barbarian" category. Iron tools placed a society at the top of the barbarians, but only a written language lets a society enter the ranks of the "civilized."

Morgan's evolutionary scheme had much merit to it. The control of fire, the domestication of plants and animals, iron tools, and writing do indeed yield potential benefits for a society. If this were only a technology rating, it would be hard to object to it. However, this threefold categorization of *savagery, barbarism,* and *civilization* had broader and more unpleasant implications about aspects of human behavior that had little to do with technology. That evolutionary categorization was frequently used to justify the enormous inequalities of the time. As these more popularized evolutionary schemes became more grandiose and self-serving, they also became more inconsistent and sometimes factually inaccurate. Thus, in the area of marriage, one set of writers saw the evolutionary sequence from "savagery" through "barbarism" to "civilization" as involving a shift from group marriage to polygamy to monogamy. Another set of writers, however, saw the sequence as moving from promiscuity through matriarchy to patriarchy. Unfortunately for all of them, there was not much correspondence between these stages of marriage and Morgan's more defined technological ones. For example, people with very simple technology often had monogamous marriages. For religion, a similar pattern developed. One set of writers argued that the "savagery" to "barbarism" to "civilization" progression was seen in the shift from magic to religion to science. But how could they themselves, who were supposed to be "civilized," still be religious and attend church each Sunday? Another set of writers thus argued that the transition was from animism (a general belief that there are spirits) to polytheism to monotheism. As with marriage patterns, however, these sequences did not directly match what was found in the field. Technologically simple cultures often had what appeared to be monotheistic views.

Boas: Cultural Relativism

Although the specific arguments of the best of the evolutionists—such as Tylor and Morgan—had much merit, the degradation of social evolutionary ideas into crude stages of savagery, barbarism, and civilization caused a negative reaction among many of those interested in this new field of anthropology. This reaction created North American anthropology as we know it today, and it was most forcefully seen in Franz Boas (1858–1942). Boas, with his training in physics, went to Baffin Island in 1883 to study its arctic geography. Once on Baffin Island, he became intrigued by the people. He wrote as follows in his journal, and I quote at length since his comments provided a manifesto for subsequent American anthropology.

> I often ask myself what advantages our "good society" possesses over that of the "savages." The more I see of their customs, the more I realize that we have no right to look down on them. Where amongst our people would you find such true hospitality? Here, without the least complaint people are willing to perform every task demanded of them. We have no right to blame them for their forms and superstitions, which may seem ridiculous to us. We "highly educated people" are much worse, relatively speaking. The fear of tradition and old customs is deeply implanted in mankind, and in the same way as it regulates life here, it halts all progress for us. I believe it is a difficult struggle for every individual and every people to give up tradition and follow the path to truth. The Eskimo are sitting around me, their mouths filled with raw seal liver (the spot of blood on the back of the paper shows you how I joined in). As a thinking person, for me the most important result of this trip lies in the strengthening of my point of view that the idea of a "cultured" individual is merely relative and that a person's worth should be judged by his heart. This quality is present or absent here among the

Eskimo, just as among us. All that man can do for humanity is to further the truth, whether it be sweet or bitter. Such a man may truly say that he has not lived in vain.[5]

Boas was setting a new tone for anthropology. As with the evolutionists, anthropology was for Boas about all aspects of the lives of all people. For him, however, those lives were to be understood not as stages in some grand evolutionary scheme, but rather as the common attempt of all people to achieve their full humanity. Boas's phrase "merely relative" should be underlined, for it, like Tylor's invocation of "that complex whole," is now a standard anthropological dictum: cultures must be understood on *their* terms, not ours, whether or not we happen to agree or approve. Thus to the invocation of holism from the evolutionists, Boas added the invocation of *cultural relativism*.[6]

In addition to this commitment to human diversity and human equality, Boas also emphasized the importance of fieldwork. No longer was information to be processed into schemes by "armchair" anthropologists. Rather, anthropologists were now to go to where the people lived to understand the details of their histories and the wealth of their material, social, and ideational culture. Boas, after all, did not have his great insight at home, but out in the field. He would in his later career personally train two generations of anthropologists, who would first spread out across North America to document in detail the Native American experience. That task had priority since these early American anthropologists feared that many Native American cultures might soon disappear entirely. Later, American anthropologists would move outward to more distant places to describe other cultures and to consider what lessons those other cultures might have for us. But here, with the young Boas, the core commitment was made. As with the evolutionists, all aspects of all people's lives were included. However, with Boas that inclusion was to be based on the premise of human equality and achieved through detailed fieldwork. The label "historical-particularist" thus rings with two exhortations as relevant to North American anthropology today as then: "all people have their own history" and "the details matter."

RADCLIFFE-BROWN AND MALINOWSKI: STRUCTURAL-FUNCTIONALISM
Boas and the other North American anthropologists were not the only people who reacted against the excesses of evolutionism. The British structural-functionalists

---

5   As quoted in George Stocking, "From Physics to Ethnology," *Journal of the History of the Behavioral Sciences* 1 (1965): 61.

6   Cultural relativism can be defined in many ways, but the gist of the idea is to understand human behavior in the context of the culture in which people live. It does not imply either judgment or nonjudgment, but it does invoke the importance of understanding why people do what they do (whether good or ill) in terms of how they themselves are thinking their way through life.

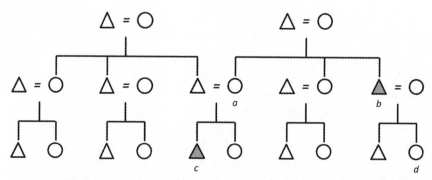

FIGURE 1.4. The mother's brother. Unlike the situation in patrilineal societies, the closest male relationship by blood in a matrilineal society is between a man (*c*) and his mother's brother (*b*) to whom he is related through his mother (*a*) (see the two shaded triangles). Note that one preferred wife for the man is often the mother's brother's daughter (*d*).

had a similar response. They too were wary of grand evolutionary schemes, and they too emphasized detailed fieldwork. A. R. Radcliffe-Brown and Bronislaw Malinowski, the two most prominent of the structural-functionalists, provide an interesting contrast. Radcliffe-Brown (1881–1955) was very much the theoretician, whereas Malinowski (1884–1942) was very much the fieldworker. Indeed, Malinowski's work in the Trobriand Islands during World War I is often considered as the model for modern anthropological fieldwork. The personal styles of the two men were quite different. Radcliffe-Brown was a rather proper native-born Englishman who wrote books with titles like *The Natural Science of Society* and *The Andaman Islanders*. Bronislaw Malinowski was a flamboyant Pole who subsequently moved to England. His titles included *Argonauts of the Western Pacific*, *Coral Gardens and Their Magic*, and *The Sexual Life of Savages*, and, yet again to titillate the populace, *Sex and Repression in Savage Society*.

Despite their differences, both Radcliffe-Brown and Malinowski saw societies as working systems that were logical on their own terms. For them history was less important than it was to the Boasians. It was not that all cultures had their own *histories* but that all societies were working *systems*. Those systems needed to be understood on their own terms as they existed in the present. One classic example of their approach involves "the mother's brother" (see figure 1.4). At the time they were doing their research, the relationship between sons and fathers was frequently described as innately tension filled. Freud's view, for example, was based on issues of the son's repressed sexual feelings toward his mother and consequent competition with his father. What both Radcliffe-Brown and Malinowski observed, however, was that these ideas were based on the particular family structure of European society. In European society at the time, inheritance was generally patrilineal (that is, the line runs through the father). Thus sons inherit from their fathers. In other societies, however, Radcliffe-Brown and Malinowski noted that inheritance did not run from fathers to sons. In matrilineal societies inheritance is generally from mothers to daughters. When there is inheritance between males in matrilineal societies, it is through female connections: thus from a mother's brother rather than from a father. Radcliffe-Brown and Malinowski could also point out that the relations between fathers and sons in matrilineal societies were different in tone from what they were in European societies. In matrilineal societies the relationship between the father and son tended to be warm and flexible. By contrast, the relationship between a male and his mother's brother reflected stress and competition. There are two fundamental lessons to be drawn from this example. First, it is essential to always consider the full range of options in different kinds of societies. For kinship, for example, comparison of matrilineal and patrilineal societies is extremely valuable—and will be pursued at several points in this text. Second, it is always wise to examine the simple and observable aspects of life (such as who inherits from whom—as in, who gets what?) before launching into more complex explanatory theories.

The early history of anthropology can be summarized as follows. From the evolutionists comes the basic sense of inclusion: that all aspects of all people's lives belong on the record. From both the historical-particularists and the structural-functionalists come the emphases on fieldwork and understanding societies on their own terms. For the historical-particularists, "on their own terms" emphasized the history of a people, and for the structural-functionalists it emphasized the practical logic of their social arrangements. The subsequent history of anthropology rests on these foundations. Many current debates can be anticipated from this early work. One is the problem caused by the broad scope of "all aspects of all people's lives." How do you manage that amount of information with that level of detail? Another is the problem caused by the length of fieldwork. It is practically difficult and requires personal wealth or some kind of funding. Fieldwork will also inevitably create a complex relationship with the people studied. Living that closely over many months and perhaps many years, anthropologists will inevitably become personally involved and no longer "objective" outsiders.[7] That will benefit their understanding,

---

7   "Objective" generally means from an outside and supposedly accurate perspective whereas "subjective" generally means from an inside and personalized perspective. As an example, a social science survey of an immigrant group would generally be classified as objective while a novel by a member of that group would be considered subjective. Beyond that, however, the meaning of the two words becomes contorted and contested. The objective survey, for example, is based on formulated questions that are often quite subjective and culture-bound. The subjective novel, by contrast, may for many readers present a far more real view. For anthropologists both are important: watching attentively and listening attentively—and perhaps also imagining attentively.

but it may also introduce problems of how to analyze information that is so strongly and personally channeled.

ADAPTATIONS, STRUCTURES, MEANINGS

Anthropology is a broad, cross-cultural, integrative discipline concerned with human biology; the environments in which people live; and the material, social, and ideational culture that serves as a buffer between human biology and the environment. Out of that broad framework comes three general sets of issues. These are addressed in the three parts of this book.

The first part, "Adaptations," focuses on understanding human societies in terms of how they react to and utilize the environments in which they live. The chapters in part I introduce the standard variations of foraging, horticulture, agriculture, pastoralism, and industrialism. Each of these adaptations creates a society with particular tendencies: large kinship groups for some but nuclear families for others; peace for some but frequent war for others; relative equality for some but sharp disparities for others. The goal of part I is to provide a sense of the variation in human societies and to what degree that variation reflects a people's relationship to their environment. You will find a bit of Lewis Henry Morgan's interest in technology here, and much of Franz Boas's early fascination with the environment and how people adapt to it.

The second part, "Structures," focuses on social organization. For anthropologists the most important organizing principle of human society is kinship. Ties of blood and marriage are the most predictable and reliable of human ties. The anthropological record shows immense variation in how kinship ties are created, perceived, and used. Anthropologists also look at other ways in which human beings are wound and bound together. Some are political, some economic, and some a combination of these. Religion is also included in this part of the book since much of its effect is to provide a structure for relationships among people—and between people and a wide range of spirits and other supernatural entities. The goal of part II is to provide a sense of the basics of human social relations and what the options are in organizing people by ties of kinship, politics, economics, and religion. You will find many echoes in part II of the structural-functionalists, including discussion of matrilineality, patrilineality, and the famous "mother's brother."

The third part, "Meanings," addresses how people perceive, create, re-create, and express the lived meanings of their lives, sometimes through thought and emotion, sometimes through language and communication, sometimes through play, sometimes through the arts, and sometimes through practical action. The discussion begins with thought (cognition) and emotion, with emphasis on how our minds and bodies organize the world for us. Part III then turns to language, including some basics about how our speech and writing organize the world, and then to other ways people express themselves, whether in play or art, through physical objects and activities, or through modification of their own bodies and environments. Part III concludes with a discussion of how the human search for meaning is faring in a contemporary world beset by economic and political forces—often global in nature—and by an increasing human control over the human body and over the environment that tilts the framework of biology-culture-environment in new and unpredictable ways.

WARNINGS AND PROMISES

In reading this book, a few disclaimers need to be made. First, in order to meet the specific purpose of this volume as a supplement to courses that emphasize more detailed ethnographic materials (whether reading them, watching them, or writing them), the approach here is indeed abbreviated. I cannot do justice to the complexity of many issues, nor can I invoke more than a little of the vast anthropological literature that now exists. My decisions about what to include generally have been to emphasize the basics of anthropology rather than anthropological debates about those basics. This is not to say that the debates are unimportant but that they provide a poor place from which to begin an introduction to anthropology.

Second, I have aimed to introduce key ideas first, and only then—and sparingly for reasons of conciseness—give short case examples at the end of chapters. I saw no other choice without lapsing into a more extended narrative format leading to a longer (and more expensive) book. The purpose here is to provide basic guidance so the ethnographic detail of other course materials can take center stage. I have done my best to streamline the presentation and keep the arguments as jargon-free as possible—except for topics such as kinship and linguistics, for which the technicalities are crucial.

Third, despite that need for conciseness, I realize this book may also be used as a reference guide—a kind of concordance for terms and ideas. To that end I have provided some additional resources. The extra references listed at the end of the chapters should help guide you to the next level of detail on each subject. There is also a glossary that will help in identifying terms. In addition, the frequent textbook convention of italicizing significant words is also used. There are also occasional footnotes to explain issues that seemed too technical for inclusion in the main text, including some special terms or references that may be useful but are probably not essential in an introductory class.

Good luck. Anthropology is a terrific field—and a terrific undergraduate course, minor, and major. It is a terrific field because it helps illuminate people's lives and because, since it is such a personal discipline, it also helps activate the minds and

Margaret Mead (1901–78), probably the twentieth century's most famous American anthropologist and one of the last students of Franz Boas. (Credit: NYWT&S staff photo by Edward Lynch, courtesy of the Library of Congress)

Franz Boas (1858–1942), the first academic professor of anthropology in North America and teacher of an entire generation of anthropologists. (Credit: Popular Science Monthly via Wikimedia Commons)

spirits of the people who do the research. So enjoy learning about how interesting people can be. But also learn from anthropologists as they attempt to do the impossible: to be objective, to be fair to the people they study, to be true to themselves, and to write it up in a reasonably engaging way.

You might also consider how useful the anthropological model can be in a variety of real-world situations. As Tylor himself emphasized, anthropology moves immediately to the practical affairs of the world. As the world becomes ever more interconnected, anthropology's emphasis on inclusiveness makes ever greater sense. Anthropologists' experience in other places becomes increasingly relevant, whether in business or government. Also worth noting are the practical values of the anthropological attention to tools and tool use, to the way people use and play with language, and to an anthropological method that is increasingly used in other disciplines and more practical contexts. Anthropology is, for example, a very strong introduction to the logic and practice of organizational and management studies, much less to governance. The nature of anthropology as an overarching vision of the world has always been alluring but daunting. In the contemporary world it may also be inexorably necessary.

SOURCES

For general overviews of theory, three useful volumes are Marvin Harris's *The Rise of Anthropological Theory: A History of Theories of Culture* (Thomas Y. Crowell, 1968; Alta Mira Press, 2001), which is both detailed and argumentative; Philip Carl Salzman's *Understanding Culture: An Introduction to Anthropological Theory* (Waveland, 2001), which is a more recent and succinct approach; and H. Sidky's more detailed *Perspectives on Culture* (Prentice-Hall, 2004). For recent reconsiderations of theory and methods, see James. G. Carrier and Deborah B. Gewertz (eds.), *The Handbook of Sociocultural Anthropology* (Bloomsbury, 2013); Hilary Callan (ed.), *The International Encyclopedia of Anthropology* (Wiley-Blackwell, 2017); and the journal *Anthropological Theory*. For earlier sources see L. L. Langness's *The Study of Culture* (Chandler and Sharp Publishers, 1987) for its extensive quotations, which give the flavor of early theoretical arguments. For more detailed historical work on anthropology as a discipline, the work of George W. Stocking is essential, especially his *Race, Culture, and Evolution: Essays on the History of Anthropology* (University of Chicago Press, 1982). Adam Kuper's *Anthropologists and Anthropology: The Modern British School* (Routledge, 1996) is an entertaining look at anthropology across the Atlantic. There are various compendia on methods, but the heart of anthropological method is probably clearest through autobiographical accounts. For example, Hortense Powdermaker's *Stranger and Friend:*

The Way of an Anthropologist (W. W. Norton, 1966) and Margaret Mead's *Blackberry Winter: My Earlier Years* (Kodansha, 1995) provide classic accounts that will take you into the heart of the anthropological approach to field research. Finally, a good sense of anthropological practice can be gained from *Practicing Anthropology*, a career-oriented publication of the Society for Applied Anthropology.

The film series *Strangers Abroad* (1985), though a bit dated now, still provides good introductions to six of the major figures in early anthropology. All the segments are sound, but the ones on Margaret Mead and Bronislaw Malinowski are especially useful in introducing, respectively, the flavor of American anthropology and the issues of fieldwork. The segment on Franz Boas is also useful, but the film on Boas from the earlier *Odyssey* series is more informative. Watching the first half (thirty minutes) of that film will help underline the range of Boas's contributions. A useful film that conveys a more recent vision of the discipline is *The Anthropologist* (2015).

Part I
ADAPTATIONS

2

Introduction to Part I

Anthropologists are concerned with the interaction of our own biology (what we are capable of); the environment (which facilitates and constrains what we do); and our culture (which through its tools, social arrangements, and beliefs serves as a buffer between us and the environment). While human beings share roughly the same biological capabilities, they live in a range of environments. One key anthropological question is how human societies vary in terms of their adaptation to these different environments. From that examination we can learn what is common to all people and also better appreciate the full range of human possibilities. That issue of adaptation to the environment is the focus of part I, for which this chapter provides a brief introduction. There are four main issues to be addressed: (1) the different ways humans interact with a range of physical environments, (2) four crucial factors in understanding adaptation to these environments, (3) some basic human characteristics that emerge in all of these adaptations, and (4) the general plan for how the examination of adaptations will be organized in the following chapters.

INTERACTING WITH THE ENVIRONMENT

The environments in which human beings live are extremely diverse. They range from the arctic to the tropics in terms of temperature, from the desert to the rain forest in terms of precipitation, and from the heights of the mountains—the Andes and Himalayas, for example—to the seas. Most of those human environments also have seasonal variation in terms of temperature and precipitation. Those seasonal variations, in turn, affect the kinds of plants and animals in the environment at different times of the year, further influencing the way human beings can live in that environment.

In examining human beings in this wide range of environments, anthropologists divide the way people live into five adaptations to these environments:

With *foraging* (or *hunting and gathering*), people largely live off what the environment provides. Whether in the desert or the forest, the arctic cold or the tropical heat, they move through an environment whose plants and animals provide their food and whose raw materials often provide their shelter.

With *horticulture*, human beings make some adjustments to the natural environment. They domesticate a variety of plants and usually some animals as well—especially pigs. The reorganization of nature into gardens permits a more settled lifestyle and larger social groups. However, declines in the productivity of gardens over time often require clearing new fields and sometimes moving to new territory entirely.

With *agriculture*, human beings further develop the domestication of plants, usually specializing in a few crops (especially grains such as rice and wheat) that respond well to more intensive cultivation. With irrigation and use of a plow, the land can produce more and with greater consistency. The result is a very settled society with a surplus that permits the growth of towns and larger urban areas.

With *pastoralism*, the specialization is in terms of animals. Although pastoralists often grow some crops, their emphasis is on a few animals (cattle, sheep, and goats in particular) that provide a broad range of products: from meat and dairy for food, to hides for clothing and shelter, to bone for tools. Unlike agriculturalists, pastoralists are usually very mobile as they accompany their herds on the search for grazing land and water.

With *industrialism*, human beings are involved in a broader range of manual, technical, and intellectual work that produces a more complex array of products. Some of these products—such as agricultural tools, tractors, chemical fertilizers, and new crop varieties—enhance the productivity of the agricultural work on which industrial society is based; others underpin a new, increasingly urban society. Here, people must adapt to a new kind of environment: one that is to a large degree made by people themselves.

FOUR KEY THEMES

Part I of this book will examine each of these five adaptations in more detail. The issues at stake will range from kinship to ecology, from social control to war. There are, however, several key themes that will emerge in discussing all of these different kinds of society. These are outlined below.

CONTROL

The first theme is control. Different societies take differing degrees of control over the environment. Hunters and gatherers, for example, make only modest changes to their environment, while industrial societies extract resources from the earth that can never be renewed. Increased control over the environment may make greater productivity possible, but it may also put a society at risk if that control is mishandled or any mistakes are made in foreseeing its effects. Specialization in a particular food, for example, may initially make more calories available. Yet that specialization may make it easier for disease to spread among plants or animals, raising the possibility of lack of food—perhaps even famine. Generally speaking, there is an increase in control over the environment from a minimal level among foragers to its maximum among industrialists.

DENSITY

The second theme is *density*. With increased control over the environment, there is usually increased density in human settlement. The presence of more people makes a profound difference in human interaction. With relatively small groups, for example, frequent face-to-face interaction yields a society in which people know each other well on a personal basis. In larger, denser settlements—such as modern cities—that personal contact is replaced by frequent interaction with strangers. The denser the population, the more human activity must be directed toward managing the affairs of the people rather than managing the relationship to the environment. Generally speaking, there is an increase in density from foragers to industrialists, but with two important exceptions: pastoralists (with relatively low density) and agriculturalists (with far higher *rural* density than is the case in industrial societies).

COMPLEXITY

The third theme is complexity. With increased control over the environment and increased density of settlement, there is usually an increased complexity in formal social organization. Simple, common-law understandings of what is proper behavior, for example, yield to complex legal codes. Face-to-face exchanges of goods and services yield to impersonal catalog and Internet sales. Even building one's home becomes enmeshed in governmental regulations about zoning, insurance, taxation, and various kinds of building, plumbing, and electrical codes. Generally speaking, there is an increase in societal complexity from foragers to industrialists, but with a caveat. Some aspects of life among foragers and horticulturalists are quite complex (marriage and kin systems, for example).

MOBILITY

The fourth theme is mobility. Some adaptations put a premium on stability; others put a premium on mobility. For example, if there is intensive investment in agricultural land, there is a decided tendency to *not* move. On the other hand, if there are better resources in other places, such as water for the herds of pastoralists, then mobility is a benefit. Mobility does not change in a linear way from foraging to industrialism. Horticulturalists, for example, are sometimes quite mobile and sometimes quite stationary. It is one of the great ironies in the contemporary world that as we search for a good comparison to the mobility of our lives in an industrial (or *postindustrial*) society, the best examples are not the agricultural societies that provided the basis for industrialization but the foraging societies that are so sharply different in the other key themes of control, density, and complexity.

SOME CRUCIAL HUMAN CHARACTERISTICS

In considering how these four themes of control, density, complexity, and mobility play out in different human adaptations, it is also important to factor in some basics of human nature. Human beings have essential, biological features that affect how they adapt to all environments. For example, human beings *age*; what they are capable of changes greatly over the course of their lives. They require enormous care as infants, spend many additional years completing their physical growth, and yet longer in achieving their full intellectual and social development. Any society must account for the different kinds of people of different ages. These people will be categorized in various ways. Sometimes it will be in terms of age itself, but often it will be in terms of generation. People in one's parents' generation, for example, are viewed differently from people in one's own generation or in that of one's children. In some societies all people in one's parents' generation are actually called "mother" and "father." The issue of age in society is thus partly biological but also partly cultural.

Equally important is *sex*. Although societies differ greatly in the extent to which they structure separate male and female roles, it is hard to escape some division of labor based on sex. Women, after all, continue to produce the society's children and tend to have primary responsibility for children during their early years. That responsibility for childcare in the early years is partly biological (nursing, for example) and partly cultural (though changing greatly in recent years). In order to understand any human adaptation to any environment, it is necessary to consider both the biological implications of sex and the more cultural aspects of *gender* roles. In most societies the socially accepted gender roles for women and for men go far, far beyond the basic biological distinctions between them.

It is also important in looking at all human societies to consider the bases on which people group together. Perhaps most important is *kinship*. Human beings require an extensive period of nurturing as they grow, and a strong bond is formed between children and those who take care of them. The initial caretaker for the child is usually (though not always) the mother. That mother/child pair, however, is usually supplemented by a father, producing a *nuclear family*. Ties of kinship, however, go well beyond the immediate nuclear family of father, mother, and child. When children are born, they have not only parents but also grandparents, brothers and sisters, uncles and aunts, and cousins.

Another option for creating links between people involves *location*. People who live near each other come to know each other. Through cooperation, they become friends or work partners. If their fields are irrigated from the same river, for example, they have to agree on how that water flows into each of their fields. In larger societies in which people cannot trace their kin relations, physical location becomes an alternative way to decide who belongs to what group. As location becomes the major basis for political organization, political borders between countries can undermine the kinship connections of those on opposite sides of the border.

One more element must be added to human variation by age and sex and to the organizing principles of kinship and location. That is *skill*. Individual people have different capacities: some have better physical skills; others have the ability to absorb new technical information; yet others are adept at social interaction. Some skills may be innate; some may be learned; most are a combination of the two. Those individual skills are important to the society as a whole, and societies have different ways to recognize relevant skills, to nurture and develop them, and to reward them.

UNDERSTANDING HUMAN ADAPTATIONS

Understanding the relationship of people to their environments hinges on two steps. The first is an appreciation of the specific environment, what it requires and what it permits. What resources are available, and what are the most effective ways to obtain and use them? There may well be options. Thus, for example, a river valley is a good place to hunt and fish, but it is also a good place to grow crops.

The second step is assessing how such basic characteristics as age (and generation), sex (and gender), kinship, location, and skill relate to that particular environment. For example, in an environment that requires great mobility to hunt wild game, the elderly may have a far more limited role than they would in a society that stayed in one place. Gender roles may be flexible in a society in which men and women cooperate in their work, but sharply divided in societies in which men are gone for long periods of time—grazing herds and hunting animals far from home. Location may be an effective basis for social organization in a settled society but a poor basis compared to kinship for societies that are highly mobile over the course of a year.

Having completed those two steps by making a general match between environmental options and constraints on the one hand, and human options and constraints on the other, it is possible to discuss more broadly the material, social, and ideational aspects of any given society. From that discussion it is possible to generalize (but with caution) about the likely tendencies of different adaptations to the environment. There are many issues that might be noted, but nine key items are selected below because they are crucial both to understanding how a society operates and to considering what we might learn from that society. The anthropological record is the broadest knowledge base we have about human beings in their full range of lived experience. We can look to it both to understand what other cultures are like and, through that understanding, to reconsider what we as human beings have been, are now, and can be in the future.

What is the basic division of labor? For example: Are there sharp differences between the work of men and women? Are there differences by age? Are there people with special skills for certain tasks?

What is the importance of territory to the society? For example: Are people's ties to the land very strong or rather weak? Do they feel free to move during the course of the year or perhaps move permanently to another place?

What are the specific kinds of family and kinship ties? For example: Are there large, formal kin groups in the society? Are certain kin more important than others?

How is social conflict resolved? For example: Are there formal authorities to resolve disputes? If people resolve problems without such formal authorities, how do they do so?

What is the degree of equality? For example: Are men and women relatively equal? Are there class distinctions between people who have property and people who do not?

What kinds of religious beliefs do people have? For example: Do people's religious beliefs include the natural environment? Do their beliefs focus on their own ancestors?

Is the society ecologically sound? For example: Does the society do permanent damage to the environment? Does the benefit from using the environment in a particular way match the efforts people put into it?

Is the society secure? For example: Can people make it through periods of seasonal shortages? Are they protected against catastrophic events such as floods?

Is the society prone to peace or war? For example: Does the society have to fight off outsiders? Can it avoid conflict with others?

STRUCTURE OF THE CHAPTERS IN PART I

Each chapter in part I discusses one of the five major human adaptations: foraging, horticulture, agriculture, pastoralism, and industrialism. Each chapter begins with a consideration of the environment in which the people live and their basic strategy in adapting to it. The central questions are what resources are available and how are they used. Each chapter then considers how the basic human elements of age (and generation), sex (and gender), kinship, location, and skill relate to that strategy. For example, what are the implications of age in a horticultural society? How are gender roles structured in pastoralist societies? What is the influence of physical location on ties between neighbors in agricultural villages? The overall emphasis in the early part of each chapter is on how biology, culture, and environment mesh together. The next section of each chapter then addresses the nine questions above about the nature of that society. The questions are the same in each chapter and will be presented in the same outline format. After consideration of these nine questions, each chapter concludes with two brief case examples. They are chosen to represent the variation in how a particular adaptation works under different conditions. A "Sources" section then provides brief suggestions on further readings and film.

What you can gain from these chapters is an understanding of the variations in human societies as they adapt in different ways to different environments. That, in turn, may help you understand what is predictable and what is unpredictable about individual societies. It may also help you consider how alternative human societies might be created with new ways of extracting resources and new arrangements of the human basics of age, sex, kinship, location, and skill. Such a consideration is essential in a contemporary world where political relations are uncertain, social values are changing rapidly, humans are exercising increasing control (and damage) over the global environment, and humans are also increasingly able to modify their own bodies through surgery and genetic editing. The more we are in control of this new world, the more we need to understand what our potential is in managing it. Only the full anthropological record can show us that potential in both its positive and negative aspects.

3

Foragers

Foraging societies rely on what is available in their environment. Although they may have an impact on the environment, they do not make the extensive changes seen in other types of adaptation. Instead, in their search for food, they use the plants and animals that already exist in their environment. They thus exercise relatively limited control over the environment and are spread out in relatively sparse numbers. Their social and cultural organization reflects the opportunities and constraints provided by this adaptation to the environment, especially by its requirement for flexibility and mobility in the search for food—whether by hunting or gathering.

The discussion in this chapter begins with the nature of foragers' relationship to their environment, particularly to the core requirements of mobility and flexibility. The discussion then turns to general social organization with an emphasis on the implications of age, sex (and gender), kinship, and location. The chapter then addresses the nine key questions raised in the previous chapter. Those same key questions will be addressed in all chapters of part I. Likewise for all the chapters in part I, there will be two concluding case examples that show something of the range of possibilities in each kind of adaptation. For this chapter the two case examples are the Mbuti of central Africa and the Yolngu on the northern coast of Australia.

RELATIONSHIP TO THE ENVIRONMENT

Natural environments vary greatly. Human beings have managed to survive and often prosper in environments ranging from the arctic to the tropics, from the jungle to the desert, from good soil to poor, from the mountains to the sea. Foragers respond to what is available in these varied environments. They may hunt anything from the largest animals to the smallest. They may also gather anything from fruits and berries to wild roots and tubers. As they hunt and gather, they will also have to protect themselves from the elements, keep predators at bay, and raise the next generation.

Mobility

These varied environments are often abundant in what they provide—surprisingly so even in such harsh environments as deserts. In most environments there are animals to hunt, nuts and berries to gather, and roots to dig up. Fish are plentiful in rivers and along coasts. Insects, grubs, and worms also have their place—and a nutritious one. However, that abundance is not in a single place but spread out broadly over the land and water. Thus the first requirement for most foraging societies is mobility. The food is not coming to you; you are going to it.

This requirement to go after the food raises two problems. The first is that all the food is unlikely to be in one place. Thus you have something of an organizational problem for the daily food quest: you have to figure out an itinerary that takes you to the different places where the different foods are. The second problem is that you may not even know before the fact exactly where those places are. Whether you are hunting game, finding ripe berries, or locating beehives for honey, you will need to devote time and effort to figuring out what the places on the itinerary should be. You may need to assess your odds carefully. Part of the problem is that what is abundant and good today may be gone or rotten the next. Nuts that are plentiful one day may have been eaten by game the next; berries that were plentiful yesterday may have gone bad—or to the birds—the next. There are also seasonal shifts: fish that run plentifully in spring are absent in other seasons. Thus the requirements of hunting and gathering will vary from day to day and through the seasons. You must be ready to move to get the resources you need.

Flexibility

Even when particular foods are available, they often pose organizational problems in how to gather or hunt them. If there are large numbers of nuts or berries that need to be gathered quickly, it may make sense for people to function like an agricultural labor crew that conducts a harvest of the nuts or berries. In other cases such large group efforts would make little sense. Honey, for example, is usually distributed widely, so the best strategy is to spread people out over a large area to find the hives. If the berry bushes or the nut trees are not in patches or groves, then it also makes sense to spread people out in small groups or as individuals. Thus, depending on the food, people must modify how they work together or separately.

Such demands are especially clear in hunting. Compare, for example, hunting midsize game (such as deer or antelope) in a forest to larger game (such as elephants or buffalo) on the plains. With bow and arrow—or even spear—the hunting of forest game is likely to require stealth, cunning, and patience and is likely to be most successful when done by individuals or small groups. A single person can easily bring down the game, and the presence of other people would probably make the hunt more difficult. In the pursuit of big animals on the plains, the situation is different. Single individuals—no matter how patient, skilled, and tireless—are unlikely to bring down a large animal, such as an elephant, on their own. Here, then, the most efficient hunting method requires a larger group. If the hunt is not for a single animal but a herd, the requirements change again. If the hunt is to be conducted as a drive with the goal of running a set of animals over a cliff, into a pit, or into a net, an even larger number of people will be needed. These people will have to be well coordinated in what will be almost a military maneuver.

The crux of hunting and gathering as an adaptation to the environment is this combination of mobility and flexibility. To utilize the full range of the natural resources in their environment, foragers will have to follow those resources to different places and according to a schedule that will vary across the seasons and often from day to day. Depending on the specific resource, hunters and gatherers may need to work alone, in small groups, or in larger groups. On any particular day, members of the community may find themselves wandering off in small groups to gather scattered fruits and roots, or going out in a large group to take advantage of a big harvest of berries or nuts. Men and women, old and young, might well be cooperating—or they might be separated for different tasks. During any particular season, that range of daily options will also shift. Spring may find men and women cooperating on group fishing with nets. An arctic winter may find men alone at their ice holes fishing for seal. Fall may find all together—men and women, the oldest and the youngest—harvesting acorns.

SOCIAL ARRANGEMENTS

This low-control, low-density adaptation to the environment thus requires great mobility and great flexibility. How would you structure a human society that met these requirements and also permitted the raising of a new generation? The answer lies with how the human basics of age, sex, kinship, locality, and skills are organized.

AGE AND SEX

Age is an essential feature of human biology. People are born, mature physically, learn socially and culturally, and eventually die. For foragers, the crucial problem is that the frequent need to move from place to place requires that people of *all* ages be physically self-reliant. The young are thus encouraged to be self-reliant at a very early age. Carrying them around while gathering, or especially while hunting, is distracting and potentially life-threatening. The alternatives to taking them along are not very good either: leaving children on their own can be dangerous, and leaving a caretaker with them robs the community of an extra pair of hands. Likewise, even the elderly will need to be physically self-reliant. If the entire group moves some distance—which is likely on at least a seasonal basis—the elderly must also be able to move. If people cannot move under their own power and with good speed, they become a serious liability to the group. Although their wisdom may be appreciated, their physical limitations preclude their full participation in the group.

Differences by *sex* are also important in foraging societies. Women are the ones who give birth and, because of breastfeeding, are almost inevitably the primary caregivers for children's early years. Women are thus less mobile in a society in which mobility is important. Much hunting, for example, precludes bringing along small children, so young mothers are likely to be excluded from those activities—especially if they involve extensive time in travel. Furthermore, the group as a whole would want women to avoid any dangers in hunting. Women are, after all, the future of the society. Men are more expendable. In a foraging society, then, one can expect some division of labor between men and women. Men are likely to do the longer-distance and more dangerous part of the food gathering, and women are likely to do food gathering that involves shorter distances, permits the addition of children (gathering berries, for example), and is less dangerous. There is thus a tendency for men to be the hunters and women to be the gatherers.

On the other hand, the core requirement of flexibility suggests that strict distinctions by sex (and by age) can be counterproductive. While the pursuit of some food sources might benefit from a division of labor between men and women, in other cases the inclusion of both sexes is more practical. Thus, while women certainly hunt less than men, they are (usually) not precluded from it when there is a need for a larger group. If a hunt involves chasing animals into a net or over a cliff, for example, women and even children may be included with men. More people produce more noise to drive the animals toward and over that cliff. Conversely, men also participate in gathering. If they are on the move, for example, why not do some gathering along the way? In foraging societies, then, there may well be significant overlap of tasks between men and women. Men may be more the hunters and women more the gatherers, yet men also gather and women also hunt.

Kinship and Location

These issues of age and sex suggest something of the character of foraging societies, but they do not fully explain how the need for flexible groups is addressed. Here, however, another basic aspect of human relations suggests an option: the links among people based on kinship. People know who at least some of their relatives are, and it makes sense that they should draw on those relatives for the tasks at hand. If a hunting party is needed, who better to trust than a relative? Thus *kinship* is likely to be important in foraging societies. On the other hand, the different tasks required on different days and in different seasons may require different numbers of people and different skills. One older aunt might be a good companion in a search for a beehive—since she can read the forest signs very well. Yet on another occasion, a set of cousins might be a better choice: for example, to go berry picking. You already know where the berries are, need more people, and your cousins are just more fun. So although all kin are important, the dictates of foraging suggest that you might want to keep your options open about exactly which kin to use for which task.

Kinship is also the basis for the relatively small residential kin groups among foragers. For procreation the old-fashioned way, it takes two adults: one female and one male. It also makes sense to keep that couple together for child-rearing since both are invested in the child's well-being. In foraging societies it also generally takes two for daily life, especially when there are children. If there is some difference in what men and women do—what resources they can produce—then a man or woman alone lacks access to the resources produced by the other sex. In a foraging life, that lack can be decisive. So the basic residential kin group in most foraging societies is the nuclear family: husband and wife need each other for daily life, as parents they need each other for the children, the children need the parents, and the society needs the children.

Another basic aspect of human society is *location*. Human relationships are often built from ties of shared locality. For hunters and gatherers, however, mobility limits the effectiveness of ties of locality. A move in camp means that a former neighbor may not be a neighbor anymore. The relationships that last through such geographical moves are those of kinship. Move two miles—or a hundred—and your brother is still your brother, your mother still your mother. Blood ties carry well over distance; ties of locality less so. Thus with a foraging society that depends on mobility, kinship is a far steadier basis for relationships. Shared locality is not unimportant, but unless those living next door are your kin, you probably cannot count on them as well as you can count on kin.

THE NATURE OF SKILL

The final core human characteristic is *skill*. There are three crucial aspects of skill in foraging society. First, most skills need to be held by virtually all people. If the size of daily task groups is so variable and the tasks are so flexible, everybody needs to have most of the basic skills needed to survive, including extensive knowledge of the environment. Second, most of these skills are apparent to everybody else. People's skill levels are public knowledge from daily observation. There is little that is hidden about people in foraging societies. These people know you and you know them. Third, the need for special skills (beyond those held by everybody) is generally task specific and temporary: a good leader for a hunting party one day, a knowledgeable healer the next day, perhaps a prophet at a time of uncertainty, and certainly a midwife. In foraging societies, then, all people (or at least all men and all women) are learning much the same skills, know quite objectively how good they are at different tasks, and, when they do have special needs, seek out somebody they know and who has demonstrated that specific skill in the past.

NINE KEY QUESTIONS

Overall, then, foragers interact with a largely natural environment that requires them to be mobile and to be flexible in group size and composition, depending on the task and the season. The basic relations of age and sex reflect that as do the reliance on kinship, the relative lack of reliance on ties of locality, and the transparency of people's skills. The answers to the nine key questions about this adaptation follow from those key characteristics and appear below in the format that will be used throughout part I.

Division of labor. All human societies have some division of labor. In hunting and gathering societies, however, that division is relatively simple and task oriented. There are important differences between men's and women's work and between people at different stages of their lives. There are also likely to be a few specialized roles. However, the varying requirements of the day and season suggest the need for flexibility. Thus the division of labor is likely to be neither harsh nor rigid.

Territoriality. Because resources are spread out over a large area, foragers are highly mobile. They may return to a favorite area but, even then, they may well have to make new shelter. There is thus no sharp commitment to a particular piece of territory or to the improvements made to a particular piece of territory. Instead, foragers are likely to have a diffuse commitment to a broad range of territory both on a daily and seasonal basis. This gives them some advantages over people who are tied to place and to property that cannot be easily moved from place to place.

Kinship. Foragers are largely organized on the basis of kinship ties. The need for frequent moves puts the emphasis on the nuclear family. A man and a woman are not only a reproductive unit but the smallest group that has access to most of the basic skills of the society. The need for larger groups on some occasions, however, suggests the need for a broader pool of kin from which to draw as needed. The result of these two pressures is residential emphasis on the nuclear family combined with flexible relations with a broader range of kin.

Social control. Because foragers have shifting needs from day to day and season to season, it is vital that they be able to draw on other people for cooperative efforts. It is thus essential to avoid enduring conflicts. When conflicts do arise, they are typically resolved through informal means. Members of a foraging society, after all, know each other well, interact on a daily basis, and are frequently kin. They can thus talk problems through. Since people are mobile, there is also the possibility of avoiding conflict by going somewhere else for a while, letting issues cool, and then returning later. Good time for a fishing trip.

Equality. While there is some division of labor in foraging societies, all people need to have roughly the same skills to survive in the environment. That implies a basic equality. That basic equality of skills is enhanced by the fact that people generally have equal access to resources. More game, more plants, and more space are usually available. Access to equivalent resources is a solid basis for equality. The result in foraging societies is usually a general equality among women, a general equality among men, and at least a relative equality between men and women compared to the sharp stratification by sex and gender that will be seen in other kinds of environmental adaptations.

Religious beliefs. The religious beliefs of foragers—as of all people—are highly variable. Yet two central points stand out for foragers. First, they live close to the natural world and are in constant interaction with it. This tends to be associated with a sense that there is spiritual power in nature itself. Second, since foragers are self-reliant and relatively egalitarian, their access to the spiritual world is likely to be personal, rather than mediated through others.

Ecological soundness. Foraging societies make good ecological sense. They rarely deplete the environment since their very survival depends on the environment continuing to replenish itself. Since they depend on a wide variety of food sources, their effect on any one resource is likely to be limited. Furthermore, this relationship with the environment also works well for the people. Studies of the time spent in the food quest by foragers indicate relatively modest expenditure of effort. At its best, foraging is thus an adaptation that is hard neither on the environment nor on the people.

Security. Although many foraging societies have been pushed to extinction by other societies, on their own terms they are relatively secure. The pressure they place on the environment is usually low, and the environment itself thus remains as their "surplus." Their reliance on a broad range of food sources makes them relatively immune to the disappearance of a single food source. That also creates a diet that is nutritionally well balanced. Nevertheless, since food resources are usually not spread evenly across the year, foragers may face scarcity during some seasons.

External conflict. Since foraging societies have a broad territorial range through which they move, they may well come into contact with other groups. Since they have little valuable property to defend and can generally find other sources of food, such contact does not necessarily lead to serious conflict. The foragers have the option of moving on. This does not mean that foragers are always peaceful. Because of their mobility, they can be effective raiders if they so choose or if their usual resources are taken by others. Nevertheless, foraging societies probably have more options for peace than do the societies to be discussed in later chapters.

CASE EXAMPLE—THE MBUTI: IN THE FOREST AND OF THE FOREST

The Mbuti are often described as "pygmies" in early accounts. They live in the central part of what is now the Democratic Republic of the Congo, formerly Zaire, and have been badly affected by the war and turmoil through that region in recent decades. From preturmoil accounts, however, we know that they lived in relatively small groups that varied over the course of the year in size and location. Sometimes they moved out into clearings, where they were, at least temporarily, much like the horticulturalists to be described in the next chapter. Yet they also moved from those clearings deep into the forest to gather fruits, berries, and nuts, and to hunt. Hunting relatively small animals—such as antelope—was sometimes a solitary pursuit for men armed with bows and arrows. Usually, however, men cooperated in

Spear fishing in a Sri Lanka lagoon (Credit: Patrick Morrow/Shutterstock)

small groups. On other occasions, larger groups of men and women beat the bushes, driving animals forward into nets. That flexibility in group size and composition is perhaps the most distinguishing feature of foraging societies.

Flexibility in group size and structure was matched by a relative equality of the Mbuti. All had access to roughly the same resources of the forest, and all lived roughly the same lives. The frequent movement resulted in few material possessions—by definition no more than they could easily carry. Their houses were constructed rapidly from available materials, especially the large *mongongo* leaves that were used in overlapping fashion, like tiles. There was a clear division of labor by sex: men did the majority of the hunting, and women did the majority of the gathering. Women were also in charge of "the home." If there was a leak through the *mongongo* leaves during the night, it was they who had to get up to fix it. Yet there was also much overlap in tasks. Men sometimes gathered, and women sometimes helped in hunting. The result was a relative equality and mutual ease between the sexes.

The feelings of the Mbuti toward their environment were positive and deeply held. Although they lived deep in a forest that the neighboring villagers viewed with distrust and fear, the Mbuti saw the forest as a place of light and beauty. The forest was imbued not only with life in the natural sense but also in the spiritual sense. If things were bad, they only needed to wake up the forest, which was innately good. The Mbuti love of song was directly tied to the forest. The *molimo*, the trumpetlike instrument that accompanied their singing, was heard as the voice of the forest. The Mbuti and the forest thus sang together.

The Mbuti still survive, although in a shrinking forest and an area of ravaging civil war. (Credit: Sergey Uryadnikov/Shutterstock)

One of the first things the Mbuti did when they began to accept Colin Turnbull—who went to live with them a half-century ago—was to cut lines in his forehead and place dirt from the forest floor into those cuts. That simple ritual—conducted extemporaneously with a razor, much to Turnbull's chagrin—meant that he now carried the forest with him and would inevitably return to it. Such a mixture of blood and dirt, implanted within the body, remains a powerful image of the union of people with their environment.

CASE EXAMPLE—THE YOLNGU: FORAGING, DREAMING, AND RECONCILIATION

"Yolngu" means "people" in the languages used by the aboriginal peoples along the northern coast of Australia. Prior to colonization, they—like other aboriginal Australians—created their living by foraging from an often difficult land. Along the coast where the Yolngu lived, however, were bountiful ocean resources: crab, squid, octopus, whale, cuttlefish, stingrays, and sea cucumber—the last such a valuable delicacy that in precolonial times, fleets of ships from Sulawesi (in modern Indonesia) would come each year to trade for them. The importance of the sea was marked in all aspects of Yolngu lives—even in such personal names as "Stingray," "Squid," and "Coral Reef." In addition to the sea, there were also marshes and swamps (with crocodiles whose skins would become an important trade item) and freshwater streams and springs with yet other food resources. Life on the coast was thus less harsh than on the interior. Population density was correspondingly higher and life more settled. With a settled life, technology was more developed because, among other reasons, there was less need for tools to be easily portable. The Yolngu, for example, used a wide variety of nets and fish traps.

The social life of the Yolngu was elaborate. Society was divided into two major marriage groups with numerous clans. Religious life was rich and strongly integrated into daily life. Spiritual forces could be seen both in the living animals of the sea and in the marks on the land made by the beings who existed at the beginning of time. Central to religious life was what is usually translated as *the Dreaming*, a kind of reenvisioning of the world as it originally was. That reenvisioning permits the contemporary world to be reformed and reordered according to that primal world. What emerges in the Dreaming is thus "a charter of absolute validity" that allows people to stand outside current events (to see them for what they are) and to "find some purpose in the whole human situation."[1]

The Yolngu did not live an isolated life. They were actively interacting with other peoples. Their experience with traders from Sulawesi was reflected in their technology (for example, the ready availability of iron). It was also reflected in their Dreaming. One particular being who emerged in the Dreaming was Birrinydji, the man of iron, who represented both the Yolngu and the Sulawesi traders who visited them each year. Here was a being who could bridge the divide between aborigines and outsiders. As Ian McIntosh studied the general nature of *reconciliation* in Australia between whites and aborigines, he found that the Yolngu had in Birrinydji their own indigenous basis for cooperation with outsiders. While the new masters of Australia might, like the Sulawesi traders, have great material resources and wealth, still there was a bond between them and the Yolngu, a spiritual charter through which reconciliation could be pursued. Sometimes this Yolngu view of reconciliation was portrayed in graphic ways. Thus one Yolngu leader devised a new flag for a united Australia that included on it both the Union Jack and a picture of Birrinydji. If both the indigenous people and the *balanda* (the nonindigenous people) were bound together through Birrinydji, then other more practical kinds of reconciliation could also take place. Adoption was one such option. The Yolngu would adopt Australian *balanda* into their clans, giving them a full Yolngu social identity. The person adopted, in turn, could be a valuable ally for the Yolngu by helping them navigate the broader Australian society.

---

1   W. E. H. Stanner as quoted in Ian S. McIntosh, *Aboriginal Reconciliation and the Dreaming* (Needham Heights, MA: Allyn and Bacon, 2000), 38–39.

As McIntosh observes, the situation of the Yolngu is not typical of Australian aborigines. The Yolngu were spared the worst of the bias of Australian policy toward indigenous groups. They retained much of their land when other aborigines were losing theirs. Their children were not taken from them when other aborigines saw their children disappear into government-run boarding schools that separated them socially and linguistically from their parents—what has come to be called the "stolen generation." In addition to being spared such problems, the Yolngu also had the advantage of previous experience with the broader world. Thus when Australian society moved toward reconciliation with indigenous groups, the Yolngu were able to make a strong contribution to that process. Their contribution had much to do with practical matters, but it also rested on a spiritual view of the world that was broad enough to encompass black and white, forager and farmer, Yolngu and *balanda*.

SOURCES

Hunters and gatherers have generated great interest and great debate among anthropologists both in terms of their contemporary lives and in terms of what they suggest about early human societies. Much of that debate has been about the relative importance of meat and plants to their diet and the relative contribution to the food search by men (who do the majority of the hunting) and women (who do the majority of the gathering). Good summaries of the range of foraging adaptations are provided in Robert L. Kelly's *The Lifeways of Hunter-Gatherers: The Foraging Spectrum* (Cambridge University Press, 2013) and Robert L. Bettinger's *Hunter-Gatherer Foraging: Five Simple Models* (Eliot Werner Publications, 2009). Or try browsing the *Cambridge Encyclopedia of Hunters and Gatherers*, ed. Richard B. Lee and Richard Daly (Cambridge University Press, 2004).

For the Mbuti, the classic source, and still an excellent volume for class use, is Colin Turnbull's *The Forest People* (Touchstone, 1968). As an alternative, Elizabeth Marshall Thomas's *The Harmless People* (Vintage Books, 1989) considers the related !Kung, who live not in the forest but in the great Kalahari Desert. That book can be supplemented by any number of excellent films on the !Kung. The Yolngu example comes largely from Ian S. McIntosh's *Aboriginal Reconciliation and the Dreaming* (Allyn and Bacon, 2000). Two useful comparative sources on more traditional aborigine society (including the Yolngu) are W. H. Edward's *Traditional Aboriginal Society: A Reader* (Paul and Co., 1998; 2nd ed.) and Ian Keen's *Aboriginal Economy and Society* (Oxford University Press, 2004). The 2000 feature film *The Yolngu* (Australian Children's Television Foundation) uses an all indigenous cast in exploring coming of age in contemporary Yolngu society.

4

Horticulturalists

Horticulturalists often use the same plants and animals as do hunters and gatherers. However, there is a fundamental difference. Horticulturalists take increased control. They rearrange natural resources into a more convenient, productive, constructed environment: the garden. Plants and usually some animals are domesticated, meaning that they are brought within human control; the "wild" plants and animals are tamed. The basic logic of horticulture is thus different from that of hunting and gathering. Increased control can produce very good yields and permits a far more settled lifestyle and increased density of settlement. That, in turn, has implications for the complexity of social organization.

As in the previous chapter, discussion begins with the relationship of the people to the environment. The central considerations will be how soil, water, and sun are managed; how plants are supplemented with the domestication of animals; and how the limits of the horticultural system sometimes force the people to move on to new territory. That is followed by consideration of the basic social arrangements in horticultural societies, with emphasis on the increasing complexity of social relations and the way kinship systems are used to manage that complexity. Then, in turn, the same nine key questions posed in the last chapter will be addressed (division of labor, dispute resolution, ecological soundness, and so on). The two case examples for this chapter involve the Trobriand Islanders, a settled horticultural people living off the east coast of New Guinea, and the Hmong, a highly mobile people of highland Southeast Asia (many of whom have moved to North America as refugees).

RELATIONSHIP TO THE ENVIRONMENT

People who live close to the natural environment readily notice the diversity of plant life. They learn from their own personal experience and from that of other people that certain plants are edible, where those plants grow, and how they grow. They will certainly note that some plants thrive with more sun and others with occasional shade; some grow best in wet ground while others do better in drier or better-drained soil. They will see some young plants sprouting from other older plants or growing where seeds or nuts have dropped. They will probably also note that plants do especially well when they have the benefit of nutrients such as decaying vegetation or excrement.

With such observations, people can consider how the way plants grow can be duplicated and even improved through human intervention. One important advantage of doing so is to locate plants more centrally, thus avoiding the constant daily and seasonal movement that characterizes foraging societies. If people can grow the plants—if they can duplicate nature—then they can also decide where those plants will grow. It may also be possible to improve the way the plants grow. The new central location of the garden can be chosen or improved to maximize control of sunlight, water, and soil.

Sun, Water, and Soil

On a small scale, managing the three elements of sun, water, and soil might not seem difficult. But there are potential problems, and many of them are serious. Too little *sun*, and plants will not grow; too much sun, and they may wither and die. Exposure (north, south, east, or west) may be crucial. Fields with an eastern exposure, for example, receive morning light but less afternoon heat than fields with a western exposure. Preservation of some shade may also be essential. This issue of sunlight is relatively easy to resolve in many cases. In forested areas trees can be cleared for more sun or partially preserved for some shade. It is even possible to create the proper kind of sunlight for particular crops: morning sun, for example, but afternoon shade. *Water* also presents problems and often more intractable ones: too little water or too much water may be fatal to the plants or sharply affect yields. The choice of site will be important but so also will be accuracy in predicting when rains will come. Flooding and drought remain great dangers. Finally, good *soil* is essential. Although the consistency of soil is important, the more crucial issues involve such nutrients as nitrogen, potassium, and potash. In some cases soil is naturally rich in these nutrients. In other cases animal droppings can have a good effect on soil that is not itself very fertile. Many horticulturalists use one fertilizer that is excellent at leaching rapidly into the soil. It is ash. Why not, then, burn the forest, thus simultaneously clearing the land, letting in light, and laying in some good, fast-acting fertilizer just before you plant your crops?

SLASH AND BURN

Many horticulturalists use exactly this "slash and burn" type of cultivation, which is technically called *swidden*.[1] They pick an area of forest that is in a good location and conduct a controlled burn. These controlled burns clear out the undergrowth but usually leave the larger trees. Those can either be cut down or—perhaps with some additional pruning—left in place. The burn leaves a layer of ash that leaches into the ground fairly rapidly. The field is then ready for planting. Sometimes horticulturalists plant only a few crops, but usually they plant a wide range of crops, which mature at different times. Thus the gardens are not like most agricultural fields in which a large crop has to be harvested at one time. Instead, different crops become available at different times and can be harvested as needed or as desired. Some root crops—such as manioc—may survive for long periods of time in the ground and provide a useful food reserve if other, more desirable foods are not available. Depending on the crop, the process of planting may involve little more than scattering some seeds, sticking a piece of a root in the ground, or poking a hole in the ground with a stick (usually called a *dibble stick*), dropping in a seed, and then kicking some dirt over the hole. These gardens may require some weeding, but since the crops get a head start in the newly cleared fields, that weeding is usually quite limited. Some effort up front thus yields a garden that will last for many, many months with relatively little need for upkeep.

BETTER CROPS; MORE PIGS

Horticulturalists thus rearrange nature into gardens over which they exercise some control, particularly in preparing the ground and planting the crops. As they do so, they can also often improve those crops. They see which plants grow the best and can select seeds or roots from those for the next year. Furthermore, since they are now more settled in one place, they can also domesticate some animals. After all, if they have created their own rearranged nature in the gardens, why not have animals too? Animal excrement is useful on the fields, and the animals benefit from grazing on the remains of the fields after crops have been harvested. Pigs are a particularly good choice. They are good scavengers, are good to eat, and can bulk up nicely as a sort of walking food reserve. That is why pigs are such an important ceremonial food in horticultural societies and often the best measure of a person's wealth and worth.

---

1   The term *swidden* derives from the old English word for "to singe."

Soil Exhaustion and Moving On

The slash-and-burn version of horticulture has much to recommend it. As long as the burn is controlled, there is little damage to the land, and the fields will eventually regenerate. The gardens themselves are an efficient combination of a wide range of foods in a better, more convenient location. That combined and convenient location means that people can live a more settled life. That increasingly settled (or *sedentary*) life permits domestication of animals that, in turn, permits a more predictable access to protein and an effective food reserve "on the hoof." There is, however, one fundamental limitation in this system. The fertilizer that makes all this possible begins to lose its value over time. The effect of the ash will be strong in the first year, less so in the second year, and in continuing decline thereafter. It will be a long time before the forest regenerates enough for a second burn. In some cases it may be possible to rotate the fields around an enduring village. However, if fields are more scattered and it takes longer to reach them, it may be time to move on to an entirely new area and begin again, abandoning the old gardens to their regeneration.

Horticulturalists, then, extend their control over nature by selecting particular plants and animals, domesticating them, and rearranging them into a system of gardens. The result retains some of the advantages of foraging, especially a diverse diet and a lack of environmental damage, but adds some new benefits. Relocating plants to a garden provides much convenience in the daily round and the possibility of a settled life. It also provides the basis for larger populations and increased density. The limitation lies with the length of time that the fields remain productive. Lacking full control over water and especially lacking alternative fertilizers, horticulturalists may well have to periodically sacrifice their settled life for a move to new territory.

SOCIAL ARRANGEMENTS
Increased Complexity of Social Arrangements

Horticulturalists' expanded control over the environment has important social implications. Since food is now more centralized in the gardens, horticulturalists are not required to be as mobile as hunters and gatherers. They do not need to move as far on a daily basis, and they do not usually need to shift residence with the seasons. Thus the foraging requirement for small, mobile groups does not apply. The steadier, more repetitive pace of horticulture also reduces the requirement for flexibility in group size. The requirements for this more sedentary society—aside from the possibility of large-scale moves in search of new fields—are thus different. A more settled social order is needed. Furthermore, because gardens are so productive and so centralized, they also permit greater density of people. That, in turn, increases the complexity of social relations.

A more sedentary lifestyle also permits an increase in material goods that would be too cumbersome for foragers. Houses are likely to be more elaborate. There are fences for gardens, pens for animals, and more tools of all kinds. There is thus more physical *property* than there is for foragers. The gardens themselves are property, and their harvests belong to those who planted the fields, not to anybody who happens to wander by. And, of course, there are the pigs. All these kinds of property may be good and valuable, but they can also be sources of conflict. They can be an especially complicated source of conflict when the owner of the property dies. Property inevitably raises the issue of *inheritance*. When somebody dies, who gets the gardens? Who gets the pigs? More property means more problems.

In horticultural societies, compared to foraging societies, there are more people living together, living together more closely, and having more to argue about. One result is potential conflict. Yet horticultural societies also require cooperation. Burning the fields, for example, needs to be a group effort. The labor may be done by the young, but the practical experience of the older people is also needed to manage the burn and to synchronize it with the rains. If nothing else, everybody needs to be available in case—despite all precautions—the fire starts to get out of control. Cooperation is also needed to resolve the many kinds of conflict that can arise: who has the right to the best land, who decides when and where to move the entire village, whose pig wandered into somebody else's house and perhaps ended up as their dinner?

Expanded and Formalized Kinship Systems

Horticultural societies thus face the problems of social organization that we ourselves face. The result, for them as for us, is a society with more formal structure and leadership than for foragers. That structure and leadership, however, do not usually involve the creation of separate economic, social, political, and religious organizations. Instead, horticulturalists largely rely on the framework of *kinship*. For kinship to work as such a framework, it must be far more defined than it is among foragers, with their nuclear families and rather diffuse set of other kin.

Such a more defined kinship system must have rules about two issues: first, who is related to whom and, second, who has authority over whom. Part II of this book will discuss kinship in more detail, but some brief comments are needed here on these two issues of *membership* (who belongs to what group) and *seniority* (who's in charge among the members of the group). In terms of membership, the basic options are that a child belongs either to the group of the father or to that of the mother. The former is *patrilineal* (the line of the father); the latter is *matrilineal* (the line of the mother). Both systems work well in establishing membership, and both systems are used by many horticultural societies.[2] In terms of seniority, age and generation are crucial: those of an older generation have priority over those of a younger generation and, within generations, those who are chronologically older have seniority. The relative seniority of men and women is more variable. In patrilineal societies males have clear seniority over women, often even if the women are older. In matrilineal societies women's status is at least relatively higher.[3]

With rules for membership and seniority decided, kin groups provide an effective means of social organization. Everybody knows in which group they belong and who within that group has the authority to make decisions. Such a structure has added value in horticultural societies that have to make large-scale moves. Horticulturalists may live in relatively clustered settlements, so the possibility of developing ties based on close residence—as neighbors or covillagers—exists. However, if the entire village is to move, then kinship is a better and surer basis for that organizational task. Kinship, after all, is portable and enduring. Neighbors may come and go, but blood ties continue. In those horticultural societies that move the most frequently, there is often a particularly complex and formal kinship organization—usually patrilineal as with the case example of the Hmong at the end of the chapter.

NINE KEY QUESTIONS

Overall, horticulturalists have some sharp differences from foragers. With increased control over the environment come increasing density and increasing social complexity. Most of the complexity is organized through formalized and extended kinship systems. These kinship systems have clear rules about who belongs to what group and who has relative seniority within those groups. Such kinship groups are especially helpful in addressing one of the most distinctive features of many horticultural societies: the alternation of a rather sedentary lifestyle with periodic moves in search of new fields. These key characteristics of horticultural societies reappear below in response to the usual nine key questions.

Division of labor. In horticultural societies, the division of labor is usually sharper and more extensive than it is in foraging societies. Differences between men and

---

2   Both systems also have a difficult point of transition when people are married. Should one of them give up their membership in their own kin group to be part of the spouse's group? This issue is discussed in some detail in part II. It is a critical issue and the one that makes patrilineal and matrilineal systems rather different in tone even though they are so similar in their logic.

3   The relative age of the connection in the prior generation may also be a factor. For example, it may be more important that your mother was older than her sister than that you are younger than your mother's sister's child (your matrilateral parallel cousin). You may be considered "senior" because your mother was.

women may be heightened, particularly if some gardens are relatively distant and tended by men and others are nearer and tended by women. In such cases the daily lives of men and women become more separate. Beyond the basic divisions of gender and the increased importance of seniority, there is likely to be relatively little in the way of special roles in horticultural societies except for such tasks as healing, midwifery, and contact with the spirit world.

Territoriality. Horticulturalists are linked to the land they cultivate and the places in which they live. However, since the exhaustion of the soil may force them to move on, those links are not unbreakable. Horticulturalists have often had the opportunity to move on to new land that has not been claimed by others because it is too mountainous, inhospitable, or remote. As long as there are such new opportunities, horticulturalists are not likely to be highly territorial. In that sense they, like foragers, have the option of moving on. If they do not need to move, by contrast, they may develop ties to territory more similar to the agriculturalists of the next chapter.

Kinship. With increased density of settlement comes an increased need for cooperation and coordination. Kin are the most reliable resource for such mutual assistance, and large kin groups make practical sense, especially if they are tightly organized. Furthermore, since there is considerable property (pigs, houses, tools), there is also a need for rules about how that property is passed on when people die. Again, a tightly organized kinship system has distinct advantages—whether matrilineal or patrilineal. Overall, kinship among horticulturalists tends to be central to the society, highly structured, and extensive.

Social control. In horticultural societies there are more people with more to argue about. Land itself may not necessarily be of long-term value, but current gardens are. Disputes that arise may be resolved between the people themselves but, if not, resolving them will be of direct interest to their broader kin groups. Leaders of those groups may not have any formal authority beyond their status as kin seniors, but that is likely to be enough to enforce their decisions. Social control through kinship is the hallmark of most horticultural societies.

Equality. With horticultural systems, the access to resources is no longer as broad as it is for foragers, but, unless land is scarce, people have the option of starting their own individual gardens. There is thus relatively equal access to resources and, in that sense, relative equality among people—or at least equality among men and equality among women. The degree of equality between men and women, however, is highly variable in horticultural societies and has much to do with the structure of the kinship system. In matrilineal horticultural societies, for example, women's access to resources is likely to be enhanced—thus producing a greater relative equality between men and women. In patrilineal societies the prospects for relative equality between men and women are dimmer.

Religious beliefs. In horticultural societies people are likely to acknowledge a wide range of spiritual forces. With larger kin groups that are more formally structured, ancestors are likely to be remembered more intensely and for longer periods of time. Since horticulturalists are dependent on the land for its productivity, spirits of the land are also likely to be important. Rain is crucial, so spirits of the sky may well be important. In most cases religious specialists will be people who have had individual experiences with these spirits. In some cases, however, a person's formal status may be important: for example, contact with the ancestors is likely to be the responsibility of the senior person in a kin group.

Ecological soundness. Horticulturalists make a variety of changes to their environment, but the effects are usually not permanent. The burning of the forest itself does little (if any) long-term damage, and the fields will generally regenerate into forest. Horticulturalists may even aid this process by leaving some midsize trees alone, thus speeding that process of regeneration. As with hunters and gatherers, there is the added benefit of relatively moderate working hours. Studies of the time used for growing food suggest that horticulturalists are efficient and thus have the benefit of considerable time for other activities, such as a more elaborate ritual life. Horticulture thus appears as a sustainable adaptation from the perspectives both of the environment and of the people themselves.

Security. The horticultural adaptation is generally quite secure. The cultivation of a range of crops, for example, provides good nutritional balance. That range also provides protection against the loss of any single crop from disease or theft. Even if someone or some animal raids a garden, for example, the raider is likely to take only what is currently ripe. The result may be hunger today but not famine tomorrow. The range of crops (especially root crops that will last a long time in the ground) and the domestication of animals (especially pigs) provide good buffers against lean times.

External conflict. Horticultural societies may be of some interest to outsiders for their land (which may have other uses for intensive agriculture) or because of some of their property (especially food that can be seized, such as pigs). But that interest is usually limited. It makes little sense, for example, to take over somebody's gardens if you then have to wait around for each crop to ripen. From the horticulturalists' point of view, there is also limited value in conflict with outsiders, unless there is a strong need for additional land for gardens. Conflict thus tends to be small-scale: raiding, for example. The greatest danger lies with the arrival of agriculturalists and industrialists who, as the next chapters will demonstrate, can make more intensive use of the land.

CASE EXAMPLE—THE TROBRIANDERS: MATRILINEALITY AND WOMEN'S WEALTH

The Trobriand Islands, which lie off the coast of Papua New Guinea, became famous as a result of Bronislaw Malinowski's writings from the period when he was stranded there during World War I. Those writings are viewed by most anthropologists as the first major demonstration of the value of long-term field work. Malinowski was enormously lucky in finding himself in the Trobriands. The elaborate *kula* exchange of ritual necklaces and bracelets is one of the most influential images in anthropology and sociology.[4] The Trobrianders also have a rich array of magical practices, a relatively relaxed standard of sexual relations among the young, and a matrilineal kinship system. Malinowski made the most of these advantages in his writing. The Trobriands made Malinowski famous.

The Trobriand Islanders are horticulturalists. Their main gardens are for yams and use a modification of the swidden (slash-and-burn) system. The undergrowth is cut first, along with the branches of the larger trees. Then the undergrowth and branches are burned, providing the nutrients for the soil. Compared to other crops, yam cultivation is relatively demanding. The soil needs to be worked well before planting, the plants need to be staked as they grow, and a solid fence must be built around the fields to keep the pigs out. Most of the work is done by men. However, during the most difficult part of the preparation of the fields, men and women work together—often putting in long days.[5] These yam gardens, much like the agricultural fields to be discussed in the next chapter, produce a large harvest of a single valuable and storable crop. Piles of yams in a field are the sign of a good garden; piles of yams in a storage house are a sign of wealth.

The yams are a crucial element in a complex Trobriand system of social interaction. Although men do most of the work in the yam gardens, neither the gardens nor the yams belong to them. The gardens are owned by women, who inherit them from female relatives. Since the women own the gardens, the product of those gardens also

---

4   The *kula* exchanges are discussed later in the text in more detail. The central image is of two kinds of objects being exchanged in opposite directions around a large circle of societies trading with each other for both practical and ritual reasons. One set of ritual objects goes clockwise in this circle and a different set of objects goes counter-clockwise.

5   Although these yam gardens are the main gardens, there are also general household gardens, which, unlike the yam gardens, are the responsibility of women.

Trobrianders perform a welcome dance for a National Geographic expedition ship. (Credit: Mickrick/iStock)

belongs to them and thus not to the men who till their gardens. As it happens, this is a matrilineal society, and the men tilling their fields are their brothers. Even married men work the fields of their sisters and give them the yams that they produce. Those yams are consumed by their sisters and their sisters' families, which include their husbands. A man, then, does not eat the yams he himself has produced, but eats the yams that belong to his wife and were grown by her brothers. This is a typically Trobriand way of doing things. Instead of eating their own food, they find a way to make food itself into a social interaction that weaves people together in ties of exchange.

Annette Weiner, who studied the Trobriand Islanders some fifty years after Malinowski did, analyzed these patterns of kinship and gender in detail. While men were hardly insignificant in this matrilineal society, women did have their own wealth and it was often considerable. When death occurred, it was women who organized the large mourning feasts and competed for status based on their wealth. That wealth was evidenced by how much they could give away. Gifts included large numbers of bundles of banana leaves and skirts they produced themselves or obtained from others in trade. In their quest for status, their husbands were obliged to aid them. After all, a Trobriand man's identity rested on the women in his life: his mother and sisters for the land they had, his wife for the food produced on her land by her brothers, and his mother's brother for any formal titles he might inherit.[6]

6   The importance of the mother's brother will be explained in more detail in the chapters on kinship. The crucial point to remember is that men *are* important in matrilineal societies, but which men are important differs from the case in patrilineal societies. The male authority figure for children in a matrilineal society is the mother's brother rather than the father.

The Hmong cross many national borders—here some Hmong children are in the highlands of northern Vietnam. (Credit: Bradley Audrey Ralph/Shutterstock)

CASE EXAMPLE—THE HMONG: PATRILINEALITY AND AN AMERICAN WAR

The Hmong are a highland people whose ancestral home lies in China but who have moved over the centuries along the mountains into Southeast Asia, particularly into the mountain areas that form the boundary between Vietnam and Laos. In the mountains, the Hmong are shifting cultivators who use controlled forest burns to clear the fields and plant a variety of crops. Their practices mirror those described earlier in the chapter. Unlike the Trobriand Islanders, however, the requirement for new fields has been a persistent demand in the rugged highlands and resulted in frequent moves.

Given the great mobility of the Hmong, it is not surprising that the Hmong kinship system is extensive and highly structured. That tight structure has been valuable to the people in managing their movement along the hills and in interacting with other horticulturalists in those hills and with the politically stronger agricultural peoples of the lowlands: the Thai, Lao, and Vietnamese. As is true of most tightly organized kinship systems, the Hmong base kinship membership on the relationships among men—and their patrilineal system includes large clans that have powerful leaders. A Hmong man is thus who he is because of his relations to, and descent from, other men.

The Hmong are in some ways relatively typical shifting horticulturalists. However, as is almost always the case in the contemporary world, the Hmong do not live in isolation. Two outside factors—one economic and one political—greatly changed their fate in the second half of the twentieth century as they were drawn into the wider world. The economic factor was opium. Horticulture far off in the mountains is an ideal way to grow a crop that requires considerable attention by its growers but considerable isolation from political authorities. Thus the Hmong, who themselves used opium only moderately, found themselves with an extremely valuable cash crop that drew them into economic exchanges with the wider world. The political factor was what Americans calls "the Vietnam war" and what the Vietnamese government calls "the American war." Suddenly, these isolated areas on the border between Laos and Vietnam became strategically significant. Since the highlands were inhospitable territory for both Americans and Vietnamese, they inevitably turned to the highland groups as military proxies along the border. To the Americans, then, the Hmong were a well-organized people in a strategically located area. Consequently, many of them were recruited into the war on the US side. They worked particularly with the US Central Intelligence Agency in the so-called secret war and were, by all accounts, very effective fighters.

With the collapse of the American-supported government in Vietnam in 1975, the situation of these Hmong shifted. Once again, their strong kinship system came into play as they migrated, this time not for new fields but for safety across the Mekong River in Thailand. There they remained for several years until a combination of pressure from Thailand and lessened hope for return to Laos propelled many of them to the United States. The fate of the Hmong in the United States has not always been a kind one. Despite some attempts, it has generally not been possible for them to re-create their horticultural lifestyle. Yet the ability to rely on a kinship system—rather than a territorial arrangement—has enabled them to move in large numbers from place to place in the United States just as they moved from place to place in China and Southeast Asia. Large numbers of Hmong, for example, moved from their initial resettlement locations in the United States to California's Central Valley, with more modest numbers moving to such places as North Carolina and Minnesota. These migrants of the mountains thus become international migrants to the United States and then regional migrants within the United States.

SOURCES

There is some debate in anthropology about the extent of the difference between horticulture and agriculture. I have emphasized the difference because the two have become such clearly competing ecological adaptations in many parts of the

world. For more general discussions of horticulture and agriculture, see Daniel
G. Bates's *Human Adaptation Strategies: Ecology, Culture, and Politics* (Allyn and
Bacon, 1998) and Bernard Campbell's *Human Ecology* (Aldine, 1995). The issue is
addressed in most full-length anthropology texts.

For the case examples, see Geddes's *Migrants of the Mountains* (Clarendon Press,
1976) as the standard source on the Hmong in Southeast Asia. It may also be useful
to look at Gerald Hickey's *Sons of the Mountains* and *Free in the Forest* (both from
Yale University Press in 1982) for information on other highland groups in that
same general area.[7] Anthropologists have been greatly interested in the experiences
of the Hmong in America. Anne Fadiman is not an anthropologist, but her *The
Spirit Catches You and You Fall Down* (Farrar, Straus, and Giroux, 1997) is exceptionally well written and so intuitively synchronized with anthropological interests that it is well worth reading (I regularly used it in upper-division classes). The
film *Becoming American* (1982) is somewhat dated but provides a sound introduction to the Hmong in Southeast Asia and in the United States. For the Trobriand
Islands, there is a particularly useful pairing of the classic works by Malinowski and
the more recent work of Annette Weiner. For the former, *Argonauts of the Western
Pacific* (Waveland, 1984) is the most frequently read, but *Coral Gardens and Their
Magic* (Routledge, 2001) gives more of the detail of horticulture itself. Weiner's *The
Trobrianders of Papua New Guinea* (Holt, Rinehart, and Winston, 1988) is essential
reading, and the film *The Trobriand Islanders* (from the *Disappearing World* series)
is very engaging (Weiner was the consultant for the film and appears in it). Some
sense of Malinowski in the Trobriands is provided by the Malinowski segment of
the *Strangers Abroad* film series.

---

7   It may be worth noting how important highland Southeast Asia has been in shaping the views of anthro-
    pologists about how relatively large, kin-organized groups can shift in political identity and action—as
    seen particularly in Edmund Leach, *Political Systems of Highland Burma* (London: Athlone Press, 1986).

5

Agriculturalists

Agricultural societies share many of the features of horticultural societies. Both horticulturalists and agriculturalists rely on a range of domesticated plants and, usually, some domesticated animals as well. For both, the domestication of plants permits a more settled life and a greater density of people. Compared to horticulturalists, agriculturalists have increased control of water and fertilization and tend to specialize in a few major crops. Their increased control and specialization yield a surplus that can support additional economic and political activities in the agricultural communities themselves and in the towns and cities that they support with this surplus. Since agricultural land is very valuable, issues of ownership are crucial. If land is limited, the result is likely to be social difference between those with land and those without it.

As usual, the discussion in this chapter begins with the basic relationship to the environment, for which the crucial considerations for agriculturalists are specialization in particular crops and the increase in yields from the land. The succeeding discussion of social arrangements focuses on the importance of land, how kin and territorial ties are interlinked, and the need for some kinds of specialized labor. Following the discussion of the nine key questions, the chapter concludes with two case examples: Vietnamese villages practicing wet rice cultivation and an Aztec cultivation system that, despite the absence of a plow, had high and reliable yields.

RELATIONSHIP TO THE ENVIRONMENT

The story of agriculture involves the same elements as the story of horticulture: a range of plants that benefit from varying amounts of sunlight, water, fertilizer, and attention. The difference between the two involves agriculturalists' sharply increased control over nature. In a swidden garden, for example, a variety of crops are planted with an initial layer of fertilizer from the forest burn and hopes for rain at the right time. With agriculture, however, there is increased specialization in particular crops, longer-term solutions to the need for fertilizer, and increased management of water resources.

SPECIALIZATION IN CROPS

Peoples' experience with a range of crops shows that some grow more easily than others and often require little human care after planting. Some grow more reliably, producing roughly equivalent yields year after year. Some provide a bigger payoff at harvest, store more easily without rotting, and respond more dramatically to increased water, fertilizer, and sun. Finally, some crops respond more readily to attempts to domesticate them. A crop that is hardy, reliable, easy to grow, storable, and improvable is thus a good candidate for specialization. The result of that quest for an ideal crop is usually a grain. In the Middle East it was wheat or barley; in the Americas it was maize; and in Asia it was rice.

WATER, FERTILIZER, AND A PLOW

With predictable rains, horticulturalists and agriculturalists may fare rather well. But the unpredictability of rainfall may cause crops to fail from lack of water, from too much water, or simply from the timing of rainfall. One more promising situation occurs along the banks of rivers, where seasonal flooding may bring water to fields. Later, receding water levels drain the fields. If annual flooding replenishes the soil, such seasonal flooding can spare even horticulturalists the need to rotate fields. The crucial improvement in agricultural societies is to control this flooding and extend its benefits farther up and down the river, and ultimately to fields more distant from the river. Upstream, the development of irrigation channels enables water to be brought to new fields that were not previously flooded. Downstream, irrigation dikes help control the timing of the flooding and reclaim agricultural land from the marshes that characterize river deltas.

In terms of fertilizer, the initial ash from a swidden horticultural burn provides an excellent immediate supply of fertilizer, but the effects wear off. Rotation of fields without burning is an option. However, if the land is to be used year after year with high productivity, additional fertilizer is essential. One solution is to put organic material on the soil and let it leach in. Previous crops or animal droppings will help. However, a more convenient solution lies with the river flooding already described. Water flowing downstream contains silt. When the river water flows out onto land along the riverbank, it slows down, and the silt then settles out of the water. As irrigation systems control the direction and speed of the flow of water, they also provide an important new mechanism for ensuring the continuing fertility of the fields.

One further improvement completes the agricultural picture. Although flooding of fields may bring in fertilizer, getting the fertilizer into the soil requires additional effort. Hoes may be used, but that is a slow and laborious process. If soil is compacted as a result of a long dry season, hoeing may be impossible. With a plow, the ground can be tilled more thoroughly. As a result, both fertilizer and air can be worked deep into the soil. Since a plow is hard to pull (although human-powered plows do exist), draft animals such as oxen, horses, and water buffalo are highly valuable.

LARGER, MORE PREDICTABLE YIELDS

The implications of these improvements in water, fertilizer, and plowing can be illustrated with data on yields from three different ways to grow rice. In Southeast Asia, rice is a good crop and is grown in a variety of ways. It can be grown in exactly the kind of swidden gardens described in the previous chapter. It can also be grown by plowing fields and then scattering ("broadcasting") the seed. Finally, it can be grown through the more intensive process of growing seedlings in a special plot of land then transplanting the seedlings into larger fields, where the amount of water can be controlled. That water not only seeps into the soil but also physically supports the rice plants as they grow. The fields and connecting ditches and canals also provide a good aquatic environment in which fish and microorganisms grow and further enrich the soil.

Historical data from Southeast Asia show that all three types of cultivation are productive. *Swidden* cultivation produces a yield of about .65 tons per acre—though this declines over the years as the soil becomes exhausted. *Broadcasting* is less productive in yield per acre (.59 tons) than swidden but requires only about a fifth of the effort to plant each acre. It is thus far more efficient *in terms of human labor*. Furthermore, with broadcasting it is not necessary to rotate fields. Finally, *transplanting* requires somewhat less work per acre than the swidden system[1] but results in a yield per acre (.98 tons) that is far higher than either of the other two systems. It

---

1   If all infrastructure costs—especially maintaining irrigation systems—are included, transplanting takes much more effort than the swidden systems.

is thus, by far, the most productive system *in terms of land*.[2] Far more people can be fed from each acre of land, and population density can thus be much higher. Based on historical data, the swidden system provides a population density of 31 people per square mile, the broadcasting system a density of 255 people per square mile, and the transplanting system a density of 988 people per square mile.

The key to understanding the enormous potential of agricultural production is the way fields can be used year after year to produce a crop that is hardy, reliable, relatively nutritious (at least in raw calories), and storable. Increased efforts on irrigation and drainage systems produce higher yields. Additional labor increases per-acre yields. Transplanting, for example, requires much more labor but produces a larger harvest. The result is that intensive agriculturalists win the numbers game. There will ultimately be more of them on any given piece of land, at least if that land can be cultivated at all.

SOCIAL ARRANGEMENTS
THE IMPORTANCE OF LAND

As agriculturalists improve the fields and the fields respond with better yields, there is little incentive to move and much to stay. Since good agricultural land can produce indefinitely, people do not have to leave their land. Consequently, existing agricultural land is unlikely to become vacant and available for other people. The only ways people can expand fields are to find or develop new land, or to displace other people from their fields. There are usually limited options for moving somewhere else and starting again. Much of the world's best agricultural land has been taken up for over 2,000 years, some of it for much longer.

The value of agricultural land and what it produces shape the social relations of agricultural societies. Since land is so valuable and in limited supply, the potential for conflict is high. To avoid such conflict, rules are needed about who has what rights to what land. Concerns about *ownership* and *rights of use* also affect *inheritance*. Since the improvements to a field are permanent, then the rights to use the fields should be permanent as well. That requires a mechanism to transfer those rights to the next generation. Within families, it must be decided which of the children gets how much of the land. In the broader community it must be decided how much of the land should be collectively owned and how that collective ownership should be passed on over time.

The nature of the agricultural product from this land also has implications. The harvest for a grain crop, for example, is a large quantity of food that is storable and

---

2   Contemporary yields are higher by a factor of two to three. That reflects improved rice strains and the increasing use of fertilizer.

transportable. Most grains dry readily and will remain viable for long periods of time (at least with modest attempts to avoid moisture during storage). These bags of grain can be used for a variety of purposes. Some are saved for consumption, but, at least in a good year, some can also be exchanged for other foods, for tools, for paid labor to help at harvest time, or perhaps even to buy land from someone whose fortunes have fallen. This agricultural *surplus* is also of interest to those outside the immediate area. A raiding party might find it of interest, as would outsiders trying to build their own economic or political power. These bags of grain could support their communities and feed their workers. The development of agriculture is thus linked to the growth of cities and political states. It is the misfortune of agriculturalists to be locked into land that is valuable both to them and to others. They live out in the open, usually in accessible river valleys and plains, and are vulnerable precisely because they cannot leave their land. Their friends and their enemies know exactly where they are, the value of what they produce, and the long-term value of the land that they inhabit.

AGE AND SEX; KINSHIP AND LOCALITY

This settled lifestyle, increased population density, valuable property, and storable, transportable agricultural surplus have important implications for social relations. At the most basic level, relations of age and sex, generation and gender, tend to be different from those in horticultural and foraging societies. Although men and women may, on occasion, work together, agricultural life tends to create separate male and female work domains. The increasing importance of property may force a distinction between male and female rights to ownership and inheritance. If women own the land and pass it to their daughters, then female prerogatives will be protected. However, the density of agricultural settlement argues for structured kin groups, and, as will be discussed in part II, patrilineal systems tends to be more tightly structured than matrilineal ones, and they tend to predominate in agricultural societies. Relations by age also tend to become more rigid in agricultural societies. The elders of the community not only accrue practical and social knowledge that makes them the experts, but also hold the property on which everyone depends. As family elders, they will hold private land; as village elders, they will control access to public land. Differences by both sex and age are thus usually sharper in agricultural societies than among horticulturalists or foragers.

Relations of kinship are important in all societies, but in agricultural societies the size of kin groups is likely to be greater and their formal structure more rigid. After all, there is greater population density and thus a greater need for social control and organization. Since people do not move, large numbers of kin are likely to reside in close proximity. These kin groups help organize and protect their members. They also frequently serve as the framework for the broader community. Such ties of blood are often complemented by ties of locality. Neighbors are crucial. Their cooperation is essential in developing land, allocating water to it, and managing times—such as harvest—when extra labor is needed. Irrigation systems, for example, almost always require collective effort to build and collective restraint to administer in an equitable way.

Specialization of Labor

In some ways the issue of skills is similar in agricultural societies to the other societies already discussed. As with foragers and horticulturalists, virtually all people must be proficient at a common set of skills. In agricultural societies, however, this issue of skills has two wrinkles. First, because of the density and social complexity of agricultural societies, and the frequent need to deal with outsiders, some special assigned political roles are likely to be necessary—such as village head or chief. Second, because of the increasing technological complexity of agricultural life, there is also a need for people trained for particular jobs, whether that involves iron working, trade, accounting, or engineering. Agricultural villages will need plows, goods from other places, a way to record information for tax and inheritance purposes, and the ability to develop and maintain irrigation systems. Fortunately, the production of an agricultural surplus makes it possible to support people engaged in such nonagricultural activities.

NINE KEY QUESTIONS

Overall, agriculturalists not only adapt to a given environment but actively change that environment through their clearing, plowing, irrigating, and cultivating of the land. They are highly sedentary, and the increasing yield from the fields permits ever-denser settlement. Ownership of land is a crucial issue that is likely to introduce social divisions into the society. Kinship tends to involve large and tightly structured groups. However, since nonkin living nearby are also important, other kinds of social organization develop based on ties of locality. The dense, sedentary settlements of agriculturalists thus show mixed and overlapping ties of blood and land. The productivity of the land produces increased and more reliable yields, but the land may be owned by only some of the people. Those without land may not benefit very much from those better yields. These characteristics of agricultural societies underlie the answers to the nine key questions posed in each of these chapters.

Division of labor. In agricultural societies the division of labor is sharper and more extensive than in foraging or horticultural societies. Differences between the sexes may be heightened as the flow of activities and rights of ownership shift. Differences in activities and property rights may also sharpen by age. There is also increased division of labor by occupation. At the village level, specialized occupations may be only part time: for example, a farmer who also repairs tools or does some trading in the agricultural off-season. Beyond the village, the possibilities brought by an agricultural surplus almost inevitably result in such workers as builder, engineer, tax collector, soldier, bureaucrat, or teacher. For such tasks an ad hoc emergence of competence over time is often inadequate. Instead, people will have to be specifically trained for jobs either through formal education or apprenticeship.

Territoriality. Good agricultural land is an immensely valuable resource. It will not be easily or often given up. So agriculturalists are strongly linked to the land. Indeed, the resource of land may become more valuable than the resource of people. More people can be easily produced, but more land cannot. With agriculture, then, people are locked into the land. The land is not only their past and present, but their future as well. Without ownership of land, one's children will be destined for poverty and one's family line for possible extinction. Only the combination of poor land at home and new opportunities elsewhere is likely to dislodge agricultural people from their homes. The discovery of the Americas by Europeans was one such new opportunity. Such opportunities are rare.

Kinship. With increased density of settlement comes an increased need for cooperation and coordination. Kin remain the most reliable resource, and large kin groups make especially good sense in agricultural societies. Furthermore, with increasingly valuable property comes the need to determine who will have future rights to that land. As a result, kinship tends to be more strictly defined in terms of status and inheritance rights, and usually takes on a patrilineal slant. Kinship among agriculturalists is thus important, highly structured, and very extensive—*unless* new land elsewhere lures people away and the advantages of the mobile nuclear family again become relevant.

Social control. There is much to argue about in agricultural societies. Land is valuable, and there are also valuable houses, agricultural tools, and draft animals. Disputes that arise may be resolved within the kin group. However, since there are likely to be different kin groups in agricultural communities, some bridging authority is needed. Frequently, this will be a set of village elders drawn from the main families of the village. They are likely to have some formal authority and some ability to enforce their decisions. One of the functions of those elders will be to deal with outside political forces that wish to control the local community for their own purposes.

Equality. With agricultural systems, the access to resources is no longer as broad as it is in foraging and horticultural societies. Land—especially good, improved land—is likely to be in short supply. Consequently, some people will have more and better land; others will have little or no land. Those without land may work as laborers or tenants on the land of those who are better off. The result is social inequality between the "haves" and the "have-nots." However, the "haves" usually need the "have-nots" for extra labor, so attempts will be made through personal patronage or communal land to ensure that all members of the community have at least a marginal livelihood, that there is some kind of "safety net."

Religious beliefs. In agricultural societies people are likely to acknowledge a wide range of spiritual forces. With kin groups in the same place over many generations, the ancestors have a lasting presence. The fields they improved, the houses they built, and their burial grounds are a part of the everyday scene. Spirits of land and water are also likely to be important. In larger agricultural societies that are more formally organized, there may as well be spirits representing the political order. Finally, since agricultural societies are inevitably involved in trade and in state formation, they will be exposed to major world religions and may convert to them.

Ecological soundness. Agriculturalists, unlike foragers and horticulturalists, make permanent changes to the land through plowing, irrigation, and deforestation. The breaking of the land by the plow (as in the American West) can permanently change the landscape as once stable grasslands become subject to erosion by wind and water. Irrigation systems in river deltas result in the loss of wetlands; conversion of highland areas to agriculture creates soil runoff. Agriculture also imposes burdens on people. Agriculturalists usually work harder on a daily basis than do foragers and horticulturalists—though they may benefit from a lull in work after harvests are in.

Security. One of the great advantages of agriculture is its ability to improve yields in quantity and predictability. However, as population increases and the infrastructure becomes more complex, the potential for further improvement becomes more limited. Furthermore, there is risk that any failure in the system will have catastrophic implications. Drought and flood take a horrendous toll, even in modern-day agricultural societies. Crop disease can also have catastrophic effects. Specialization in a single crop puts the system at great risk. The Irish potato famine of the mid-nineteenth century was an extreme example.

External conflict. Agricultural societies are of interest to outsiders because of the value of their land and because they produce a harvest that is storable and transportable. Bags of grain can feed other people: enemies, friends, and one's own government. Agricultural societies are also easy to find and relatively easy to control. It is virtually impossible for agricultural societies to be free from external conflict. As they become part of state systems, they will be acutely aware of the trade-offs between the protection they receive from the government and the taxes they must provide to that government.

CASE EXAMPLE—VIETNAMESE VILLAGES: A LONG HISTORY BUT A NEW FRONTIER

Agriculture in northern Vietnam's Red River delta developed some 2,500 years ago along the middle stretches of the river, where there was some annual flooding but not marshy conditions that required extensive drainage. The first capital of an identifiable Vietnamese state (Van Lang) was built along this stretch of the river. From these initial footholds for rice cultivation began a long process of expansion. Hanoi, the later capital, is located down the Red River from the original settlements at a bend in the river that requires dikes to avoid flooding. Only in recent centuries was the land fully drained further downstream in what was originally a marshy delta.

The Vietnamese villages that developed in the Red River delta of northern Vietnam were compact and usually surrounded by tight bamboo hedges. The production from the fields, supplemented by vegetables from gardens and a smattering of chickens and pigs, permitted a well-settled life. For these villages there was generally a kinship nucleus, with the leaders of dominant kin groups functioning as village elders. Those kin groups were patrilineal. The orderly inheritance of land was important to the national government, and formal laws governed it. For example, the legal codes specified that sons were generally to receive equal shares of the land while daughters and widows were to receive half-shares. The codes even specified that a portion of the inherited land was to be put aside as "incense and fire" money for the veneration of the ancestors. That portion went to the eldest son. Although kinship was crucial to village structure, the village was an important social unit in its own right. The village had its own spiritual entities represented in temples, and its own founding ancestors were recognized by tablets in the village community hall. Prominent in that hall would likely be the royal edict that had officially established the village many centuries in the past. The village also usually held some land collectively on behalf of all the villagers. That collective land was used to support general village responsibilities, including being offered to poor landless villagers to help sustain them. The welfare of all was crucial to the village.

In Seoul, Korea, rice plants are brought to the central part of the city so people can remember their agricultural roots. (Credit: D. Haines)

Over the centuries, the density of the population in the Red River delta increased. As new land was wrenched from the Cham (in central Vietnam) and then the Khmer (in southern Vietnam), many people from the heavily populated areas in the north sought new lives farther south, first along the narrow coastal strip that links northern and southern Vietnam, and then in the vast delta of the Mekong River in the south. In these southern areas, villages took on a different shape. They were not compact, secluded, and bounded by bamboo hedges, but instead were strung out along the rivers and canals that formed the region's irrigation and transportation system. Indeed, it was not always easy to tell where one village's territory ended and another began. Sets of houses would spring up in the middle of fields, at a road crossing, or a waterway. These small hamlets would then be organized together as a village. The scenic elements of rice, houses, tombs, and clumps of trees are similar in the north and south, but in the southern areas have a distinctly more scattered and open look.

In the south as in the north, kinship was vital in village structure. Sometimes hamlets and sections of bigger villages in the south might include neighbors who were all close kin. Yet in other places, neighbors might not be kin. For these Vietnamese, life in the newer areas on the frontier often meant smaller family groups and a less rigorous imposition of formal kinship rules. There is an interesting parallel between

The ancestors and their tombs are always close in rural Vietnam. In this mostly Buddhist country, there are Christians as well. (Credit: Joel Carillet/iStock)

the North American experience of moving west to new lands and the Vietnamese movement south to new lands: the famous "Go West, young man" of the American nineteenth century and the "southern advance" (*nam tien*) of Vietnamese tradition. In both cases the new frontier societies were noticeably more open and flexible.

Neither the dense, long-settled villages of the Vietnamese north nor the string-like frontier villages of the Vietnamese south existed in isolation. Whether it was the dikes that prevented flooding of the Red River in the north or the extensive canals that controlled the backwash of the more tidal Mekong in the south, it was public work and oversight that enabled the cultivation of rice. Villages might have significant autonomy, but they were also subject to central government control. The national government, for example, frequently had a hand in designating the village chief, since that person had to function both as representative to the central government and as a representative from it to the local community. The national government—whether under the ancient Vietnamese kings, the current socialist republic, or the former South Vietnamese republic—always understood the crucial importance of villagers as farmers, but also as tax payers, as workers on dikes and canals, and as soldiers.

CASE EXAMPLE—THE AZTECS: AGRICULTURE WITHOUT A PLOW

In the Americas a wide range of foraging and horticultural societies existed before the Europeans arrived. Central to most of those societies was maize. Extensive archaeological work has documented the domestication of wild maize and its gradual development from small ears to large ears similar to what we know today. None of these societies was agricultural in the specific sense of using plow agriculture, yet several developed exactly the kinds of state systems and urban settlements that we generally associate with fully developed agricultural systems. A consideration of how they managed that process is instructive.

The most fully developed of these agricultural systems in the New World were those in central Mexico. Both before and during the Aztec period, fields were capable of producing good yields of maize continuously over time, thus meeting the essential requirements of fully sedentary life and creating a significant agricultural surplus. Historical accounts suggest that these agricultural systems reached their fruition under the Aztecs in roughly the two centuries prior to the Spanish conquest. Tenochtitlán, the major Aztec city, was itself situated on an island in the middle of a large lake. The city had to be protected from floodwaters from other lakes during the rainy season, so a ten-mile dike was built along the exposed eastern side of the city. The agricultural fields themselves were often along the borders of the lake, and were extended by reclaiming shallow waters with sod brought from the mainland and soil piled up from the shallow waters themselves. The result was a series of ditches that separated field areas from canals that both brought in water and allowed transportation. Most of the maize was germinated in seedbeds (often on floating rafts) and then transplanted to the fields themselves.[3] At least for the Lake Texcoco area of Tenochtitlán, the salinity of the water also required aqueducts that brought in freshwater from higher land. Farmers thus had to simultaneously resolve problems of drainage, protection against saline water, and access to fresh water.

The fields, called *chinampas*, depended on multiple kinds of fertilizer. Some nutrients could be expected from the water itself. To these were added organic fertilizers in the form of water plants growing in the canals. These plants were applied as a heavy mulch. Finally, mud from the bottom of the canals, which contained good nutrients (including fish feces), was placed on the fields. Even without a plow, the resulting soil was sufficiently rich and replenished frequently enough to permit good, continuous yields. As in the rice paddies of Asia, the fields not only used water but became a full aquatic environment in which fish and microorganisms could grow and further enrich the soil.

Some *chinampas* continue to be used in selected areas today, particularly in Xochimilco, a few miles south of Mexico City. The Mexican government has spent considerable money to protect them and maintain what is a significant tourist draw,

---

3   Those floating seed beds are probably the cause of the erroneous impression that the fields themselves were floating.

including for ecotourists interested in the *chinampas* as a model for sustainable, organic agriculture. The fields are still productive, though they have increasingly been turned toward growing flowers. Their effectiveness is clear from that current use. Historical records also document how efficient this plowless agriculture could be. At the time of the Spanish arrival, Tenochtitlán was one of the world's major cities. It supported an extensive nobility, a wide range of craft specialists, a large army, and a highly developed religious system, including an estimated 5,000 priests. Only with this agricultural base was the Aztec state able to sustain a large government and extensive military campaigns.

SOURCES

The literature on agriculture ranges in topic from the origins of agriculture (and horticulture) to the very latest in genetically engineered crops. For the classic discussion of the political implications of agriculture and irrigation, see Karl Wittfogel's *Oriental Despotism* (Yale University Press, 1957). Lucien Hanks's *Rice and Man* (University of Hawaii Press, 1992) remains a wonderfully accessible introduction to the subject (and is the source for the Southeast Asian data on rice yields); Robert McC. Netting's *Smallholders, Householders* (Stanford University Press, 1993) provides a broad overview of the implications of intensive agriculture; and a visit to the website of the International Rice Research Institute (www.irri.org) will yield a wealth of information about the enormous improvements in yields that have been made for the world's single-most-important food crop.

For further information on the Vietnamese case example and for the essential review of early Vietnamese society, see Keith Taylor's *The Birth of Vietnam* (University of California Press, 1983). Gerald Hickey's *Village in Vietnam* (Yale University Press, 1964) remains the crucial source for the southern areas of the country, and it is also a good reminder of how technically detailed anthropological *monographs* can be. An interesting compilation of work on various northern Vietnam villages is provided in *The Traditional Village in Vietnam* (The Gioi, 1993), and a more extended single case example is provided in Hy Van Luong's *Tradition, Revolution, and Market Economy in a North Vietnamese Village, 1925–2006* (University of Hawaii Press, 2010; rev. ed.). For the Aztecs, a good introduction is provided by Frances Berdan in *The Aztecs of Central Mexico* (Wadsworth, 2004; orig. 1982), and more detailed discussion is available in Michael E. Smith's *The Aztecs* (Wiley-Blackwell, 2011, 3rd ed.) and Richard Townsend's *The Aztecs* (Thames and Hudson, rev. ed., 2000). Miguel Leon-Portilla's *The Broken Spears: The Aztec Account of the Conquest of Mexico* (Beacon Press, 2007, rev. ed.) taps Aztec accounts for a more inclusive assessment.

6

Pastoralists

Pastoralists provide an interesting comparison to other adaptations. Unlike horticulturalists and agriculturalists, who expand and refine the use of plants, pastoralists expand and refine the use of animals. Usually choosing one or two animals that are hardy, herdable, breedable, and the source of multiple products (meat, milk, bone, skin), they organize their lives around the lives of those animals. In many ways they are like foragers, except that they are foraging for food for their animals and not for themselves. Like foragers and many horticulturalists, they are frequently on the move as they search for food and water for their animals. Finally, like agriculturalists, pastoralists have property that has great value to others. Unlike an agricultural commodity, however, their herds are mobile and can be led away by would-be thieves. Constant vigilance is required.

In reviewing the characteristics of pastoralist societies, this chapter emphasizes the logic of building a life based on the needs of animals. The first section of the chapter concerns the pastoralist relationship to the environment with particular emphasis on the value of animals and the way they are managed in herds. The next section is a consideration of social arrangements, particularly the issues of mobility, property, and skills. That, in turn, is followed by a discussion of the nine key questions asked in each of these chapters of part I. The first case example at the end of the chapter is about the Nuer, a cattle-herding people living in the southern Sudan. The second concerns the Mongols, herders from central Asia who swept out of their homeland to create the world's largest empire.[1]

RELATIONSHIP TO THE ENVIRONMENT
THE VALUE OF ANIMALS

The logic of pastoralism is in one vital way similar to that of agriculture. Pastoralism hinges on specialization. Just as agriculturalists tend to specialize in a few crops, so pastoralists specialize in a few animals. The reasons for choosing the crops or animals in which to specialize are also similar. For agriculturalists, a good crop is one that is hardy, responds well to cultivation, and has a good yield. Likewise, pastoralists seek an animal that is hardy, breedable, and has a good yield.

Above all, an animal should be *hardy*. It should not easily sicken and should be able to endure at least some hardship. It should be hardy both when young and as an adult. An animal should also be *breedable*, both in the general sense that it breeds easily and in the sense that improvements in the stock can be made by controlling that breeding. The animal should also have a good *yield* much as a crop does. Furthermore, it helps if the animal has a good yield in a variety of ways. Animals can be eaten as meat, of course, but their ability to provide dairy products may be more important because it is a continuing product, not a one-time reckoning. Animal by-products such as skin (hide) and bone are also important as clothing and tools respectively. Many pastoralists go beyond those basics to other by-products: hair as brushes, blood as food, urine for washing (since it is sterile). Finally, there is one additional requirement. The animal must also be *herdable*. Intelligence may be less important than docility, but it might be nice to have both.

For pastoralists, the search for a good animal usually narrows to a choice (or combination) of three animals: cows, goats, and sheep. All three are good as meat; all three provide dairy products; all three provide hair and hide. The value of wool is an extra bonus for sheep; horns are a bonus for cattle. This does not mean that pastoralists are restricted to these animals, but other animals usually serve to help in managing the core animals. Thus in raising cattle, it would be good to have another animal that would help you herd the cattle (thus the value of horses). In raising sheep, riding a horse might also be valuable, but a well-trained dog might also do well. Horses and dogs are thus part of the human team that herds the animals—and, in many societies are specifically off limits as food.

---

1   There is some debate about whether it was the biggest, largely because there was some autonomy among the different segments of the empire. But the appellation seems fair to me in terms of physical territory and also in terms of percentage of the world population under Mongol control.

Managing Herds

In caring for their animals, pastoralists must come to terms with the environment, not for their own direct needs but for those of the animals. Like foragers, they will probably have to move on a seasonal basis. Those seasons may be characterized by temperature. Thus herds are taken farther up the hills during the summer and back to the valleys during the winter. Sometimes the seasons are characterized more by precipitation. Thus herds move to higher ground in the rainy season and down along the rivers in search of water in the dry season. Even in the absence of seasonal changes, movement will probably be needed to avoid overgrazing the land.

One important factor in pastoralist life is the size of the herds. There are practical advantages in herding relatively large numbers of animals together. There are also difficulties. One difficulty is that during seasonal movements a particular resource, such as water, may be limited. The larger the herd, the more pressure there is on that resource. This poses a central dilemma in the lives of pastoralists: they may not need any particular food or water source all the time, but when they do need it (e.g., water in the dry season), they *really* need it. The result can be, as it was in the American West, that agriculturalists fence off their fields near a river so their crops are not trampled by the herds. The pastoralists might not care about that for most of the year, but during the dry season, when their cattle are thirsty, they might well cut those fences and trample those crops if that is the only way to get the water. That conflict over fencing was a fierce one in the shaping of land use in the western parts of North America.

SOCIAL ARRANGEMENTS

Mobility and Organization

Pastoralism is an adaptation quite distinct from those already discussed. Yet it resembles them in certain ways. Like foragers, pastoralists are almost inevitably on the move, but unlike foragers, their movements are more on the behalf of their animals than for themselves. Like agriculturalists, pastoralists have a useful commodity that may raise covetous sentiments among their neighbors, but unlike agriculturalists, they themselves are mobile and can thus move more quickly and aggressively to protect their interests. Pastoralists are unique in this combination of mobility and large, well-organized groups for herd management and protection. That has important implications for pastoralist society. The high degree of mobility is accompanied by reliance on kinship and, since the need for formal order is high, reliance on patrilineal kinship. More problematic, however, are the pastoralist relations to territory, to property, and to equality.

The Defense of Territory and Property

In terms of *territory*, pastoralists have the challenge of maintaining their rights to use resources at multiple places at different times of the year. They may have settled homesteads during one season of the year (say, winter) but more scattered camps during another season (say, summer). They do not need the summer camps in winter, but they do need to know that the summer camps will be there and available the next summer. They cannot afford to have someone else move into that area during the winter and stay the next summer. Likewise, they may have little interest in a river that is on the way to the summer camps except for a brief period on their path there when their herds are thirsty. They cannot afford to have someone take control of that river during the time they are not there and then deny them water the next year. They must protect their rights to future use of places and resources that may, right now, be far away and of little concern. Likewise, when they are at the summer camp, they cannot afford to have someone move into their winter quarters. Pastoralists must therefore defend places from which they are currently away but to which they will return in the future. In that nearly impossible task, they will need the ability to move rapidly and to work effectively in large groups.

In terms of *property*, pastoralists have a valuable commodity in their herds. That commodity itself is mobile. Most of their money is, so to speak, on the hoof and self-propelled. Theft is thus a constant danger. If some other group is quick enough and daring enough, they can have your herd on its way before you can react. To counter that threat requires an ability to react quickly and in well-organized force. Within one's own group there are also potential problems. Individual herds are likely to be merged at some times during the year. The result may be that it is difficult to tell which animal belongs to which person—or at least to *prove* which animal belongs to whom. That requires not only organization but also trust. You cannot afford to work with anybody who might steal. If anybody does try to steal your animals, it is vital—and usually a matter of personal honor—to make sure they do not succeed or, if they do succeed, that they are punished so severely they will not ever try it again. In the code of the old West, then, cattle rustling is a hanging offense.

Equality and Inequality

Pastoralists tend, in some ways, to be very egalitarian. As men work with the herds, they must rely on each other. Each man must be able to do almost all tasks and, when necessary, to actively help defend the herds from outsiders. This tends to breed a rough equality and independence among men, even though they must also cooperate well together. On the other hand, the nature of the pastoralist life tends to separate men from women during much of the year and to allocate them to different tasks. Men may take care of the herds while women watch the home—and perhaps cultivate some crops. Or men may take care of one set of animals and women the other. In either case men are likely to be more mobile and more often away from any settled homestead. Although such a sharp division of labor by sex does not necessarily rule out equality, it certainly does not help foster it. Thus, among pastoralists, there is often simultaneously a great degree of equality among men yet sharp inequality between men and women.

NINE KEY QUESTIONS

The answers to the usual nine key questions follow from these basic points about the environmental and social aspects of pastoralist societies.

Division of labor. In pastoralist societies the division of labor is minimal in some ways yet sharp in others. Differences between the sexes are often sharp in terms of the flow of daily and seasonal activities. Such differences may also sharpen by age. Men beyond their prime physical years, for example, are likely to have a harder time in pastoralist than in agricultural societies. Aside from such division of labor by age and sex, little other formal specialization is likely to exist except for the more occasional need for healers, war leaders, or prophets.

Territoriality. Pastoralists are in the difficult position of requiring rights to use a broad range of territory. There are likely to be times of the year when resources are limited and pastoralists must have access to them. Thus pastoralists will be committed to the full extent of this territory even though they are only using part of it at any particular time. Pastoralists will be determined in their defense of their rights to use that range of territory. They cannot survive without it.

Kinship. With increased mobility and larger groups to manage the herds, there is a strong need for cooperation and coordination. Kin remain the most reliable resource for that, and large kin groups make practical sense. Since patrilineality provides a surer basis for large and tightly organized kin groups, pastoralists are indeed usually patrilineal.[2] Furthermore, pastoralists have valuable property that requires clarity of ownership and inheritance. A well-defined kinship system also helps resolve such problems.

Social control. There is much to argue about in pastoralist societies. The herds themselves are valuable, and there may also be other kinds of property. Many

---

2   Patrilineality and matrilineality will be compared in more detail in the chapters on kinship. For reasons that will be discussed there, patrilineal systems tend to be more rigidly structured for both men and women. That rigidity of structure has both positive and negative consequences for both males and females.

disputes that arise can be resolved within the immediate group. However, since various kin groups will be interacting during at least some times of the year, some additional authority is needed. This might be a set of the heads of major kin groups working together as a leadership council. There may well also be intermediaries—perhaps religious leaders—who can help arbitrate disputes but who have limited formal authority.

Equality. In pastoralist systems access to resources is relatively similar for most males. Thus pastoralist societies often show remarkable equality among men. Similarly for women. However, the nature of those resources and the need to move frequently tend to create separate lives for men and women. Such separateness does not inevitably cause inequality, but it can have that effect. Although some pastoralist societies have relatively balanced relations between men and women, many pastoralist societies have extremely sharp control by men over women.

Religious beliefs. Pastoralists are likely to acknowledge a wide range of spiritual forces. As with agricultural societies, the importance of large kin groups suggests an important place for the ancestors. On the other hand, the extent of mobility and the rough equality that pervades relations among men suggest the relevance of a more individualistic and universalistic religion—a religion that will travel well. Shamanistic practices are frequent based on individual connections to spirits. Broad-ranging gods or forces (for example, the "eternal blue sky" of the Mongols) are likely. In recent times there has been a tendency for pastoralist groups to convert to Islam and Christianity. Both provide a universalistic vision that travels well and allows for individual access to spiritual help and power.

Ecological soundness. Pastoralists, by definition, need the same resources in the coming year that they have this year. Thus, like foragers, they cannot afford to exhaust the resources they use. In that sense, pastoralism is ecologically sound. Furthermore, the intensive use of animals ensures that there is little waste. In theory, then, pastoralists—unlike agriculturalists—make no permanent, severe changes to the land. Nevertheless, extensive grazing may well cause changes, and overgrazing may occur if herds become too large or are confined to areas that are inadequate for them.

Security. One of the great disadvantages of pastoralism is exactly its specialization. Thus, as with agriculture, specialization raises the risk of catastrophic loss. A drought, for example, may put the herds at risk for water. Even worse, disease can wipe out major portions of the herd. Aside from that catastrophic possibility, and the frequent threat from other human beings, the pastoralist adaptation has much to recommend it. The "surplus" is on the hoof and—at some risk to the future of the herd—can be eaten if needed as a last resort.

External conflict. It is the misfortune of pastoralists to be at risk for two main reasons. First, their herds are valuable. Other pastoralists might wish to take them and may well have the speed and enterprise to do so. Agriculturalists would be interested as well: they have a relative lack of livestock, since their land is too valuable to be used for grazing. Second, pastoralists must protect a range that includes places that may be far away from their current location. If any of their range is suitable for agriculture, for example, they run the risk of permanently losing access to that land. In that kind of conflict with agriculturalists, they will have the initial advantages of speed and organization. But the agriculturalists will, sooner or later, have the numbers.

CASE EXAMPLE—THE NUER: CATTLE ON THE UPPER NILE

The Nuer are cattle herders who live in the upper reaches of the Nile River in the southern Sudan. The twentieth century was difficult for them, beginning with a great loss to the herds from rinderpest, a highly infectious viral disease of cattle and some other hoofed animals. There was also colonial control by the British, and—at the end of the century well after independence—one of the world's longest civil wars that pitted the Nuer and the related Dinka, who had largely converted to Christianity, with the Islamic northern part of the country. That, in turn, has been followed by civil war within the new Republic of South Sudan. These wars have taken their toll on the people, on the cattle, and on the lifestyle that hinged on both. Nevertheless, the basic structure of the Nuer life appears to remain similar to what we know from earlier accounts.

For the Nuer, pastoralism revolves around cattle. The cattle are used for their full range of possibilities: from milk to blood to meat for nourishment, and from hides to hair to bone for tools. The cattle are the focus of much Nuer imagery and the currency through which social arrangements are made. They are also the focus of yearly migrations, which are determined by water: a wet season (that roughly corresponds to our summer) and a dry season (that roughly corresponds to our winter). During the rainy season, the Nuer move to higher ground to avoid flooding. On that higher ground— think of low rolling countryside—the Nuer plant crops and place their cattle in *byres* (corrals). During this time of the year, the cattle are fed rather than let out to graze. After the rains end the rivers begin to recede, and wild grasses grow in the drying earth. At this time, some of the Nuer—especially young men—break camp and move the cattle to lower ground where they can graze and have access to water. As the dry

Cattle on the move in the southern Sudan. (Credit: John Wollwerth/Shutterstock)

season progresses, larger groups of Nuer begin congregating at the places where there is still adequate water. Finally, as light rains begin, the Nuer move back toward higher ground in order to have crops in the ground by the time the heavier rains begin.

These Nuer movements across the land and through the seasons require a variety of social and political interactions. During the wet season, when the Nuer are on higher ground, they live in settled clusters of houses. During the dry season, however, the Nuer first break apart into smaller groups to graze. Those smaller groups are initially male. Later on, the Nuer coalesce into larger groups around water sources. All members—men and women, old and young—are once again together. The Nuer social system must thus be adequate to the demands of relatively dense villagelike interaction in the wet season; more dispersed, and often age-specific and sex-specific, groups in the early dry season; and larger concentrations at the height of the dry season.

The Nuer answer to that call for a portable, flexible, social framework is an extensive patrilineal kinship system. Since the groups vary so much in size and structure at different times of the year, that structure is expansive enough to include all Nuer but also flexible enough for smaller groups to function independently at different times of the year. The size of the resulting kinship framework of the Nuer, which includes hundreds of thousands of people, has generated the phrase "headless government." The argument is that the Nuer kinship system accomplishes many of the purposes of formal government but without any formal political leaders. The flexibility of that kinship framework has also been noted among Nuer who have come to the United States as refugees from the civil war. Although many of them are without relatives in the United States, and without the pastoralist lifestyle of the Upper Nile, they have shown resourcefulness in creating new kinds of kinlike networks—and sometimes in putting their pastoralist expertise to good use as workers in meat-packing plants.

A mixed herd of sheep and goats spills out onto a highway in Mongolia. (Credit: D. Haines)

CASE EXAMPLE—THE MONGOLS: FROM HERDING TO CONQUEST

Most people fly into Mongolia from the south. The days are often clear, and it is easy to see the gap as you leave the relative green of northern China, including inner Mongolia, for the desert. Beyond the desert there are hills and again some sprinkling of color as you land in Ulan Baator, the "Red Hero" city named during the Soviet domination of the country. The city is bustling now with businesspeople from all over the world. Yet even in this rapidly developing city, there are neighborhoods still composed of yurts, the circular felt tents that are the traditional Mongolian homes. If you leave the city, you are more fully in that traditional Mongolia. Herds graze the hills and valleys, and the occasional structures are as often yurts as "modern" buildings.

The herds are large. Mongolians will tell you how many more animals there are in Mongolia than people. And there are many different animals. The largest of the herds are a mix of sheep and goats. They graze well together because the sheep will move on before eating the grasses to their roots. The goats, by contrast, would eat to the roots and destroy the vegetation if left to themselves but, being with the sheep, move on with them before that happens. There are cattle as well, and some yaks. And, of course, there are the horses, and as many horses in Mongolia as there are Mongolians. Without the horses it would not be possible to manage the herds. These are not big horses, bred for speed or power. They are small and very, very tough. The horse races of Mongolia, for example, are not short track affairs, but tests of raw endurance as both boys and girls, men and women, launch on courses that are often around twenty-five miles long. There is now even a 1,000-kilometer Mongol Derby.

With its horses and herds, this pastoralist society is built for mobility, and for mobility over great distances. Pastures here are far from fertile, so the grazing animals have to cover significant distances. The Mongols have a housing structure—the yurt—that can be packed up quickly but is nevertheless sufficient against the bitter cold of Mongolian winters. Flash back in history and you find that people from this area have been flooding out into the rest of Asia and Europe for millennia. Here is a place that in many ways and at many times has been very much at the center of the world. In 1206 began the greatest of the Mongol conquests. At that time, Genghis, one of many competing Mongol chiefs, enlisted the formal support of the other Mongols, became Khan, and embarked on Mongol expansion. Recent climate research suggests that during this period there were unusually good rains and thus food for expanding herds of animals. So the homeland was more than self-sufficient, making his plans far more feasible.

Genghis Khan was a brilliant strategist and methodically expanded his control in all directions. While he relied on his sons as generals, he relied on his daughters as administrators, often marrying them off to local leaders, creating distinctive "son-in-law" kingdoms that were controlled more by his daughters than by their husbands.[3] One daughter went north to Russia, securing the northern border. Another went south first, establishing a Mongol territory on the south side of the desert. From there, the Mongols advanced until they controlled all of China. Their path in that direction only stopped when they faced effective resistance from the Japanese and the Vietnamese. To the west, they extended all the way along what is usually called the Silk Road—although it was actually a set of multiple paths from China to the west. One result was an economic boom as goods now could flow freely from Asia to Europe because of Mongol control of the entire route. The Mongol expansion continued into Europe, with enormous loss of life to those who dared resist. Budapest in Hungary fell to the Mongols, and they were only stopped just short of Vienna.

Eventually the Mongol empire collapsed, though some of its pieces lasted independently. Many reasons are suggested for the collapse: overextended control that made internal communication difficult and environmental changes in the homeland that weakened it. Jack Weatherford suggests another reason: Genghis Khan's success lay in the strong personal and political alliance that he had with his wife

---

3   Genghis Khan actually had many wives and many children both within and outside those marriages. His primary marriage, however, remained strong, and it was the children of the primary marriage who became his main agents for military campaigns and civil governance.

and a set of capable daughters to whom he could entrust control of the inner part of the Mongol empire, thus freeing his (less capable) sons to expand the empire at its perimeters. But later Mongol leaders tended to exclude women and that, he suggests, was their downfall. "Genghis Khan created the nation and inspired it, but the queens gave it life. Like their father, these dedicated queens did not waste time, effort, and emotion building monuments; they built a nation."[4] When the nation later excluded them from power, it unraveled.

SOURCES

Pastoralism is an intriguing adaptation and rather more varied than I have been able to present here. Some sense of the diversity of pastoralism can be obtained by looking at such edited volumes as P. Nick Kardulias (ed.), *The Ecology of Pastoralism* (University Press of Colorado, 2015); John Galaty and Douglas Johnson (eds.), *The World of Pastoralism: Herding Systems in Comparative Perspective* (Guilford, 1990); or Joseph Ginat and Anatoly Khazanov (eds.), *Changing Nomads in a Changing World* (Sussex Academic Press, 1999). A good pairing of case studies might be Fredrik Barth's classic *Nomads of South Persia* (Waveland, 1986) and Dawn Chatty's *Mobile Pastoralists* (Columbia University Press, 1996). *The Kirghiz* (1975), a segment of the Disappearing World series, is a reasonable film introduction to a nomadic group, especially valuable on the nature of political leadership and the implications of being denied the full extent of a traditional migratory range. Those sources will also give a good sense of how pastoralists are challenged in state systems that tend to restrict free movement of herds. When free movement of the herds is restricted, there can be ecological problems caused by overgrazing. For a more recent North American example, see the depiction of Montana sheep-herding in the film *Sweetgrass* (2009).

Regarding the case examples and for the classic discussion of their livelihood and their politics, see E. E. Evans-Pritchard's *The Nuer* (Oxford University Press, 1969). Sharon Hutchinson's *Nuer Dilemmas* (University of California Press, 1996) provides a more recent view of the Nuer, and Jon Holtzman's *Nuer Journeys, Nuer Lives* (Allyn and Bacon, 1999) discusses the Nuer as refugees to the United States. The film *The Nuer* (1971) is a beautiful portrayal of traditional village life. It is long and mercifully free of narration. Even watching a short segment will provide some sense of the physicality of Nuer life. For the Mongols, Jack Weatherford provides a rousing discussion of the great Khan in his *Genghis Khan and the Making of the Modern World* (Broadway Books, 2004), but an even more enjoyable read is his *The*

---

4   Jack Weatherford, *The Secret History of the Mongol Queens: How the Daughters of Genghis Khan Rescued His Empire* (New York: Broadway Books, 2010), 276.

Secret History of the Mongol Queens: How the Daughters of Genghis Khan Rescued His Empire (Broadway Books, 2010). For an interesting discussion of Mongolian shamanism, try *Sky Shamans of Mongolia: Meetings with Remarkable Healers* by Kevin Turner (North Atlantic Books, 2016).

7

Industrialists

Industrialism is a broad label that applies to a wide range of technologically complex societies that have developed in different ways. Technology and society have also changed sharply since the early days of industrialism. Indeed, many people would argue that we are now in a postindustrial society. Nevertheless, certain broad patterns emerge in all these societies that differentiate them from other kinds of human adaptations, including the agricultural societies from which they originally developed. With industrialism, control over the environment is greatly expanded—expanded so much that most of life is spent in engineered rather than the relatively natural environments in which humans originally lived. That extended control over the environment is associated with enormous increases in the density of urban life and in the general complexity of social organization. It is also accompanied by significant mobility as people move from place to place where their labor is needed.

This chapter provides an outline of industrial societies with emphasis on their differences from the other adaptations already discussed. The first section discusses the unique relationship to the environment that characterizes industrial societies—especially their span of control and the mobility of their populations. The succeeding sections outline the social organization of industrial societies and how such societies fare in terms of the same nine questions addressed in previous chapters. The first case example at the end of the chapter concerns China, a country that is now undergoing massive industrialization. The second example is drawn from my own experience and concerns the evolving relationship between people and information technology.

RELATIONSHIP TO THE ENVIRONMENT
RESOURCES, TECHNOLOGY, AND LABOR

Industrialism is a story of new ways of harnessing power and the tools used to do so. Those tools permit the manufacture of more powerful and more numerous products. Those products range from simple consumer goods (clothing, for example) to military goods (better guns and more of them) to machines themselves (from the small ones that run household appliances to the large ones that run nuclear power plants and, increasingly, to the minute nanotechnologies that underlie computerization). These tools radically change the logic of production, but also the logics of exchange and consumption. It is horsepower without the horses, manpower without the men, human control and interaction through non-human means.

The changes wrought by industrialism can be seen in many areas. As an example, compare crop production in agricultural societies with crop production as it develops in industrial societies. In agricultural societies a mix of technology, resources, and labor are combined in the production of the crop. Agricultural societies are not, after all, without technology. They have plows, and those plows usually have iron tips. Somewhere, then, there must be a source of iron, a mining operation to extract it, and a production system to produce the desired tool. The main resource in an agricultural society, however, is land. Improvements to that land—especially with irrigation—make it far more productive. To that improved land and the basic agricultural technology of the plow is added the labor of the people and of their field animals. A distinctive feature of intensive cultivation is that additional labor on the land can produce a bigger harvest. Thus investments in further labor can achieve increased yields.

The situation in agricultural societies is diagrammed in the top part of figure 7.1. Resources (land) are utilized by people (using human and animal labor) through technology (plow) to produce an agricultural crop such as rice, wheat, or corn. If there is more land, productivity can be increased by cultivating that new land. However, most of the good agricultural land was taken up long ago. Further increases in production must thus be through technology or labor. If technology is limited, then increases must come largely through labor. Thus agricultural societies can and do become dense in population. "More people" is the mechanism to have more goods.

An industrialized version of agriculture is possible by changing the relative input of technology, resources, and labor. That alternative is shown in the bottom part of figure 7.1. Technology is the crucial issue. Machinery, for example, can transform the land in ways that human labor cannot. Hills can be leveled, swamps drained, land reclaimed, and water diverted across large distances through canals. The fields

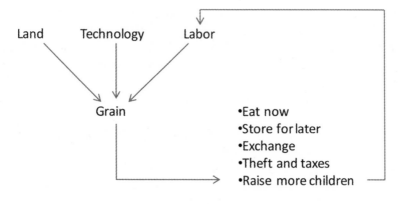

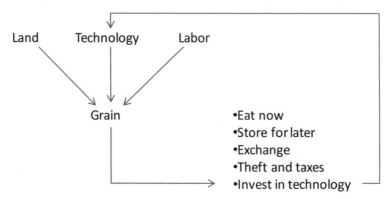

FIGURE 7.1. Two models of grain production

themselves can be made more productive with machine rather than human labor, tractors rather than animals pulling plows. Other technology-derived factors include more productive fertilizers (produced in factories rather than gathered locally) or improvement in the crop itself through research and, ultimately, genetic engineering.

What industrialism provides is not simply a modest change in this formula of technology, resources, and labor, but a huge one. Part of the change has to do with yield: for example, better fertilizers and new strains of crop that can increase yields. Another part of the change involves an increase in the productivity of human labor. If human labor is joined by machine labor (tractors, threshers, harvesters), then far, far less raw human labor is needed, and the human role increasingly becomes one of managing the machines. The net result is that the same fields produce more crops and with only a fraction of the human labor.[1]

The success in increasing production in the fields hinges on increasing production of the new tools needed in the fields. Just as resources (especially land), labor, and technology go together in producing the crop, so they also go together in producing the tools and machines that make it possible to produce the crops. While an iron tip for a plow might be hammered out by a local blacksmith, a tractor and its engine are not going to be produced locally in every community where they are used. Tractor production will occur in more centralized locations that best meet the logistics of moving resources to factories and goods from factories to their consumers. That web of logistics itself becomes increasingly complex and, ultimately, globalized.

SPAN OF CONTROL AND MOBILITY OF LABOR

The changed balance of technology, resources, and labor has many implications. Two are of particular importance for the understanding of human life in industrial societies. First is the increase in the span of control needed for industrial production and exchange. In industrial societies it is necessary to have access to an increasingly wide range of goods that support your own particular work, whether you grow crops or make products. For example, if you are running a farm with tractors, harvesters, and threshers, you need gasoline. Furthermore, you have to make sure that supplies of gasoline exist now and *also* will exist in the future. When war comes, for example, you now have two battlefields to avoid: your own territory and the territory that has the oil fields that are the source of your gasoline. Therein lies much of the history of the twentieth century, including problems in the Middle East and the Japanese attack on Pearl Harbor—the Japanese were desperate to secure access to oil in Southeast Asia.

Second, in industrial societies labor is often in the wrong place. In an agricultural society, it makes perfect sense that most people are working the land. Their effort is productive. Once human labor is supplemented and eventually largely replaced by machinery in agricultural production, then that logic changes. There are too many people on the rural land and too few options for them. At the same time, however, factories producing the agricultural machinery (among other products) will be expanding and need more workers. If a tractor factory happens to be in a rural agricultural area, people could switch from one line of work to the other without moving.

---

1   Although the increase in productivity of labor is the larger factor, still it is worth noting how great the increase in productivity per land unit can be. In the discussion in the chapter on agriculture, for example, rice yields per acre approached 1 ton for the transplanting system. These days, however, rice yields per acre are higher in almost all countries and are far higher in countries that have switched to new crop varieties and have mechanized rice-growing: for example, Japan and the United States (both at 2.9 tons per acre) and South Korea (3.1 tons per acre).

That has long been the argument for locating new production facilities in rural areas, sometimes by building entire new towns there. However, there are likely to be many reasons to locate factories elsewhere: closer to raw materials, closer to transportation, closer to markets, closer to other factories that use their products or that furnish them with parts for their own products. The workers have to move. Some of that movement will be from region to region. Initially, almost all of it will be from the countryside to the city, from predominantly agricultural jobs to predominantly industrial jobs. In a place such as contemporary China, that movement has involved some hundreds of millions of people over the last few decades, which is doubtless the world's largest migration of all time. In industrial societies people seem forever in the wrong place, moving not only from countryside to city, but from city to city and nation to nation.[2] In the process, they are often moving from one kind of job to another. Geographical and occupational mobility often go hand in hand.

SOCIAL ARRANGEMENTS

These two factors—span of control and mobility of labor—have pervasive implications for how industrial society is organized. These two factors give rise to two rather different stories: one for the society as a whole and one for the people within it. The society as a whole becomes more extensive, with greater integration and greater needs for stability in its resources. The people, on the other hand, become less deeply rooted in place and move frequently into different geographical areas and often different kinds of work. Their personal connections may narrow as they lose their roots in local physical communities and in extended kin groups. For people, this complex, integrated society re-creates something of the lifestyle of foragers: people who move in relatively small groups from place to place in search of shifting resources. Some further consideration of control and mobility helps illuminate these two rather different perspectives on industrialism: that of the society as a whole and that of the individuals within it.

CONTROL

Industrial society operates at a high level of control over the environment. One problem is that once control is established, it must be maintained. This is also true in advanced agricultural societies, where the success of irrigated systems lays the

---

2   The arguments for a "postindustrial" society are a simple extension of this argument. For industrialism, then, there is a displacement of labor from agriculture to industry, from countryside to city. That occurs, to simplify, because human labor is largely replaced by machine labor on the farm. The postindustrial shift has exactly the same logic. Human labor is now largely replaced by machine labor in the factories. Once again labor is in the wrong place. The fact that a different kind of labor may be needed makes the transition more difficult.

basis for catastrophic famine if those irrigation systems collapse or are destroyed. High control often means high risk. Likewise the success of productive systems created in industrial societies lays the basis for catastrophic failure if any element of the system fails. If the industrial version of agricultural production relies on oil, for example, lack of oil means the machines cannot operate and crops are not planted and harvested. All the different parts of the system (whether agriculture or mining, food production or tractor production) have to work, have to work together, and have to work reliably. Simply put, a high level of control requires new, more reliable, and more future-oriented management skills and systems.

That requirement for the maintenance of control requires specialists who know those different systems individually and collectively. Such specialization means that people will not usually understand other people's work well since it is so specialized. Lateral coordination is difficult, and some form of overall management is needed. One key question in contemporary society is who should provide that overall coordination. Some countries, such as the United States, have taken a relatively loose governmental approach to economic matters, only to find that they need to control or regulate at least some parts of the economic and financial systems. Other countries, such as China, have stressed the need for central control by the government, only to find that they have needed to loosen that control to increase overall productivity.

The specialization in occupational roles in industrial societies also has important implications for individuals. These different occupations are likely to have different characteristics: some more manual and some more mental; some more people oriented and some more machine oriented; some with control over other people and some that require following other people's orders; some requiring only limited training and others requiring extensive, specialized education. In agricultural societies a few people are specialized, but in industrial societies virtually everybody is. That may be inevitable and efficient, but it removes one of the most important bases for human connection and interaction: a shared experience of work.

Managing Mobility

The second major theme stressed here is that with the process of industrialization, labor ends up being in the wrong place. People are not in the locations where their labor is needed. In the early stages of industrialization, extra labor is largely in rural areas, where it is no longer needed. In later stages of industrialization, labor may be in an industry that was once profitable and labor intensive but has become less profitable or simply requires less labor; for example, coal and steel in the central and eastern parts of Canada and the United States and textiles in the US South. On the other hand, there is often a lack of labor in the places where it is now needed, the new places with the new products and services such as the high-tech zones around Boston, San Francisco, and Toronto. In industrial societies, then, people move. Those new places may be within a country or across national borders. The explosion of production facilities in southern China, for example, initially drew workers from the rural areas of China, but also draws people from across the border in Vietnam, where wages are now lower.

It is possible to imagine cases in which this movement could be handled in a relatively organized fashion. A factory owner might, for example, choose an area that had sufficient numbers of the correctly trained people. The bigger and more specialized the business, however, the harder that is to do. One alternative is to build an entire town around a new production facility and advertise for workers in areas that have excess labor. New workers would thus come in an orderly fashion to this new place and settle down in newly built homes and neighborhoods with their families. This has been tried, including with the planned cities for the new automobile industry in the early 1900s. But there are potential problems. It may be hard to predict how fast production should expand and thus exactly how many workers will be needed. Perhaps those people coming with their entire families will want good wages for that move and, precisely because they have families, want such "extras" as good schools for their children and good medical care for their families overall. Think of a company that offers great benefits, including the down payment on your house, and has just given your local community $10 million for a new park. That is great but it will, directly or indirectly, raise production costs.

A different business model is to *not* be involved directly in people's movement. Businesses, after all, do not really need families and communities; they just need the workers. Those workers may be men (especially if the work is heavy) or may be women (especially if employers believe that women are either better at the work or will do equivalent work for less money). Furthermore, it will be convenient if those workers are available when you need them and will go away when you do not need them: no guaranteed employment, no pensions, no unions. The work can thus be done well, done the way the company wants, and done as cheaply as possible. If people want a raise, or become sick, old, or pregnant, they can be easily replaced with others who are younger, cheaper, more tractable, and less distracted by their personal life. This approach is on the rise. Think of the millions of undocumented workers who provide agricultural and construction labor in the United States without "requiring" fringe benefits, job security, union-level wages, or community services for their families. Think also of those workers in the "gig" economy who are what were called pieceworkers in agricultural and industrial work, but who now sell a particular task (such as a ride) and are themselves responsible for putting together the components of a full job: time management, communication, tools, insurance, retirement, health care.

Mobility, Families, and Individuals

The nature of mobility in industrial society has varied over time. In earlier periods the move might be a one-time event: from a rural area to a city, for example. Increasingly, however, the movement involves a chain of events with unpredictable futures. A person may move from a rural home to a city to a different part of the city, then to another city (perhaps overseas). With such constant and often unpredictable movement, the logic of a foraging lifestyle reappears: the smaller and more flexible the groups, the easier to move. The advantages of the nuclear family are impressive. It is the smallest possible unit that bridges the genders and the generations. It is thus not surprising that the kinship systems of industrialized societies resemble those of hunters and gatherers rather than those of horticulturalists, agriculturalists, and pastoralists. Yet the force exerted on people to move can fracture even the nuclear family. If both spouses work, for example, their current jobs or future career development will pull them in different directions. If they live in two separate places—and commute between them—they may postpone having children or choose not to have them at all.

In the face of such mobility, families may start to look like liabilities to people and to those who employ them. From the perspective of the people who face a job move, family obligations are expensive, the ability to meet those expenses may be unpredictable, and the negotiations on who will move where (or commute for how long) may be aggravating. From the employer's perspective, why pay one person enough to support a family when you can probably hire an individual at a lower wage—at least if there is no government regulation and no effective labor union. Even if you cannot reduce the salary, you can save substantially on costs for supplementary benefits (health insurance, maternity/paternity leave, family sick days) and have employees who will give you more of their time and attention—and maybe even be willing to work unpaid overtime.

This potential loss of family ties has important implications for the society in terms of marriages (or other unions) that do not occur, that are delayed, or that end in separation. The result is generally fewer children. In most advanced industrial societies, birth rates are plunging below replacement level. There is currently great concern (and sometimes outright panic) in many industrialized countries about this decline in the number of children. For some countries it is immigrants to the rescue, whether as short-term workers (especially common in Europe, the Mideast, and parts of Asia) or as permanent new settlers (largely in Australia, Canada, New Zealand, and the United States). Thanks to these various forms of international migration and a society that is relatively tolerant of childbirth outside marriage, Canada and the United States have so far avoided the economic problems caused by demographic decline.

NINE KEY QUESTIONS

As in previous chapters, comments on the nine key questions follow below.

Division of labor. In industrial societies the division of labor is extensive. For many specialized jobs an ad hoc emergence of competence over time is inadequate. Instead, people will have to be trained for specific jobs through formal education and structured experience on the job. Such occupational specialization may be structured around age and sex, particularly in early industrialization. However, the logic of assigning different jobs by age and sex is enormously reduced in advanced industrial societies. Thus while the division of labor is far more complex in general, the division of labor by age and sex is generally lessened, though still quite variable by country.

Territoriality. Good agricultural land continues to be an immensely valuable resource in industrial societies. However, it is joined in importance by other kinds of natural resources. Previously unimportant land may suddenly become important if resources (gas and oil, for example) are discovered on or below it. Even access to resources beyond one's own territory becomes vital: petroleum and shipping lanes, for instance. For industrial societies the link to territory is thus a combination of the different kinds of territoriality seen in other societies: actual full-time occupation of some territory in addition to periodic access to a broader range. Industrial societies as a whole are strongly territorial, both about the territory (and resources) within their borders and about their access to territory (and resources) beyond their borders. While the society as a whole is thus fiercely territorial, for individual people the links to specific locations may lessen as they move from place to place.

Kinship. With mobility of the kind needed in industrial societies, kinship is greatly narrowed in scope. As with foragers, the nuclear family tends to predominate. Furthermore, the experience of the highly industrialized countries of Europe, North America, and East Asia suggests that the nuclear family itself may be fracturing: increased divorce, decreased marriage, fewer children. Such a narrow and often fractured kinship system provides limited support for people in times of need, thus the importance of general societal "safety nets." One of the dilemmas of industrial societies is that ties of kinship and ties of locality are narrowing at the same time. As the two prime components of human community—ties of blood and ties of place—weaken, other kinds of community connections develop that are more episodic, tied to transitional institutions like schools, or built through virtual worlds of social media and gaming.

Social control. For industrial societies, with their dense settlements of people who are often strangers to each other, social control requires a more formal system. Consider disputes as an example. There is an enormous amount to argue about in industrial societies. Land continues to be valuable, but there are also many other kinds of valuable property, both physical (cars, houses, money) and virtual (reputation, intellectual property). Disputes that arise may involve people who know each other, but many of the disputes involve strangers or people with whom interaction is limited. Informal ways of resolving disputes are less likely to be successful, and there are few larger kinship or locality groups that can help. Instead, industrial societies have specialized rules and institutions for social control. Those institutions have their own power to enforce decisions. The result is a complex system of laws, police, judges, jails, and inevitably the lawyers to explain and navigate this complex, specialized system.

Equality. With industrial societies, the issue of access to resources—which is fundamental to equality—is complicated. On the one hand, the sheer variety of useful resources and ways to attain them suggests that people may have expanded options for improving their lives. Furthermore, much of the rationale for differences by age and gender disappears. On the face of it, job qualifications for most jobs would not seem to require men rather than women, or the younger rather than the older—as long as the candidates happen to have equivalent preparation for the jobs. All that argues for equality. On the other hand, much of the work of industrial societies is done by machines and could not be done without them. Getting the resources to produce and fuel those machines is expensive. Money is important, and that gives an advantage to those who already have it. In that sense, access to resources is not equal, separating those with property from those who have only their labor to sell. And inequality is indeed on the rise by most standardized measures.

Religious beliefs. In industrial societies people acknowledge a wide range of spiritual forces. However, localized kinds of spiritual forces tend to be less common. Relatively unstructured nuclear families, limited memory of earlier generations, and simple distance from family grave sites suggest that ancestors are unlikely to be very important. Likewise with spirits of the land. When people are mobile, such spirits are harder to access and less useful on a day-to-day basis. As is also true for pastoralists, people in industrial societies need a religion that travels well and that can be with them as individuals, as well as members of families or other groups. World religions make much sense. They provide an ever-present and everywhere-present deity, and portable scriptures. On the other hand, there is also a secularizing trend in industrial societies that may undermine religious beliefs, segment them into a private sphere, or completely disavow them as irrational.[3]

Ecological soundness. Industrial societies exact a harsh price on the environment. Like agriculturalists, industrialists make changes to the land that are permanent. Industrialists exhaust resources that cannot be replenished: water from aquifers, minerals and metals from mines, oil and gas from wells and rocks. Unlike other human adaptations, then, industrialism is not self-sustaining in its current use of resources and will have to find alternate sources in the future. Actual contamination of the planet is also occurring. Lost resources are matched by ruined resources. One political problem with that contamination is that much of it occurs elsewhere in the world and is thus relatively invisible in North America, whether it is exported production or just exported garbage, including an increasing amount of e-waste, those discarded electrical and electronic products that are so toxic that most countries other than the United States have banned their export.

Security. The great advantage of industrialism is that it can produce almost anything, whether those goods are agricultural or industrial, necessities or luxuries, nurturing of the human spirit or just cheesy. However, as the infrastructure becomes more complex, failure in the system can have catastrophic implications. Furthermore, since industrial systems are largely powered by nonrenewable resources, they can maintain themselves only if they find new resources. If they cannot do so, there is no "Plan B." Industrialists cannot go back to a simpler, lower-density lifestyle. On the brighter side, as long as things do continue to work, the physical well-being of most people in advanced industrial societies is relatively good and their life prospects generally improving because of better medical care, public health, and sanitation.

External conflict. Industrial societies are likely to be of interest to outsiders because of the value of their resources and the wide range of products that they produce. What makes the relations of industrial societies so different, however, is that with industrialism the number and range of resources are greatly extended. Resources that once had little value, or had been buried so deeply they could not be retrieved, or had been in places that could not be reached, now have value. Fracking is a good current example, bringing oil from ground thought no longer profitable through the injection of pressurized fluids. Thus

---

3   Like others, those in North America appear to be becoming less religious. But levels of religiosity remain high in the United States, where, for example, over half pray at least daily. The Pew Research Center is especially attentive to such religious issues. See, for example, their 2014 survey *US Public Becoming Less Religious* at http://www.pewforum.org/2015/11/03/u-s-public-becoming-less-religious/.

industrial societies will be ever vigilant in protecting every piece of territory that they have. Borders will be finely drawn and fiercely protected. At the same time, industrial societies will be alert to opportunities to expand beyond their own borders for resources and markets. They will always be watching to see where other resources may lie and how those resources can be controlled—no matter how far beyond their own borders those resources lie. The raw occupations of territory that characterized classic colonialism may have ebbed, but more covert and indirect mechanisms of controlling places beyond one's own territory remain very much alive.

CASE EXAMPLE—MASS MIGRATION IN CHINA

On my first trip to China in 2000, I decided to get out of Shanghai and visit Nanjing, reputedly one of the most pleasant of China's big cities. I thought this might be a useful break from Shanghai with its masses of cranes and construction. Yet Nanjing was also in turmoil. As I walked down one street, workers were carefully dismantling, brick by brick, the houses that had taken up a full city block. The usable bricks were stacked up carefully on the edge of the street. That is the way things used to be done, especially since building materials have tended to be in short supply in China. As I walked south on a smaller road, I found myself in a new, modern plaza area where several roads converged. Looking around, I noticed that all the buildings were new. In fact they were very new. A multistory department store lay ahead. Towering above the department store—and built on top of it—was an office building or hotel (or perhaps a combination of the two). It was impossible to tell because the building was not yet finished. Yet the department store, directly below the construction, was already open. That is the new way. Somehow China was using two systems at once: hard manual labor to pull down old buildings brick by brick and huge cranes to put up new skyscrapers—and opening them before they were even finished.

One of the inherent problems in this kind of rapid industrialization is that people are in the wrong place. Originally they are rural when they need to be urban. Then they are one kind of urban (steelworkers, for example), and they need to be another kind (electronics assembly or software design, for example). China is confronting both problems at the same time. The growth in the urban Chinese population is especially striking: China's cities experienced a growth in their urban population of about 240 million people from 1975 to 2000—roughly equivalent to moving into Chinese cities the entire population (at that time) of the United States.[4] But the changes since then are even more staggering. At the time of that initial trip to

---

4   The figures on urban populations are drawn from *World Urbanization Prospects: The 1999 Revision*, prepared by the United Nations Population Division.

This ghost town in the Sierra Nevada is a reminder that jobs in industrial society, in this case mining, often disappear. (Credit: D. Haines)

China, the Chinese population in cities was about 36 percent, and the gross domestic product was about $1.2 trillion. Fifteen years later, the urban population had risen to 55 percent and the gross domestic product to about $12 trillion.[5] In that fifteen-year period, the urban population grew by another 240 million people. This is, in numbers, the greatest human migration in history.

The size and rapid growth of the urban Chinese population have caused problems. Too many people in the cities yields a surplus population that is willing to work at lower wages but strains urban resources: not enough water, electricity, sewers, schools, housing, transportation. Since the Chinese have had a strict system of residence permits that are either rural or urban, these migrants are in violation of their residence permits. Until recently, that was an actual crime. But punishment aside, the lack of proper residence permits affects access to all kinds of social services. These migrants—invaluable though they are to the Chinese economy—thus

---

5   Figures on gross domestic product vary based on the assumptions used, particularly whether the figures
    are adjusted to reflect what that money can buy within the country itself. With a lower cost of living,
    the "real" value of the gross domestic product is higher. Most statistics now factor that in and provide a
    purchasing power parity (PPP) version of gross domestic product. That figure is much higher for China.

The growth of Chinese cities such as Shanghai has hinged on massive migration from rural areas. (Credit: D. Haines)

live a kind of floating shadow life in the cities. They are easy targets for low wages and other kinds of discrimination. They may live in housing that is subject to demolition as entire city blocks are slated for renovation by the government. Their children often do not have the right to go to regular public schools. Thus China has much the same dilemma with these "illegal" migrants from the countryside to the cities as the United States has with undocumented workers from other countries. Their work is valued but not enough to grant them full rights.

The members of this floating population are not alone in their difficulties adjusting to a rapidly changing Chinese economy. They are also joined in their pursuit of work by those who have lost their jobs in industries that were once prosperous but are now restructuring. As in the old North American industrial heartland, those who worked in what were once progressive, relatively well-paying industries, such as steel, now find themselves unemployed or underemployed and living in reduced and often marginal circumstances. It is not just that industrialism is hard on people and hard on the environment during its initial stages, but that its new developments and new forms extract yet additional costs.[6] That may be progress overall, but the costs of that progress on the individual level are not borne evenly.

6   The Chinese slogan of "Study Dazhai" from the days of Mao Zedong, when it meant to ever increase production through ever greater effort, now has a different meaning as the Dazhai plants now produce not steel, but unemployed workers.

CASE EXAMPLE—COMPUTERS AND HUMANS AT WORK

Fresh from six months in Europe looking at refugee resettlement programs, I found myself back in the United States and in need of a job. A newspaper ad led me to a position in state government as a management consultant (yes, anthropologists do management consulting). That position led, in turn, to a senior management position in the state's workers' compensation commission (yes, anthropologists do management too). One part of my work was oversight of the agency's computer operations. It was time to see what an anthropologist could understand about these new tools, what they could accomplish, and how people related to them.

The good news was that the machines were generally good workers. They could crunch numbers, store large amounts of information, and pass information around quickly and accurately. Suddenly keeping track of a half-million workers' compensation cases did not seem so difficult. No longer did staff have to get the physical case file to do their work. They could just look up the case on the computer and find out—more or less—what was going on with it. Furthermore, if the agency needed to send somebody a letter, that process could be automated. Push a button, out came a form letter; the form letter was then mechanically folded and stuffed into a window envelope. So the machines did good work, and, furthermore, agency staff generally came to like working with them—especially when they could have a new computer with a good monitor, an engaging graphic interface, and a game or two. This small state agency thus benefited greatly from the manifest benefits of a new information technology era. The humans and the machines were doing well together.

However, there was also bad news. One troubling problem was how individualistic the computers were. Even within a single set of computers ordered with exactly the same specifications at the same time, there were idiosyncrasies. The individuality of the machines could be entertaining at times. Thus when the electricity went out—and it often did because of bad wiring—it was impossible to predict which computers would survive. As the lights came back on, there would be the sound of dozens of computers rebooting throughout the building. Which ones would make it? Which ones would not? I remember a distinct sense of comradeship with staff as we all waited in the semidark to know which of the computers would return from the dead to work with us another day. The unpredictability, however, was not always entertaining. The loss of a single workstation might be acceptable, but the main databases were a more serious matter. I finally came up with a system that backed up the data in three different ways so I was reasonably confident it could be reconstructed no matter what. I even created a clone of the main database in my own office upstairs to match the one downstairs in the IT department. It provided some comfort.[7]

These new tools, computers, also had some interesting effects on organizational culture. Some people turned out to have a knack for computers. That meant there was a new kind of skill that was relevant to the work—and might be a good reason to request a raise in salary. Computers thus gave at least some people new and better work options. There was also something a little revolutionary about how computers affected the interaction between management and staff. For example, the computerization of information provided some protection against arbitrary management action. In one case the agency head was missing a file and claimed, in a rather unpleasant memorandum, that this was caused by the file clerks—the lowest paid of the organization's staff. From his point of view, and his position of power, the file clerks had performed poorly; they had lost a file when it was needed. But was that actually true? Normally, the file clerks would have had to accept the accusation. Who were they to argue with the agency head? But now they had an option. A quick inquiry to the computer department provided a printout of who had actually had the file when the agency head had needed it. And, guess what, the file clerks did *not* have the file at the time in question. So there was an apology from the agency head. Score one point for the dignity of labor, thanks to computers—and computer staff.

In this case, as in many others, new technology made a positive difference. Technology can indeed improve the efficiency and quality of work. It can also provide new and improved opportunities for people—including those who are relatively underprivileged. It can even make work more enjoyable as machines become new and valued coworkers. But it does not always work out so well. There can be negative consequences of various kinds. One involves human privacy. That agency head who had apologized to the file clerks, for example, became interested in whether he could monitor the computer e-mail of those same staff and tried (unsuccessfully) to get us to do it for him. Computerization, as has become more apparent every year, provides the basis for vastly increased surveillance in the workplace and highly effective intrusions into personal privacy at home as well. And all that data can be easily stolen. Not the old-fashioned way, one item at a time, but millions of items, documents, and files all at the same time, and all instantaneously deliverable to the entire world. Very efficient, very dangerous, very different.

---

7   Any reasonable database will now do a variety of replication automatically. In the old days, however, the creation of a de facto replication was a little more difficult. I actually had to program a matching computer to think it was the primary database machine since that was the only way I could get it to test a full reload of the backup tapes. That's a rather practical example of false consciousness and its virtues in the workplace.

SOURCES

Industrialism covers a vast territory as an academic subject. Unlike many other issues in which anthropologists have an interest, industrialism crosscuts the territory of virtually every other social science. What distinguishes the anthropological approach to industrialism is its comparative approach (that is, in different parts of the world and versus other adaptations), particularly its tendency to look at the back roads and ill-lit corners of the industrial world that do not always follow the overall patterns for industrial societies. Thus anthropologists have been strongly interested in the fate of ethnic minorities; the growth of cities (thus urban anthropology); what happens to nonindustrial countries when industrial countries want something they have (thus colonial and postcolonial studies); what happens when humans and human relations are subject to large economic forces (thus interest in commodification, globalization, and migration); how people view the world when there is rapid social and economic change (thus arguments about modernism and postmodernism); and how they as anthropologists might affect all these processes (thus interests in applied and practitioner anthropology, engaged anthropology, public anthropology, and the anthropology of policy). Much of how anthropologists sort these issues out can be traced through the main anthropology journals in terms of theory (especially the *American Anthropologist* and *Anthropological Theory*) and in terms of the work that anthropologists do in the "real" world (especially *Human Organization* and *Practicing Anthropology*). Bruno Latour's *We Have Never Been Modern* (Harvard University Press, 1993) remains a good statement about why anthropologists should *not* entangle themselves in the debates about modernity and postmodernity.

For the case example on China, two earlier edited volumes provide the flavor of the enormous changes of China's initial urbanization: Elizabeth J. Perry and Mark Selden (eds.), *Chinese Society: Change, Conflict and Resistance* (Routledge, 2000); and John R. Logan (ed.), *The New Chinese City: Globalization and Market Reform* (Blackwell, 2002). Li Zhang's *Strangers in the City* (Stanford University Press, 2001) provides an invaluable interpretation of China's early floating population. For a more rural perspective, see the latest edition of *Chen Village* for southern China (3rd ed. was Anita Chan, Richard Madsen, and Jonathan Unger [eds.], *Chen Village: Revolution to Globalization* [Stanford University Press, 2009]) and Michael Meyer's wonderfully readable discussion of a northern China village: *In Manchuria: A Village Called Wasteland and the Transformation of Rural China* (Bloomsbury Press, 2015). Change in China is extremely rapid, however, so those sources should be checked for currency; the *Economist* does an especially good job on the interactions of economics and politics as they are evolving in China. The documentary *Last Train Home* provides a good sense of how the massive industrialization of China is changing people's relationships with family and place.

The computerization example derives from my own experience (see "The Promise and Perils of Computerizaton," *Journal of Applied Behavioral Research* [1999] and "Better Tools, Better Workers," *American Journal of Public Administration* [2003]), but there are many anthropologists who are concerned with similar issues. Three early books that give a good sense of anthropological approaches to new technology include David Hakken's *Cyborgs@cyberspace? An Ethnographer Looks to the Future* (Routledge, 1999), Julian Orr's *Talking about Machines* (Cornell University Press, 1996), and Diana Forsythe's *Studying Those Who Study Us: An Anthropologist in the World of Artificial Intelligence* (Stanford University Press, 2001). See also the *Anthropology of Work Review* (published by the Society for the Anthropology of Work). Finally, many anthropologists are involved in science and technology studies (STS), and an Internet search will yield a number of anthropology departments with an explicit STS focus, including discussions of the key issues involved.

Part II
STRUCTURES

8

Introduction to Part II

The discussion in part I of the basic human adaptations illustrates the logic of human society and also the extent of its variation. Another way to look at human societies is to focus less on the overall environmental and cultural context and more directly on the structures that link people together in society. That is the purpose of this second part of the book. Kinship is the most primal of such structures, and the anthropological record is clear on the importance, variability, complexity, and pervasiveness of kinship in human society. There are, however, other structures through which people are linked together, what we generally term politics, economics, and religion.

This chapter introduces these basic structures. The discussion begins with a brief review of lessons from part I, then considers some of the kinds of diversity that must be addressed in bringing people together. Managing diversity has become an increasingly important issue as larger and larger numbers of people with often disparate experiences engage with each other in the contemporary world. The chapter concludes with a brief introduction to the five chapters in part II and how they are organized.

SOME LESSONS ABOUT ADAPTATIONS

Many of the discussions and examples in part II rest on insights from part I. Several of these are worth reiterating.

CONTROL, DENSITY, COMPLEXITY, MOBILITY

Throughout the discussion of foragers, horticulturalists, agriculturalists, pastoralists, and industrialists, there have been four common themes. The extent of *control* over the environment varies greatly and is reflected in the degree of control over the society itself. Increased control over the environment yields increased *density* of settlement. The greater the density, the more people are organized into larger groups and the more frequently they must interact with people that they do not know well. They may even be dealing with total strangers. Control over nature and over society, combined with increased density, results in greater *complexity* of social institutions. This does not mean that all aspects of life will necessarily be more complex. Kinship, for example, becomes *less* complex in industrial societies than in most agricultural and pastoralist societies, as many of its functions are taken over by formal economic, political, and religious institutions. Yet, overall, industrial societies are indeed more complex in their social arrangements. The fourth theme, *mobility*, is less predictable. People in industrial society, for example, are more similar to foragers than to agriculturalists, despite the fact that industrialists are more similar to those agriculturalists in terms of the other themes of control, density, and complexity. The unpredictability of human mobility is especially important in the contemporary world as people are increasingly drawn into migration circuits that propel them to new locales, often across national borders, and sometimes back again.

CORE SOCIAL BUILDING BLOCKS

The examination of different adaptations also provides insight into the basic building blocks of human society. *Age* and *sex* are the most important. Both have a biological base but are culturally elaborated into generations (whether based on kinship or such general societal categories as Boomers and Millennials) and gender (with its increasing range and complexity of experiences). It is crucial to remember the range of possibilities in how these building blocks can be organized in particular societies. Differences by sex, for example, may be sharp or blurred: men and women may work together or apart, property may be held by, or passed through, men or women or both. There are also the key anchoring frameworks of *kinship* and *location*. These too can be organized in different ways. People's relationship to location is highly variable, ranging from strong ties of locality to the diffuse attachments of transnational elites. Kinship also varies. People in industrial and foraging societies, as noted, are almost opposites in terms of control over nature, but their kinship patterns are rather similar.

STRUCTURE AND SOLIDARITY

Part II builds on part I by emphasizing the links people have with each other rather than the links they have with the environment. In many cases the discussions in part II follow closely from part I. It will come as no surprise, for example, that agricultural societies have more elaborate political systems than do horticulturalists or foragers. On the other hand, some of the discussions in part II may provide unexpected insights. The complexity of economic relations in technologically simple societies, for example, may come as a surprise. Some of the similarities in religion among societies that seem different in how they relate to their environments may also be unexpected.

Central to the consideration of social relations in part II is the notion of *structure*. The use of that term follows directly from the insights of the early structural-functionalists. Both Radcliffe-Brown and Malinowski viewed societies as systems composed of parts arranged in structured (rather than random) ways. Furthermore, they viewed the different parts of the system as providing useful functions for the system as a whole. This does not mean that everything in a society always works well. But it does mean that it is usually far better to begin by asking how a particular society *does* work than by assuming it does not work or that its beliefs and behavior are simply left over from days gone by.

Although the discussion here is largely phrased in terms of how structures link people together, sometimes this issue is discussed in terms of social solidarity. One key distinction is between the *solidarity of sameness* and the *solidarity of difference*. The solidarity of sameness often receives more attention. It makes sense that people are together, stay together, and value being together because they are the same in beliefs, values, and behavior. That solidarity may be at the small group level ("our family"), at a broader level ("our community"; "our nation"), or even at the global level ("we are all human"). But solidarity can also grow out of difference. People may see each other as different but complementary: men and women, parents and children, soldiers and diplomats, even producers and consumers. Societies will inevitably have relationships of both kinds. One of the most interesting examples in contemporary North American society is that of gender. The extent to which men and women are the same (as human beings) or different (based on their different reproductive roles or gender identities) is very much up for discussion. The main point is to remember that what binds people together can be their similarity or difference—or both.

UNDERSTANDING DIVERSITY
CATEGORIES OF DIFFERENCE

In all societies, then, linking people together means linking those who are similar and those who are different. Given the degree of diversity in contemporary society, some further consideration may be needed of how this diversity is organized. One way is to find some similarity despite the differences: something people share, such as similar experiences or interests, or even knowing some of the same people. The more difficult case is when people really are different (no common language, for example) and unconnected on a personal basis. People then need a way of categorizing these other and different people in a way that makes sense, is easy to use, and works. Each of these points is crucial. The system of categorization must *make sense* to the people who are using it. If it does not make sense, people will object to it and the system will lose its value. Furthermore, the system must be relatively *easy to use*. If it is complex to apply, then the effort needed may be too great. This is why race, gender, and age are so often used by people in categorizing themselves and other people. The categories seem to be fairly easily determined based on quick physical observation. Finally, the system has to be *practical*. If the system persistently yields wrong conclusions or wrong results, it is counterproductive.

There are many bases upon which such systems of categorizing people can be developed. Age, class, religion, disability, and political opinion, for example, are all extremely important in how people think, act, experience life, and are evaluated by others. The categories that probably receive the greatest attention in the contemporary North American scene are race, ethnicity, gender, and sexual orientation. All aim to address a dimension of human diversity that is deemed significant, can be seen relatively easily in what people do (if not always exactly what they look like), and provides some reasonable predictive power about how best to interact with these other people. All have some internal problems and contradictions; all share the same fine line between providing a guide for more effective interaction and a stereotype or profile that undermines such interaction.

RACE AND ETHNICITY

"Race" purportedly refers to physical differences among people, but anthropologists have long contested the notion that there are any clear lines between human populations. There is thus no established breakdown of the human population into defined races. But that has not kept people from believing that racial distinctions are real, from using skin color as a visual marker for such differences, and from working very hard to impose racial distinctions. In the colonial United States, for example, the constant search for cheap labor brought a wide range of migrants to the United States in various degrees of servitude. Some were temporarily indentured servants. Others were slaves. Even though an independent United States soon banned the "import" of additional slaves, there were strong incentives to make sure slavery itself was not abolished. The economic system in the South required the labor of slaves, and white political elites were perpetually threatened by the sheer number of slaves—often the majority. Thus it was vital to maintain the ideology of racial difference to justify slavery and to make sure slaves could be easily identified and controlled. Even with emancipation after the Civil War, racial distinctions remained. The result was a system of social differentiation and control almost as rigid as slavery itself. While supporters of the system might argue that the races lived "separate but equal" lives, the economic and political reality was of racial stratification—a system in which diversity is not of groups side by side but of groups that are assigned to higher and lower strata in a controlled social hierarchy.

Compared to race, ethnicity seems a relatively benign way to categorize people. Yet it usually invokes biology as well. Ethnicity is generally considered to be carried in the blood—you are what your parents were. Ethnicity, however, also acknowledges the experiential and cultural heritage of a people—you are what you grew up to be. Ethnicity as a system of categorizing people has its strength in being based in both biology and culture but not precisely limited to either. That combination makes it appear sensible to most people. It is also eminently practical, since knowing people's ethnic background is a useful—even necessary—step toward knowing how to interact with them. Ethnicity often has clear markers that let you know how somebody fits into the system. Some of that is biological. Koreans, or Japanese, or Haitians, many people maintain, look a certain way that is not simply black or Asian. Not simply skin color, but height and heft, noses and ears. Often as important are cultural markers: kind of clothing, hair style, bearing, gesture. Ethnicity is also usually announced with sound cues—a different language with a different pace, sound, and intonation—all of which often result in a distinctive accent in English. The blending of who somebody is by biological parentage and who that person is by cultural heritage is a powerful one. That power helps explain the broad use of ethnic categories in contemporary North American society.

Despite its virtues, ethnicity shares with race some fundamental problems. One is that ethnicity can also be turned to purposes of social exclusion and control. Indeed, ethnicity is in some ways a stronger statement than race. To say that somebody is ethnically different is to say that they are both biologically and culturally different. In many countries there is not much distinction between racial and ethnic classification. For Japanese and Koreans, for example, being Japanese or Korean is something that is distinctive in cultural terms but also carried in the blood. North Americans are a bit more flexible. For example, interracial and international adoptions are common in North America. Yet even in those cases, the adoptive parents may be unsure how much of ethnicity is carried in the blood and thus how much their children have a separate heritage. The adoptive children, in turn, may seek out the "original" part of their identity. They may be American or Canadian by upbringing but something else by heritage.

Another difficulty with ethnic categories is that, as with race, many people do not fit neatly into the system. Identifying somebody as Korean American, for example, would seem to make general sense. But the range of that term is enormous. Was this person American born? Does he or she actually speak Korean? Even been to Korea? Studies of immigrants consistently show the unpredictability of ethnicity, depending on the specific person and the specific environment. Many people, for example, do not fit neatly into the existing categories because of mixed parentage. If one of your parents is native-born Korean and the other white American or perhaps American-born Filipino American, what are you? Is Barack Obama African American because biologically he has one African and one American parent or because when he moved from Hawaii to the mainland he chose to be identified as African American and married into the established African American community? Once again, a system of categorization that might seem to make sense and be easy to apply turns out to not be very reliable or informative. As with race, there is also the question whether these categories are freely chosen or imposed by force. Ethnic categories, like racial ones, can be both liberating and imprisoning.

Gender and Sexual Orientation

Biological sex, like age, is an important kind of physical human diversity. Thus it is quite predictable that people will distinguish men from women, girls from boys. There are, after all, important biological distinctions between men and women. Women bear children and are likely—for reasons of breastfeeding if nothing else—to be the primary caretakers during children's early years. Yet the actual way that men and women live and act varies by individual personality and by social and cultural context. If women do not bear children, for example, much of the logic of the division of labor by sex disappears. Thus differences between men and women are now conventionally discussed under the term *gender*, rather than sex. The term *gender* acknowledges the social and cultural ways in which "sex" is constructed. Gender, like race and ethnicity, thus encompasses both biological and social factors.

As a way to categorize people, gender would seem to make good sense. Whatever the exact mix of biology and culture in the construction of gender, the combined impact is high, and people readily explain their own and other people's behavior based on gender. Since there is a great deal at stake in the relations between men and women—control of property, access to resources, reproductive rights, and thus the entire future of the social group—it is hardly surprising that differences between the genders are often sharply drawn and sharply enforced on both men and women. On the other hand, in many contemporary societies distinctions by gender are blurring between, and expanding beyond, the traditional binary of male and female. Certainly the rationale for gender differences in most areas of employment is rapidly disappearing.

The issues of gender take on added complexity when sexual orientation is added to the discussion. The anthropological record is clear on the wide range of sexual activities and relationships in which humans engage. Sexual relations among men and among women are common in many cultures. In some cases those sexual activities go against gender stereotypes. Thus there were men in Plains Indian society—sometimes called berdache—who generally acted as female and could marry other men. That was acceptable, but it did involve a de facto shift in gender. For many other societies, however, engaging in sexual relations with someone of the same sex is a quite customary form of sexual activity that accords with stereotypic gender status. Thus, as for the Etoro, a group in New Guinea, men may have sexual relations with women for the purpose of producing children, but sexual relations with men are themselves a normal, even preferred, form of sexual activity. Somewhat analogously, among Afro-Surinamese women on the northeast coast of South America, women may engage in sexual relations with women without being seen as unwomanly and without precluding sexual relations with men.[1]

These interrelated issues of gender and sexual orientation are now undergoing change and considerable debate in North American society. The legalization of same-sex unions and then same-sex marriages has helped crystallize the combined issues into a broader social debate. The question is no longer about the range of human sexual activity but rather about the specific sexual relationship with a single person that will be formally sanctioned as a legitimate marriage in the eyes of society, church, and state. When such couples have children, as they often do, gender roles are especially challenged: what are the roles that we used to define as "fatherly" and "motherly," and how are they rearranged when both parents are of the same sex? The very distinction between sex as physical and gender as cultural is challenged when people undergo gender reassignment surgery, thus bringing the body into alignment with gender orientation rather than the reverse. Here, as in other frontiers such as genetic engineering or climate modification, human culture is no longer just an adaptation to biology and environment respectively, but an actual restructuring of them.

---

1   The classic sources are Raymond C. Kelly, *Etoro Social Structure* (Ann Arbor: University of Michigan Press, 1980); and Gloria Wekker, "Mati-ism and Black Lesbianism," *Journal of Homosexuality* 24 (1993): 3–4, 145–58.

STRUCTURE OF THE CHAPTERS IN PART II

Part II has five chapters. The first two deal with kinship. Anthropologists have spent a great deal of time studying kinship. They have done so because they have found that human beings use kinship in far more extensive and interesting ways than we would know from the Euro-American experience. As will be seen, the topic of kinship includes several related issues: how people reckon their relations with others, whom they live with and interact with on a daily basis, what broader sets of kin they interact with on at least some occasions, and whom people marry. The succeeding three chapters address economics, politics, and religion. These are somewhat arbitrary categories since the anthropological record suggests that these domains often overlap. Nevertheless, these are the conventional categories and work reasonably well in sorting out different streams of social organization that—as always with anthropologists—must somehow be put back together again to understand the society as a whole.

The structure of the chapters is more variable than in part I since it is not possible to analyze kinship, politics, economics, and religion in exactly parallel fashion. Nevertheless, each chapter has roughly the same framework and begins with two or three major issues to provide a general orientation to the topic. Each chapter then moves to more detailed considerations and more technical material—often including the specific terminology that has been developed to give precision to anthropological analysis. As with part I, each chapter concludes with two case examples. Several of those case examples are continuations from part I. The Nuer, for example, reappear in the chapter on politics and the Vietnamese in the kinship chapters.

The emphasis in part II remains with the full range of the human experience and all the different adaptations discussed in part I. There is always a temptation to begin to emphasize the particular character of recent industrial (and postindustrial) society. Yet anthropology—to invoke Tylor again—aims for an encompassing vision of human society over space and time. Human culture today, especially with its increased control over biology and environment, does have distinctive features. But to understand the implications of those distinctive features, we need to understand the full range of human potential that we see from the entire anthropological record. The one thing we can be sure of in our increasingly globalized world is it will require collective human effort to manage the future. In that effort we will benefit from knowing how we as human beings have organized human society in the past and what elements of kinship, economic, political, and religious structures have served us well and which may need to be changed.

9

Kinship: Terminology and Households

Understanding kinship has been one of anthropology's greatest challenges. What seems a simple and elemental form of human connection turns out to be highly complex and variable across different societies. Some societies recognize relatively few relatives; others recognize a large number. Some societies remember only a few generations of ancestors; others maintain lists of ancestors that cover hundreds of years. For some societies the blood relationships through the father determine who the most important kin are; for other societies the crucial blood connection is through the mother. Finally, for many societies the lines between those linked by actual kinship and those linked just by interaction become blurred, and the study of kinship becomes a more generalized study of relationships based on kin metaphors: "like a brother"; "like a mother."

This chapter is the first of a two-chapter sequence dealing with the core anthropological issue of kinship. This first chapter introduces four key questions about kinship and then addresses in more detail the first two of those questions: what terms are used to describe kin and what kin live together on a daily basis, usually in what we call a *household*. The first of the case examples at the end of the chapter returns to Vietnam for a discussion of kin terms in a patrilineal society. The second discusses household structure among the Western Apache, a matrilineal society. The succeeding chapter will then address the issues of how larger kin groups are formed and how marriage is organized.

FOUR QUESTIONS

The discussion of kinship in this and the next chapter is organized in terms of four key questions. A brief preview of these four questions may be of assistance.

First, what kinds of kin do people think they have? After all, there are many people with whom they are related by some degree of blood connection, by marriage, or by some other "fictive" kin relationship. Clearly some of these people are "closer" than others. Brothers and sisters, for example, are biologically closer than cousins, and parents are biologically closer than uncles and aunts. However, trying to prioritize different kinds of cousins, aunts, and uncles is more difficult, at least for English speakers in North America. A key anthropological question has been to actually ask people who their kin are and how they categorize those kin. That question elicits the specific terms that people use for kin in different societies and thus permits cross-cultural comparison of how people structure the world of kinship through the labels they use. This is the issue of *kinship terminology.*

Second, with which particular kin do people actually live? Some people may live in large three-generational family groups; others in smaller nuclear families of father, mother, and children. The composition of households, in turn, reflects how people are added to the group and when people leave. Many of those comings and goings are relatively predictable: children are born; older people die. However, there is one crucial decision point that charts the future course of the household, and that is getting the parents together in the first place. After all, the mother-to-be and father-to-be usually grow up in separate households. If they are to live together, somebody has to move. This is the issue of *postmarital residence.*

Third, how are larger kin groups constructed? In many societies—and certainly most horticultural, agricultural, and pastoralist societies—kin groups extend far beyond the immediate household. Those kin groups can include hundreds, even thousands, of people. Larger size requires a greater degree of organization of kinship and usually clear rules about who belongs to which larger group. This is the issue of *descent.* The largest and most versatile kin structures usually involve a specific rule about whether people belong to their mother's (and her mother's) group or to their father's (and his father's) group. Those are, respectively, the *matrilineal* and *patrilineal* options.

Fourth, how do men and women come together in marriage, and what implications does that marriage have for their relatives? Marriage is highly variable. In some societies people marry only one person at a time; in others, they have multiple spouses. Having multiple wives is rather common in the anthropological record, but having multiple husbands also occurs. The exact choice of spouse is crucial for the couple, for the families in which they grew up, and for the children they will have. For example, if a society has two large kin groups and those kin groups always marry

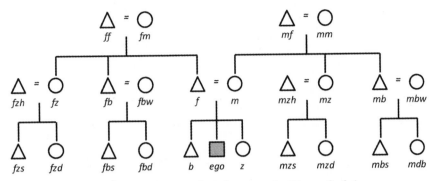

FIGURE 9.1. Kinship from an anthropologist's perspective. Notes: *f* = father; *m* = mother; *b* = brother; *z* = sister (because *s* is for son); *h* = husband; *w* = wife

people from the other group (Lees marry Smiths and Smiths marry Lees), those groups will be strongly allied to each other. They will share grandchildren—which is a strong bond indeed. This is the issue of *marriage*.

More detailed discussion of kinship terminology and postmarital residence follow below; larger kin groups and marriage are discussed in the next chapter.

KINSHIP TERMINOLOGY

The first question, then, is what people call their kin. This is seemingly a simple question and a typically anthropological one. Why make assumptions about a society's kinship system when you can just ask the people themselves? This simple question, however, yields a wide range of responses that suggest our own Euro-American system is only one of many options. Anthropologists have had to find a more specific, descriptive way of talking about kinship than using such words as "aunt" and "uncle" that reflect our own cultural categories about who our kin are. A brief introduction to this more technical way of talking about kin is thus needed.

Figure 9.1 provides a simple chart with four generations. Note the following conventions:

△ Triangles refer to men.
○ Circles refer to women.
= Equal signs indicate marriages.
| Vertical lines indicate descent.
— Horizontal lines connect multiple descendants.
☐ A box represents any person (whether male or female).

Type	Elements				
Hawaiian	Gender	Generation			
Eskimo	Gender	Generation	Core		
Iroquois	Gender	Generation		Line	
Sudanese	Gender	Generation	Core	Line	Seniority

FIGURE 9.2. Overview of kinship terminologies

Several points need to be made about this diagram.

- First, this is a simple diagram. People often have multiple brothers and sisters, for example, and multiple marriages as well. There are often missing people and replacements for them. For example, a father dies and the mother remarries a man who already has children of his own. Kinship can become very complex. This kind of diagram inevitably understates that complexity.
- Second, some reference point is needed to anchor the discussion of kinship terms. Lacking such a reference point, a particular woman might be a mother, a sister, or a daughter. The reference point is the shaded figure in the chart. That person is called *ego*. In this case the box (meaning a person of either gender) is the shaded reference point *ego*. The circle directly above the shaded box is identified as "*m*" (for mother) since she is ego's mother.
- Third, the diagram traces relationships *one step at a time*. This avoids ambiguity. For North Americans, for example, the person labeled *fb* (father's brother) would be an "uncle." But "uncle" is ambiguous since it also refers to *mb* (mother's brother) and even to the husbands of *fz* (father's sister) and *mz* (mother's sister). It is the same with people we call "cousins." In the chart they are indicated by their exact relationship: for example *fbd* (father's brother's daughter) or *mzs* (mother's sister's son).

People can, of course, refer to relatives the way anthropologists do. They can say "so-and-so" is my father's brother's wife. But societies also have their own systems of referring to relatives that select out crucial features. There are four major systems, each with its own logic. All these systems include generation and gender. Indeed, the first of the four to be discussed below *only* includes generation and gender. The systems discussed after that, including our own, add additional detail in their systems of kin terminology (see figure 9.2). But this system based only on gender and generation is the place to begin.

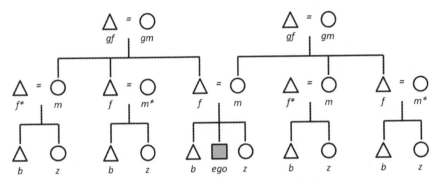

FIGURE 9.3. Hawaiian kinship terminology. Notes: *gf* = grandfather; *gm* = grandmother; * = often, but not always

Gender and Generation (Hawaiian)

The simplest kind of kinship terminology (see figure 9.3) is based solely on the two issues of gender and generation. There are separate terms for "mother" and "father." Those terms mean "female one generation up" and "male one generation up." Sisters and brothers are *not* one generation up, so they have separate terms. "Sister" and "brother" mean female and male of your own generation. Likewise (not shown in the chart), "daughter" and "son" mean female and male one generation "down." Thus one's father is called "father," one's mother "mother." Your father's brother (*fb*) is also a "father," since he too is a male one generation up. So also is your mother's brother (*mb*), and even your mother's sister's husband (*mzh*). All the males one generation up are "fathers," and likewise all the women one generation up are "mothers." All the males of one's own generation are "brothers," and all of the females of one's own generation are "sisters." This is called, eponymously, *Hawaiian kinship terminology*—even though many other societies have a similar system. The use of this system does not mean that people do not know who their immediate parents are. But the terminology is elegantly simple in its invocation of the principles of gender and generation. It has the nice implication that there is a general parental quality to all people one generation up (the *ascending* generation), a general child quality to those one generation down (the *descending generation*), and a general brotherly or sisterly quality to those of one's own generation.

Gender, Generation, and Core (Eskimo)

From a Euro-American perspective, what might seem odd about Hawaiian kinship terminology is the reference to "aunts" and "uncles" as "mothers" and "fathers" and

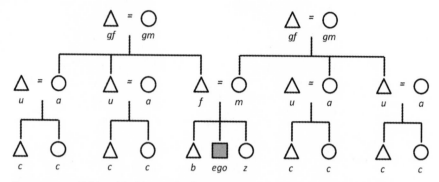

FIGURE 9.4. Eskimo kinship terminology. Notes: u = uncle; a = aunt; c = cousin

all "cousins" as "brothers" and "sisters." The terminology seems to ignore the fundamental distinction between one's actual mother, father, brothers, and sisters, and these other more "distant" relatives. The terms ignore the boundaries of the core nuclear family. For us, the solution is to add a third distinction: whether or not a relative is part of the core family. That addition produces the terminology shown in figure 9.4. Here "brother" and "sister" are reserved for the actual brother (b) and actual sister (z). "Mother" and "father" are likewise reserved for the actual mother and father. All the other relatives one generation up are not "fathers" or "mothers," and all the other relatives of one's own generation are not "sisters" or "brothers." This is, again eponymously, *Eskimo kinship terminology*. It is, of course, standard North American terminology as well. In our terms the "not mothers" are "aunts," and the "not fathers" are "uncles." For "not brothers" and "not sisters," English speakers do not even distinguish by gender; they are all "cousins."

GENDER, GENERATION, AND LINE (IROQUOIS)

Although the Eskimo system has its merits, one limitation is that terms such as "aunt," "uncle," and "cousin" cover a wide range of people, including people to whom you are related through your mother and through your father. The terms also include people who are spouses of your blood relatives rather than being themselves your blood relatives. Eskimo terminology is thus rather vague about your precise connection to relatives except those in your immediate core family. One alternative is to discard the principle of nuclearity and instead consider the principle of line—whether relatives are related to you through your mother or through your father. Such a terminology still indicates gender and generation, but with clarity about the *side* of the family for each relative. The result (see figure 9.5) has some interesting implications. "Mother" is again no longer restricted to the actual mother,

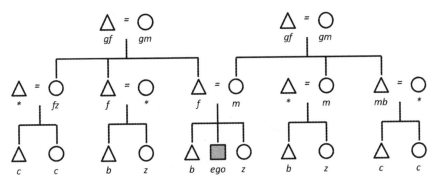

FIGURE 9.5. Iroquois kinship terminology. Notes: *c* = something like "cousin"; * = variable

but includes the mother and her sister (*mz*). This makes some sense even in Euro-American kinship because, insofar as one has a "backup" mother, the most likely candidate is the mother's sister. Likewise, the father and his brother (*fb*) are both "father." The children of the brothers and sisters of your parents now fall into two groups. Those who are the children of your "father" (*f* and *fb*) or of your "mother" (*m* and *mz*) are necessarily your "brothers" and "sisters," since they have the same "father" or "mother" that you do. The others (*mbd, mbs, fzd, fzs*) are not. This is called *Iroquois kinship terminology*.[1] It is a common kind of terminology, used both by cultures that emphasize the male line and those that emphasize the female line.

GENDER, GENERATION, LINE, AND CORE (SUDANESE)

Iroquois is a good general-purpose terminology. It separates out relatives based on whether they are linked through the mother or through the father. That is helpful if the society uses patrilineality or matrilineality as the basis for some kind of larger kin groups (as will be discussed in the next chapter). However, the result still fails to distinguish the "real" father from the father's brother and the "real" mother from the mother's sister. The system also lumps together a variety of people as brothers and sisters, including not only nuclear and nonnuclear relatives but also relatives from both sides of the family. In that sense, it seems to defeat its own purpose of distinguishing the two sides of the family. Given such problems, one might argue that it would be more precise to distinguish *both* core and line rather than choosing between them. The result is what is usually called, again eponymously, *Sudanese kinship terminology*.

---

1   There are variants of Iroquois that are tailored to match the specific needs of patrilineal and matrilineal societies. These are called, respectively, Omaha and Crow. With some reluctance, I am not including a discussion of them here for purposes of brevity. Diagrams of both of them can be easily found online.

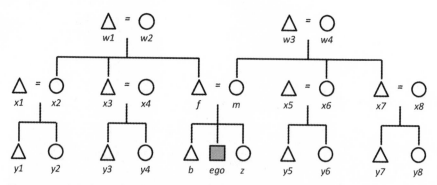

FIGURE 9.6. Sudanese kinship terminology. Note: In Sudanese-like systems, there are often combined categories for the *y* relatives.

It is also sometimes just called *descriptive kinship terminology* because it does what anthropologists try to do: precisely describe each kin relationship. Sudanese kinship terminology is diagrammed in figure 9.6. Here, the father, father's brother, and mother's brother are all clearly distinguished. Likewise distinguished from each other are the mother, mother's sister, and father's sister. In the diagram, then, all the relatives on the parental generation—x1, x2, x3, and so on—have their own separate terms.

There is also a variant of Sudanese kinship terminology that deserves mention because it is so common in strong patrilineal systems, such as the ones in East Asia. Those systems add an additional seniority principle that sharpens the hierarchical aspects of kinship, highlighting which relatives deserve the most respect and obedience. The Vietnamese kinship system is one example, and a description is provided at the end of this chapter. That indication of seniority emphasizes the authority of older relatives over younger ones. Thus, on the male side, an older brother is distinguished from a younger brother and father's older brother is distinguished from father's younger brother. That relative seniority of males is often also reflected in special terms for women that focus on their slot in the male system. In Korean, for example, one's "big mother" is not one's mother's big sister, but your father's older brother's wife.

Perhaps the most general implication of this discussion of different terminologies is the variation. Different human societies conceptually organize their world of kin in different ways. That variation reflects the human basics of gender and generation, with the addition of distinctions about whether kin are inside or outside the core family, whether they are on the mother's or father's side of the family, and sometimes relative seniority within a generation. Terminology thus provides a useful guide to the range of ways humans see their kin relations. Yet the terms are, after all, just terms. A different starting point in looking at kinship provides a contrast—one that emphasizes not kin terms but the actual kin with whom people live and interact most frequently.

POSTMARITAL RESIDENCE

FAMILIES AND HOUSEHOLDS

In most societies, most of the time, people live together in households of some sort. Those households usually have a kinship basis and provide the framework for much of daily life: for eating, sleeping, social relations, and economics. Households vary greatly in their composition. They may be big or small. Some may include only relatives, and some may include nonrelatives. They may have the same membership throughout the year and for many years, or they may shift in composition over the seasons (as with nomadic groups) or change every few years. Households also have varying physical structures: from temporary huts and camps to imposing high-rises; from small structures (in which the whole family may sleep in the same room) to large ones in which family members may be separated for much of the day in separate rooms. Finally, the boundaries of households may be firmly fixed or be relatively porous. Individual households, in some societies, tend to be part of larger compounds—and that compound may be the arena for much daily interaction. On the other hand, what seems like a single, large household may include groups of people whose daily lives are largely separate from each other. They may, for example, have multiple hearths where different sets of household members cook and eat separately.

All these various family households share one fundamental dilemma. In their midst are children who are (usually) the offspring of a married couple within that household. When those children grow up, they will then (usually) marry and have children themselves. That means two people from two different households are going to get together somehow. How they choose each other will be discussed in the next chapter. Here the focus is on a more specific decision point: if they are going to live together, at least one of them will have to move. That decision about who will move is a fateful one, for it shapes what the future household will be. This is why the issue of *postmarital residence* is so crucial.

TYPES OF POSTMARITAL RESIDENCE

There are various types of postmarital residence. The major ones are as follows:

Neolocal. One option for a couple is to set up their own household, separate from either of the households in which they were raised. The result is a new (~*neo*) household rather than the continuation or extension of an existing one. Husband and wife live together, either by themselves or with their children.

Uxorilocal. Here the couple resides with the wife (~*uxor*). This assumes that the wife has already established her own household to which the husband comes.

This occurs but is relatively rare because young women in most cultures have tended not to live alone—rather, they have remained with their original family until marriage.

Matrilocal. Here the couple resides with the wife's family. Technically, this is called *uxorimatrilocal*—specifying that the residence is with the wife's mother (rather than with the husband's mother). This is a common form of postmarital residence in many cultures and has some distinct advantages.

Virilocal. Here the couple resides at the husband's (*~vir*) household. This assumes that the husband has already established his own household. That is more often the case than with the wife, so virilocal residence has been more common than uxorilocal residence.

Patrilocal. Here the couple resides with the husband's family. Technically, this is called *viripatrilocal*—specifying that the residence is with the husband's father (rather than the wife's father). This is a common form of postmarital residence with some distinct advantages—and disadvantages—for both men and women.

Avunculocal. Sometimes the couple will reside with a different relative. This may be a matter of chance: perhaps a husband's father has died but the husband's father's brother is managing his property, and the couple goes to live with him. This form of residence also sometimes occurs as a preferred residence with an uncle (*~avunculus*), especially in matrilineal societies in which a man inherits property from his mother's brother and not from his own father.

None or intermittent. It is also possible that husbands and wives do not live together at all. In such cases men may live alone or together with other men in a separate men's house, sleeping only occasionally with their wives. It is also possible, and not uncommon in contemporary societies, that coresidence of husbands and wives is intermittent. People may travel extensively or take jobs that are far away.

NEOLOCAL, MATRILOCAL, AND PATRILOCAL: ADVANTAGES AND DISADVANTAGES

Of the above options, three deserve additional attention because they occur frequently and because they demonstrate some of the trade-offs for the individuals involved. These are neolocal, matrilocal (technically uxorimatrilocal), and patrilocal (technically viripatrilocal).

For the couple themselves, there are some obvious merits to neolocal residence. The couple starts off fresh on relatively neutral ground. They may not be far away from their parents and may interact with them on a daily or weekly basis. But the couple avoids continuous face-to-face involvement in their daily lives by parents who may well try to control them. There are, however, some offsetting disadvantages. There will be greater social distance between the couple and their parents even if they live close by and, perhaps even more importantly, between the couple's children and their parents (that is, between the grandparents and the grandchildren).

Matrilocal and *patrilocal* residence have the opposite advantages and disadvantages. The couple will retain closer ties to their parents, and their children will be closer to their grandparents. The parents are likely to have some significant assistance in their daily lives from parents (the grandparents to their children). If one agrees with Margaret Mead that cultural transmission really requires three—not two—generations, then building three generations into a single household has great merit. On the other hand, with two adult generations in a single household, there are likely to be questions about who is in charge of what. The grandparents may have the major authority role in the household since it is probably their house in which everybody is living, at least initially. The parents of the children thus lose some of their own authority as parents.

Although there are similarities in the advantages and disadvantages of matrilocal and patrilocal postmarital residence versus neolocal residence, there are also some differences between the matrilocal and patrilocal options. Consider the additional advantages of matrilocal residence. If men are gone for long periods of time, divorce their wives, or die relatively early in life (in war, for example), children are already living with their mother in her mother's house and are not subject to any great dislocation. Contrast that with patrilocal residence. If a woman leaves for any reason, she may wish to take the children with her, especially if they are very young. Thus the grandparents (the father's parents) lose the contact with their grandchildren that patrilocal residence provided. With patrilocal residence, there are thus strong efforts to control the daughter-in-law and make sure she does not have the option of leaving—no matter how bad or even abusive the marriage is. If she were to leave and take the children, that would be intolerable, for in the world of kinship, no children means no future.

The choice of postmarital residence sets the tone for the marriage and the structure of the household. With neolocal residence, households are based on nuclear families. Although other relatives may occasionally coreside, the basic structure is parents and children. Once those children marry, they move into their own households. On the other hand, if there is continued residence with one set of parents, then households have three generations together. In such cases household dynamics will be more complex since they involve more people, and there may be struggles between the parents and the younger couple, between the younger couple

Perhaps the oldest remaining Minangkabau matrilineal longhouse. The private rooms are to the left. (Credit: D. Haines)

themselves about the parents, or between the parents and their child against the child's spouse, who is the outsider. On the other hand, the broader resources of these households may yield an emotionally richer family life and a more profitable economic one. The decision about postmarital residence is indeed a fateful one.

This general anthropological analysis of postmarital residence is challenged in some ways by contemporary North American society in which marriage itself is less frequent, occurs at a later age, and is increasingly separated from the issue of having children: people who are married often do not have children, and people who are not married often do. Changing issues in marriage are discussed in the next chapter, but it is worth noting that changes in marriage itself do not greatly change this issue of residence. Whether a couple is married or not, whether they are gay or straight, they still have to decide on where they will live and whether they will live together. If they have children, whether they are married or not, they must still address the advantages and disadvantages of living with, or close by, the families in which they grew up. Their decisions will greatly affect their own lives and those of their children.

The Yurok on the west coast used houses that were set into the ground and with a narrow circular entrance—only one person at a time could get in. (Credit: D. Haines)

CASE EXAMPLE—VIETNAMESE KIN TERMS

The complaint that might be lodged against Hawaiian, Eskimo, and Iroquois kinship terminologies is that they lump too many relatives together in too few categories. On the other hand, a fully descriptive system, such as the Sudanese one, has the reverse problem: too much detail. There are, however, options in between. Vietnamese kinship terminology provides an example of one such option. It is very detailed in certain areas that are essential to the kinship system, yet in other areas lumps large numbers of different relatives together.

Vietnamese kinship is patrilineal. That is, it links kin together in terms of a blood line of males. That line goes back in time through one's male ancestors and forward in time through one's male descendants. It is essential, then, to distinguish the father's side of the family from the mother's side, and Vietnamese kin terminology is clear on such differences. At the parental generation, there is never any doubt about whether people are on the male or female side. Vietnamese terminology also distinguishes between one's actual parents and their siblings. Finally, since patrilineal kinship needs some ordering among the males, seniority is also important. That too is reflected in Vietnamese terminology.

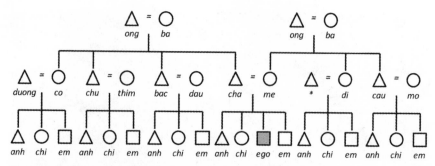

FIGURE 9.7. Vietnamese kinship terminology. Note: This is southern Vietnamese usage; there are variations in Vietnamese terminology by region.

There are actually several regional variants of Vietnamese kinship terminology that have some modest differences. Figure 9.7 shows the version that prevails in the southern part of the country. The terminology for the parental generation has distinct terms for a variety of males: your actual father (*cha*), your mother's brother (*cau*), your father's older brother (*bac*), and your father's younger brother (*chu*). Note particularly that the two "uncles" on the father's side of the family have separate terms. Father's elder brother (*bac*) is in a highly respected position, whereas father's younger brother (*chu*) can be treated with more informality. Although Ho Chi Minh, the late communist leader of Vietnam, was indeed often photographed in happy interaction with children, the English translation "Uncle Ho" fails to convey the deep respect and authority accorded to him as *bac* Ho (father's older brother Ho).

A few other points of the Vietnamese terminology deserve note. For the parents' sisters, "mother" (*me*) is not the same as either mother's sister (*di*) or father's sister (*co*). Furthermore, those women related through blood are distinguished from women marrying into the family. The additional terms for the latter include the mother's brother's wife (*mo*) and the wives of the father's older and younger brothers (*bac* [*dau*] and *thim*). For one's own generation, seniority is built into the terms for brother and sister. There is one term for older brother (*anh*), one for older sister (*chi*), and a separate gender-neutral term for younger sibling (*em*). This is thus a terminological system with considerable detail about gender, generation, line, core, and seniority.

Yet, despite the specificity about relatives in the parental generation, Vietnamese kin terms for other relatives are rather rudimentary. The sibling/cousin terminology is much like Hawaiian. All children of any of the parents' brothers and sisters are "older brother," "older sister," or "younger sibling." Both sets of grandparents are called *ong* (grandfather) and *ba* (grandmother). This does not mean that Vietnamese lack ways to specify their immediate brothers and sisters (they call them "intestinal" siblings/cousins) or to distinguish the two sets of grandparents (the father's parents are the "inside" grandparents). But in the basic kin terms, Vietnamese strikes a balance between being very specific in areas that are crucial to family organization and rather general in other areas.

CASE EXAMPLE—MATRILOCAL RESIDENCE AMONG THE CIBECUE APACHE

The Cibecue Apache are among the westernmost of the Apache in Arizona. Although their lifeways changed greatly during the course of the nineteenth and twentieth centuries, their relative isolation from the surrounding society tended to leave larger portions of their traditional culture intact. That includes a strong attachment to the land and a strong commitment to the spiritual world. Many Apache have individual connections with spirits that help guide them through their lives. Sometimes those spirits come to them, and sometimes the Apache seek them out.

The Apache are matrilineal. The relations among women as mothers, daughters, and sisters govern most of the organization of social life. Clan membership, for example, is based on who your mother is. The relations among women are also crucial to decisions about postmarital residence. Since Apache households (*gowa*) tend to exist as clusters of households (*gota*), both kinds of grouping require discussion. The household (gowa) consists of a married couple and their unmarried children. The Apache thus have nuclear family households. Since the couple sets up their own household when they get married, this is technically neolocal postmarital residence. The gowa may include multiple buildings, with the couple sleeping in a small one-bedroom house while the children are out in a *wickiup* (a brushwood hut covered with mats) or sleeping in an open-air shelter. The gowa, however, is usually part of a cluster of households called gota. These gota are matrilineal in structure. When a man marries, he does indeed set up a new household with his wife. However, that household is located among the households of his wife's kin, including her parents, her sisters, and the husbands and children of her sisters. At the level of the family cluster—the gota—this is thus matrilocal postmarital residence.

After marriage, then, a man goes to live in his own household but among the households of his wife's relatives. This is not always an easy process. The man needs to be on his best behavior, since his wife's parents will be carefully watching him. He would be wise to work hard and be respectful. He would also be wise not to spend too much of his time away from his wife and her family or spend too much time with, or money on, his own family and friends. If he is too generous with his own family or friends, that may be considered a betrayal of his wife and her kin. The young son-in-law is in a somewhat awkward position and potentially an unpleasant one. After all, the women are the framework of the system, the trunk of the kinship tree. The husbands are merely the leaves and, as the Apache put it: "The leaves drop off but the branches and the trunk never break."[2]

There are, however, benefits for the man. He will have the satisfaction of rearing his own family in his own household and having them close to one set of grandparents. Furthermore—as is common in matrilineal societies—his status in his wife's family is likely to increase over time, and eventually he may well become head of the gota—the cluster of households. A man cannot inherit such a leadership role as he would in a patrilineal society. But he can achieve it if under the watchful eyes of his wife's relatives.

SOURCES

Kinship has received a great deal of attention from anthropologists—far more than can be conveyed here. Robin Fox's *Kinship and Marriage: An Anthropological Perspective* (Penguin, 1967) remains a good guide for basic discussions of kinship and descent and is useful both for the material here and the next chapter. A more recent work that aims at a fuller integration of kinship and gender studies is by Linda Stone: *Kinship and Gender: An Introduction* (Westview Press, 2013; 5th ed.). Almost all anthropology texts provide a good overview of kinship, and most will include a discussion of Crow and Omaha terminologies—excluded here in pursuit of brevity. Crow and Omaha are important for showing how generic Iroquois terminology is adjusted for patrilineal versus matrilineal systems.

For the case examples, Hy Van Luong's work on Vietnamese kinship terminology is essential. The fullest version is his *Discursive Practices and Linguistic Meanings: The Vietnamese System of Person Reference* (John Benjamins Publishing Company, 1990). Other useful sources include Danièle Bélanger's "Regional Differences in Household Composition and Family Formation Patterns in Vietnam," *Journal of Comparative Family Studies* 31 (2000): 171–89; Minh Huu Nguyen's *Tradition and Change in Vietnamese Marriage Patterns in the Red River Delta* (PhD dissertation, University of Washington, 1998); and my own *The Limits of Kinship: South Vietnamese Households 1954–1975* (Northern Illinois University's Center for Southeast Asia Studies, 2006). See also Tine Gammeltoft's *Haunting Images: A Cultural Account of Selective Reproduction in Vietnam* (University of California Press, 2014) for a harrowing discussion of parental decision-making in the face of new biomedical technology. The discussion of the Apache is taken from the

2   Keith Basso, *The Cibecue Apache* (Long Grove, IL: Waveland, 2015), 26.

work of Keith Basso—the details coming from his early book *The Cibecue Apache* (Waveland, 2015; orig. 1970), though his *Wisdom Sits in Places* (University of New Mexico Press, 1996) provides much of the impetus for including them here and provides some useful indications of the durability of Apache society and culture. As with the Vietnamese example, I have elided the historical changes and regional variability in the society in order to provide a more cogent introductory discussion of how kinship works.

10

Kinship: Descent and Marriage

This chapter continues the discussion of kinship with an emphasis on larger groups that can be constructed based on kinship, largely through principles of descent, and the way that individuals and groups can be linked to each other through marriage or some similar arrangement. It is through the creation of larger groups and more extensive links across groups that kinship can serve as the framework for social interaction, even in quite large societies. There are advantages to using kinship as the basis for social interaction. Kinship is a relatively portable framework for social relations and one that is especially useful for mobile populations. Another advantage is that kinship can extend intimacy across distance even for settled groups. If people have a tradition of marrying people in a different village or area, then they have potential allies there. A far-off village or area is effectively and affectively "closer" than its geographical distance would suggest.

The discussion begins with the ways kin relations can be used to create larger groups, focusing especially on the options of patrilineality and matrilineality. Both are effective in organizing people into descent groups—although their implications for the personal lives of men and women are rather different. The discussion then turns to marriage—who gets married to whom and how that marriage links groups together—and concludes with contemporary social arrangements that have challenged traditional notions of what marriage is. The first case example at the end of the chapter concerns *son preference* in China and Vietnam (both of which are strongly patrilineal societies), and the other considers the implications of same-sex marriage in North America.

BEYOND THE HOUSEHOLD

Much of the story of kinship concerns the day-to-day relations of people living together within family-based households. However, kinship often extends far beyond the household. Those extensions may be by blood (often called *cognates*) or by marriage (usually called *affines*). The major forms are kindreds, cognatic descent, and unilineal descent.

KINDREDS

One kind of larger kin group can be seen in figure 10.1, which replicates (without the kin terminology) the chart for Eskimo kinship terminology in the previous chapter. From ego's point of view (the shaded square in the chart), there are two sets of grandparents and all the people descended from them, including siblings of ego's parents, their spouses, and a variety of people termed "cousin" in Eskimo terminology. These people are held together by kinship ties that make intrinsic sense to most North Americans. All the people of your own generation in this chart (your brothers, sisters, and cousins), for example, share at least one set of grandparents with you. They are also the children of a brother or sister of one of your parents. Those are close connections to people who are (usually) still alive while you are growing up. If you need to assemble some people for a specific purpose—a wedding, for example— then this set of kin will work quite well. When those people show up at the wedding, many will know each other, you will know most of them, and most of them will be inclined to be generous toward you. This set of people will also work well for other purposes. In early Anglo-Saxon common law, for example, this was the set of people who would pass judgment on you if you were accused of committing a crime.

Such groups are usually called *kindreds*. They are *ego oriented*, which means that the kin group is figured from the point of view of the individual. That is the strength of the kindred: it is the set of relatives who are closest to you. Since kindreds are ego oriented, different people have different kindreds. Your own brothers and sisters will have the same kindreds as you, but nobody else will. When you go to your cousin's wedding, you will see many people you know, but probably many that you do not. If the cousin getting married is on your father's side of the family (say your *fbd*), you will see your relatives from that side of the family and, if they are still living, one set of grandparents. But your mother's relatives (and your other set of grandparents) probably will not be there.

If the social goal is to assemble an occasional group in support of a particular individual, kindreds are an effective mechanism. However, they have three limitations. First, they do not last over time. The kindred of a particular person disappears when that person and that person's siblings die. The people who were part of your kindred

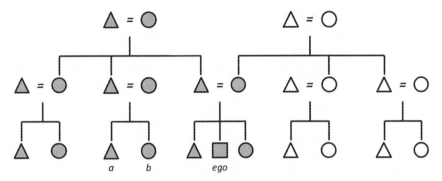

FIGURE 10.1. The kindred. Note: All of these would be in the kindred of ego and siblings, but only the shaded relatives would be part of the kindred of their cousins *a* and *b*.

may still be alive, but their connection to each other through you is lost. Second, since no people (other than siblings) have the same kindred, kindreds are not easily used as an overall framework for society, since people have overlapping membership. If more rigorous group membership is needed, for example, to work on sections of the village canal or to defend portions of a city wall, kindreds yield confusion because people belong to many potential kindreds. Third, kindreds pose problems as they become larger. Constructing a kindred based on relations through shared grandparents may not be too difficult. Trying to trace a kindred through four sets of great-grandparents is far more difficult and would produce yet more overlapping kindred memberships.

COGNATIC DESCENT

Kindreds are thus useful as an ego-oriented ad hoc mechanism to bring kin together, but they are transient, have overlapping membership, and are difficult to expand beyond a fairly modest size. One alternative to kindreds is to create groups not from ego's perspective but from the perspective of ancestors. This is called *cognatic descent* (~*cognatic* meaning related by origin). All the people descended from a particular ancestor are members of the kinship group. This has some significant advantages compared to kindreds. Above all, the anchor point of the group does not change over time or according to the individual involved. The question of membership is always the same and a simple one: Are you descended from a particular person or not? If that person is a famous person (Thomas Jefferson, for example) the task is easy. Even people who may not know the names of most of their ancestors may well know that they are descended in some fashion from this famous person.

Cognatic descent groups have the advantage of an anchor point that endures over time. For someone to know whether they belong or not requires only that their parents have told them that they have a certain ancestor—and a relatively famous ancestor is an advantage. Because they can reach so far back in time, cognatic descent groups can also become large. If you want to bring together a large set of people—for an Independence Day picnic, for example—then cognatic descent groups work well. The people may not know each other personally, but they share the memory of one original ancestor. The main problem with such cognatic descent groups is that people inevitably belong to multiple groups. You might be both a Smith and a Lee. That overlap in group membership may pose no problem most of the time. But what happens when both the Smiths and Lees are having picnics on the same day or going to war against each other on the battlefield or in the courtroom or boardroom? Which side are you on?

Unilineal Descent

The final major option is also based on descent but avoids the problem of overlapping membership by specifying only one line of descent. This is *unilineal descent*. Although you have two parents, you are considered to be formally descended from only one. This works exactly the same as the "inheritance" of family names that is still standard (though not universal) in North America. Thus if your father is a Lee and your mother is a Smith, you are a Lee. The North American convention is *patrinomial*, meaning that the name (*~nom* for name) comes from the father. The alternative of using both family names re-creates exactly the problem of cognatic descent. Names from both parents may work for one generation, but it is hard to keep accumulating them. Furthermore, you have to choose which name comes first. Thus a joint surname like Lee-Smith or Smith-Lee is plausible (but who comes first?). However, if in the succeeding generation a Lee-Smith (or was it Smith-Lee?) marries a Kim-Jefferson, then what?

Inheriting names illustrates well the central problem of descent. If descent from all ancestors on both sides of the family is acknowledged, then people belong to multiple and overlapping groups. That may have some advantages. But it will not be very helpful if there are more specific tasks to be done, property to be inherited, or people to marry. For such purposes unilineal descent has distinct advantages. At birth one becomes a member of *either* the Smith or the Lee group. That does not mean you are unrelated to the other group but only that, when the occasion calls for it, you know where you belong as your primary membership. When the call goes out for "Smiths over here and Lees over there," there are no longer any people milling around in the middle, neither here nor there, not knowing which group to join.

To place people firmly into one group rather than another, a basic rule must be established about the line (thus *unilineal*) by which people will be attached to kinship groups. The basic options are through the mother (thus *matrilineal*) or through the father (thus *patrilineal*). If a child is born into a society and is considered to belong to the mother's group, then that is a matrilineal society since the line of attachment runs through the mother to her mother, to the mother's mother, and so on. If a child is born into a society and is considered to belong to the father's group, then that is a patrilineal society since the line of attachment runs through the father. Anthropological research has shown a great variation in how unilineal descent groups are structured and has also shown that this distinction between matrilineal and patrilineal oversimplifies the options that people actually use. However, the matrilineal and patrilineal options are the predominant ones. Since they are so frequent in human society (and provide an interesting alternative to each other), they merit more detailed discussion.

MATRILINEALITY AND PATRILINEALITY

Matrilineality and patrilineality are in some ways similar options for constructing unilineal descent groups. Both provide a basic rule for deciding who belongs to what group, and that rule is automatically applied at birth. Thus in a matrilineal society when children are born, they will not only be a part of an immediate family group but also part of the mother's line. In a patrilineal society when children are born, they will be a part of the father's line. In both cases those descent lines are the basis for forming kinship groups that endure over time. Those groups are called *lineages*: *matrilineages* in matrilineal society and *patrilineages* in patrilineal society. A lineage is generally defined as a set of people descended from a known ancestor. You are thus related to anybody else who can trace their descent from that same ancestor. Lineages can be small if descent is traced only for a few generations or large if descent is traced for many generations. In some societies there are lineages within lineages. Among the Nuer, who appeared in the chapter on pastoralism and will reappear in the chapter on politics (chapter 12), there are four distinct layers of lineages ranging from a minimal lineage (tracing back four or five generations), a minor lineage (tracing back another generation or two), a major lineage (with yet another generation or two), and a maximal lineage (tracing back nine or ten generations).

When ancestors are not far removed in time, it is easy to trace the links. In a society that writes down or memorizes full genealogies, lines of descent can be traced for hundreds of years. However, unilineal systems still work well even if some of the connecting links are unknown. You can know you are a Lee or a Smith without being able to exactly trace your ancestry back to the original Lee or Smith. All you have to know is what your parents are. There is, in fact, often a leap in matrilineal and patrilineal societies from known ancestors to presumed

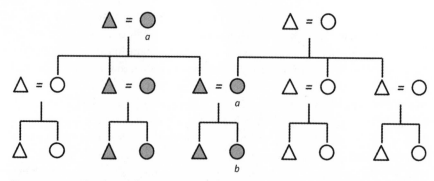

FIGURE 10.2. Patrilineal descent. Note: The *a* women will almost certainly be considered part of their husband's family; the *b* woman is certainly a member at birth but, with marriage, will move into her husband's family.

or mythical ancestors. Anthropologists often use the word *clan* to describe such a group, and sometimes the more specific words *matriclan* and *patriclan*. Exactly as with a lineage, you are born into a clan based on who your mother (matrilineal societies) or father (patrilineal societies) is.[1] A clan typically consists of a number of lineages with some presumed historical relationship. In turn, clans may themselves have relationships with other clans—perhaps a legendary connection among the clan founders.[2]

The decision at birth about whether a person belongs to the mother's or father's line thus permits the development of a wide range of groups of varying size with clearly defined membership. If you are a Lee, you *are* a Lee and you are therefore *not* a Smith. The problem of overlap in membership that occurs both with kindreds and cognatic descent groups is avoided. "Lees here and Smiths there" yields two distinct sets of people with no one wandering around in the middle. That clarity of organization has advantages for the rules of social interaction. For example, if you are a Smith man, you pass your property along to a Smith (not a Lee) and provide hospitality and assistance to any other Smith (but not necessarily to a Lee). You will (probably) marry a Lee and *not* a Smith. This does not mean that women are ignored in patrilineal societies or that men are ignored in matrilineal societies. In fact, in matrilineal societies men often

---

1   A warning is in order here. This particular distinction between clan and lineage is far from universal. Indeed, in the Nuer case Evans-Pritchard was clear that many of the units he called lineages were based on precisely this kind of presumption of relationship. Alternately, in the Chinese case many "clans" are based on actual known relationships. I maintain the lineage/clan distinction here simply because the issue of known versus presumed ancestry is an important one.

2   Such sets of clans are usually called *phratries*. Also, lineages or clans may be organized into a system that has two overall groups whose members marry each other. Such binary divisions are called *moieties*. Moieties can also exist on their own without clans.

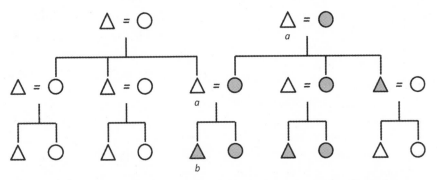

FIGURE 10.3. Matrilineal descent. Note: The *a* men may retain membership in their own original family group; the *b* man is certainly a member at birth and may stay that way.

inherit property and titles from men. But they must inherit from a man who is related to them through women. Thus it is the mother's brother who holds such an important position in matrilineal societies. But the importance of the line *does* mean that it is essential for people to have sons in patrilineal societies and daughters in matrilineal societies. Without that, there can be no future for the group: a patrilineage that produces no sons is at an end; so too a matrilineage without daughters.[3]

There is, however, one fundamental problem in matrilineal and patrilineal descent systems. It is easy to specify that a child belongs to either the mother's or father's line at the time of birth. But what happens when the child marries? Consider a patrilineal society and a marriage between a Smith man and a Lee woman. It is likely that the couple will live with, or near, the husband's family. The woman, after all, will be bearing children who carry on the Smith line. If she is unhappy with the marriage and wants to return to her family, that will be bad enough. If she has had children already and wants to take them with her, that will be a disaster. She would be taking with her the very future of her husband's patrilineage. It is hardly surprising, then, that in patrilineal societies there is much effort taken to ensure that this does not happen. The husband and his family will do their best to make sure that she is fully and irrevocably absorbed into their family. She will likely have to forsake her birth identification as a Lee and become a Smith. That process may be relatively benign or truly oppressive for the woman. The lot of the daughter-in-law in patrilineal societies is rarely an easy one.

The situation in matrilineal societies is, in certain respects, the reverse. When the Smith man marries a Lee woman, the couple is likely to reside with or near her parents. It is, after all, from her parents that they and their children (both male and

---

3   People do not just give up if they do not have the required son or daughter. There are options. Adoption is an important one in many societies.

female) will inherit property. If, after marriage, the man decides he is unhappy with the arrangement and wants to go home, however, the problem is far less severe. He is less likely to want to take the children with him. If the children remain with their mother and she with her family, far less long-term damage is done. There is no threat at all to the matrilineage, since the children are staying where they belong: with their mother and her kin. This does not mean that in matrilineal societies marriage is not valued or that a woman's family does not appreciate their son-in-law. It does mean, however, that there can be greater flexibility about marriage and about sexual relations in general. Even the notion of "illegitimate" children changes sharply. A child that is with its mother is automatically "legitimate"—the child is in the right place whoever and wherever the father might be. For this reason, the situation of the son-in-law in matrilineal society is usually more flexible than the situation of a daughter-in-law in a patrilineal society.

MARRIAGE
MARRIAGE AS A SOCIAL CREATION

In most societies marriage is important both to the individuals involved and to the families and larger kin groups to which they belong. Whether a person marries, when they marry, and whom they marry are all vitally important to these larger kin groups, and they are issues that are potentially controllable. Much of what happens to people in life is not so easily controlled. For example, people die and often neither in a predictable way nor at a predictable time. Societies may pay great attention to death and clothe it in elaborate ceremony, but there are limits to their control. Marriage, in contrast, is a social creation.

There is a great deal of variation in how marriage is carried out in different cultures. Sometimes there are rules or preferences about whom one should marry. Those rules may involve a specific relative. For example, in matrilineal societies a man might be encouraged to marry his mother's brother's daughter. Such a marriage helps tie together two people in whom the mother's brother has a direct interest: his own blood daughter (who is a member of his wife's matrilineal group) and his sister's son (who is a member of his own matrilineal group). In some patrilineal societies, on the other hand, there is a preference for a man to marry his father's brother's daughter. Here the couple are both already within the same patrilineal group and thus the new wife does not have to move to a different group, nor do there have to be exchanges of property with other groups. In many other societies there are no specific rules about whom to marry, but there are rules about whom *not* to marry. People within one's own nuclear family are inappropriate spouses, and often cousins, or at least close cousins, are also inappropriate as well. Sometimes what we call "cousins" are both good marriage partners *and* bad marriage partners depending on what kind of cousin they are. "Cross-cousins" (father's sister's children or mother's brother's children) are often acceptable while "parallel cousins" (father's brother's children or mother's sister's children) are not.[4]

Marriage Types and Variations

In order to talk about prescriptions, proscriptions, and simple preferences about marriage, a variety of terms are used. These are largely "-gamy" words (*~gamos* for marriage), just as those used for postmarital residence were largely "-local" words. The major options are as follows.

Monogamy and *polygamy*. *Monogamy* means there is only one (*~mono* for one) marriage partner. This does not mean that people cannot have more than one spouse during their lives, just that they cannot have more than one at the same time. Having multiple sequential spouses is called serial monogamy and is quite acceptable in many societies. However, some societies do frown on remarriage—especially for widows in patrilineal systems. *Polygamy* means having multiple (*~poly* for many) spouses at the same time. When a man has multiple wives, it is *polygyny* (*~gyne* for female). Polygyny is common in the anthropological record, though it has largely disappeared as a legally recognized union in contemporary nation-states, unless Islamic. When a woman has multiple husbands, it is *polyandry* (*~andro* for male). Polyandry is noted occasionally in the anthropological record but is far less frequent than polygyny.

Fraternal polyandry and *sororal polygyny*. Polygyny and polyandry pose practical and emotional management challenges. Multiple spouses may not get along and tend to advocate for their own children. One solution is for a man to marry sisters or for a woman to marry brothers. These are, respectively, sororal polygyny and fraternal polyandry. As cospouses, brothers or sisters may be better at managing their potential conflicts than would strangers, and they may have a stronger sense that the other spouse's children are related to them too. Another reason for marrying a pair of brothers or a pair of sisters is that by marrying a second person from the same kin group, you are relying on (and strengthening) the relationship you have already formed with that group.

---

4   It may be helpful to remember that in Iroquois kinship terminology, those parallel cousins would actually be called "brother" and "sister." So they are parallel to you in their relationships in the same way that brothers and sisters are. With cross-cousins, by contrast, there is something not parallel. That cousin is not linked by either a brother-brother or sister-sister relationship of your parent. The link crosses gender lines and is thus not parallel.

Sororate and *levirate*. When a woman dies in many societies, one replacement for her may be one of her sisters (called the sororate). When a man dies, one replacement for him is likewise one of his brothers (called the levirate). Both practices reflect the fundamental social fact that a man and his brother, or a woman and her sister, are the only people who are exactly identical in kin terms, who share the same relatives, and who are at the core of a shared kindred. In those senses they really are the same person. In this case as well, the new spouse reiterates the ties between two groups and may signal that the linkage between the two kin groups is a good one and worth maintaining.

Endogamy and *exogamy*. *Endogamy* (*~endo* for within) refers to marrying within a particular group, while *exogamy* (*~exo* for outside) refers to marrying outside a particular group. The terms are applied to local territorial units (for example, *village exogamy* means people must marry outside their own village) and to kin units (for example, *clan exogamy* means people must marry outside their own clan). The terms can also be used more broadly to describe issues of religion, class, ethnicity, and other social categories that continue to affect marriage choices in more complex industrial societies. Endogamy and exogamy can involve formal rules or general preferences. The effect of rules of endogamy and exogamy is to narrow the choice for marriage to those who are neither too close nor too far away in physical or social terms.

Hypergamy and *hypogamy*. Hypergamy and hypogamy refer to whether people are marrying "up" or marrying "down." If one person is marrying up, the other is marrying down so, in order to avoid confusion, the terms are always used from the perspective of the woman. Thus *hypergamy* (*~hyper* for over or above) means a woman marries up and *hypogamy* (*~hypo* for under) means she marries down. Although marrying up or down can happen for a variety of reasons, the options are clearest when comparing matrilineal and patrilineal societies. If a woman in a patrilineal society is marrying down, there can be problems. After all, she is expected to give up most—perhaps all—of her connections to her own family as she becomes fully incorporated into her husband's family. If she comes from a higher-status or richer family, she is less likely to subject herself to the new family and may feel free to go back to where things were better. Thus hypergamy makes sense—and is common—in patrilineal societies. In matrilineal societies, the argument is exactly the reverse. If the woman is marrying up, then her husband who comes to live with her and her family will be all the less likely to devote himself to his marital life. Instead he may tend to return when he wishes to visit with, or work for, the family in which he was raised. Thus hypogamy makes good sense in matrilineal societies.[5]

DEATH AND DIVORCE; REMARRIAGE AND BLENDED FAMILIES

Discussions of rules for descent and marriage must be supplemented by a recognition that sometimes things go wrong. A family in a patrilineal society may lack sons; a family in a matrilineal society may lack daughters. It is rare for families simply to give up in such circumstances. Instead they are often flexible and rather creative. A son-less family in a patrilineal society, for example, may well decide to find a good husband for their daughter and then formally adopt him as their "real" son. In more extreme situations, they may even decide to consider their daughter as a "son" and find her a "wife" who then has children. If they have a son, but that son dies before being married, they may also provide a wife after the fact in what is sometimes called a ghost marriage, since the husband is physically dead but is considered alive for the purpose of the marriage. The physical details of impregnation are easily handled (perhaps by an especially discreet kinsman), though the public explanation may involve a nighttime sighting of the dead man's spirit near the sleeping place of his new wife.

In contemporary North American society, death is a relatively rare occurrence among the young. However, divorce is extremely common. North American families are built largely on the ties of couples (whether heterosexual, gay, or lesbian), but those ties are far from durable or reliable. Divorce is not only practically difficult but is a sharp challenge to the very meaning of families, since it retroactively undoes the history on which the family is based. In that way it is more damaging than death itself. Death takes away a spouse but does not make the marriage retroactively "wrong" or meaningless; divorce often does. Although some divorced couples retain friendly or at least cooperative relations, many remain hostile—perhaps especially if divorce was based on the violation of marital vows of fidelity.

One solution to the statistical dangers of death and divorce is to avoid marriage altogether. People may live alone, or couples may decide to live together, perhaps

---

5   The issue of hypergamy comes up often in the contemporary world as women not only strategize their own futures but those of their children. Hypergamy, after all, will have the effect of the woman having children who are higher status than she was. One interesting wrinkle in the case of modern international marriage is that a woman may well marry down in terms of status when she moves, for example, from a developing country to a developed one. But the new country itself is, in some ways, "higher" status, and her children will have more promising futures there than they would probably have in her original country. For a very good collection of essays on these issues of international marriage, see Nicole Constable, *Cross-Border Marriages: Gender and Mobility in Transnational Asia* (Philadelphia: University of Pennsylvania Press, 2004).

have children, and consider marriage later—if ever. Another solution is to go ahead and marry anyway, accept the risks, and muddle through as best possible. Many people do just that. If divorce then comes, custodial parents struggle with the enormous practical and emotional problems of raising their children on their own, and noncustodial parents (whether voluntary or forced) struggle with *not* raising their children. Children, in turn, may have split allegiances between hostile parents or try to manage split residence with parents who have chosen some form of joint custody. Grandparents may find themselves cut off from the grandchildren they have grown to love, but may also find themselves once again de facto "parents" to their grandchildren while their own child (the actual parent) tries to balance a job and single parenthood. In contemporary North America as well, families are often split by migration. Especially for Mexicans crossing into the United States, tightening border controls often create families that are fractured by distance or by legal status.

Just like son-less patrilineages and daughter-less matrilineages, North American families are flexible. The childless adopt. Those who have been divorced remarry. Children who have moved away from their parents move back in with them—or the parents with the children. More distant relatives take on roles usually associated with parents and grandparents. As these people move in together or come to live nearby in active daily and weekly interaction, they bring relatives of their own. Biologically unrelated children, for example, come to be brothers and sisters. This blending of people into new families is not without stress and confusion for the children. Is your "real" father your biological father? Or is he the man who married your mother and has taken care of you since you were little? There is also stress and confusion for parents. Who has full authority over the child? Is it the original biological parent or the parent who is most frequently at home? Despite such problems, these new blended families serve as a reminder of how flexible human beings can be in constructing and reconstructing their family relationships. Indeed, the best measure of a society's kinship system may be how well it functions when things are *not* going according to plan.

CASE EXAMPLE—SON PREFERENCE IN CHINA AND VIETNAM

In patrilineal societies, families need sons to carry on the family line. If families have many children, then the odds are rather good that they will have sons. However, if families begin to have fewer children, then the odds of having sons are greatly reduced. If—as happened in China—families are only allowed to have one child, then the odds of having a son drop sharply to about fifty-fifty.[6] This puts families in

---

6 Actually the odds are slightly above fifty-fifty. The chance of the birth of a son is statistically higher all other things being equal, but not greatly so.

Korean graves are often in the countryside, but here they are in the city for royalty. The mound behind the building is the actual grave. (Credit: D. Haines)

a difficult position. If their first child is a daughter, they have lost their opportunity to have a son and thus lost irrevocably the ability to carry on the family line. One result is that once this *one-child policy* was implemented in China, a large number of daughters disappeared. Some "disappearances" were doubtless late-term abortions. Other disappearances were daughters who were not officially registered, some of whom ended up in international adoption circuits. Over time, disparity between female and male infants in China has become a disparity between young men and women. The net result is that there are tens of millions of Chinese men for whom there are, statistically speaking, no wives. These men will either remain bachelors, or wives will have to be found from somewhere else. In 2015 the Chinese government decided to rescind the one-child policy, but that will not resolve the problem. There are already some 40 million males in China for whom there are, again statistically speaking, no potential wives within China. If they had a country of their own, this would be a nation of bachelors more populous than Canada and about half as populous as Germany.

The situation in Vietnam has been different. Vietnamese society is also patrilineal, and families recognize that sons are important to continuing the family line.

Gay marriage supporters in front of the US Supreme Court in March 2013. (Credit: Purdue9394/iStock)

However, what is unofficially called Vietnam's "two-child" policy was less restrictive than China's "one-child" policy. So in Vietnam a family's desire for a son was only delayed by having a daughter as the first child rather than being ruled out as in China. That suggests that son preference might work somewhat differently in Vietnam than in China. A wide range of researchers have looked at this issue in Vietnam with a blend of ethnographic work (which is especially good at determining how people think about their options) and demographic analysis (which is especially good at determining if those social views actually correlate with data on the population as a whole).

The ethnographic research produced strong indications of son preference in Vietnam. Indeed, many of the women interviewed had harrowing tales of how much their own worth as women hinged on producing sons rather than daughters. One set of researchers began looking at contraception. They hypothesized that if son preference was strong, then it was more likely that couples who had a daughter but no son would forget to use contraception or that the contraceptive would somehow "fail." They would thus have an excuse for another pregnancy. That guess about increased contraceptive failure turned out to be true, supporting the existence of son preference.[7]

---

7 Contraception in Vietnam involves a variety of means, the major ones condoms and IUDs. Both are subject to failure.

The ethnographic research thus showed evidence of son preference. But was it sufficient, as in China, to produce a population imbalance in the proportion of male and female children in Vietnam? Here the demographers became involved, looking at several sets of data on actual births, including partial information on the parents and their prior children. The results were mixed. The data suggested an imbalance in male and female births, which supported the ethnographic findings on son preference. On the other hand, the imbalance was modest, suggesting that the strength of the preference for sons was limited. Furthermore, there was also evidence of a *daughter preference* among those people who already had a son. That would suggest that an emphasis on son preference obscures other important parental values and goals. Those other values and goals include a desire for daughters in addition to a desire for sons.

The results of this combined ethnographic and demographic analysis suggest two general points. First, general kinship structures—such as patrilineality—continue to have profound effects on the way people organize their lives in the contemporary world. Second, kinship issues often turn out to be more complex than they might seem. The Vietnamese data, for example, suggest that a preference for sons does not rule out a separate preference for daughters. A patrilineally oriented society may well value both male *and* female children. The reverse is certainly true for matrilineal societies, in which men fare very well indeed even though they are outside the formal lines of inheritance and family structure.

CASE EXAMPLE—SAME-SEX MARRIAGE IN NORTH AMERICA

In Canada, same-sex marriage was established throughout the country in 2005. In the United States the process took much longer. The creation of legalized same-sex unions in Vermont in 2000 was followed by broader actions in other places: with legality at the city level (especially San Francisco) and then formally at the state level as Massachusetts in 2004. Ultimately, the United States Supreme Court weighed in to support same-sex marriage in 2015. In Mexico the first legalized same-sex unions were only in 2009 in Mexico City, but the country's Supreme Court upheld the action and further stipulated that the Mexico City same-sex unions had to be accepted as valid throughout the country. Other local jurisdictions followed, with national action proposed by the Mexican president in 2016 and supported by both the Supreme Court and Parliament in 2017. Anthropologists have generally been supportive of same-sex marriage, since the anthropological record is clear that human beings have a wide range of sexual relationships that frequently include people of the same sex and also a wide range of formalized relationships that we would generally call marriages. These also may include people of the same sex.

Opposition to same-sex marriage has, however, hardly disappeared in North America. Some of those in opposition accept the general right of people to live together, but have hesitations about gay or lesbian couples assuming custody of children from prior heterosexual relations, and balk entirely at allowing the adoption of children into same-sex relationships. Gay and lesbian couples also have varied opinions. Some object to the basic structure of contemporary marriage, since they maintain it is inherently based on a heterosexist model. Yet they nevertheless maintain their right to enter into such a marriage on the same basis as other people. Others argue that with new reproductive technologies, the very basis for heterosexual marriage has disappeared.

Ellen Lewin conducted research on the issue and was herself in a same-sex marriage during the period when they were still illegal in the United States. Her comments on what is at stake from the couple's point of view thus carry considerable weight. She suggests two main points. First, the marriage ceremony itself provides an important *ritual* acknowledgment of the union for the couple and for their friends and relatives, whether gay and straight. Commitment is a highly valued quality in personal relationships, and its public acknowledgment for a same-sex relationship, based inevitably on invocations of love, often brings tears to those participating, including those not entirely supportive of same-sex unions in general. One argument for same-sex marriage is thus simply that without such a ceremony, people lose the right to make a public commitment that is emotionally and socially fulfilling to them and to those around them.

Second, she notes the importance of the formal *legal* acknowledgment of the union. Key practical rights are at stake. Legal spouses have access to many employment, health, retirement, and death benefits that do not apply to nonlegal partners. But more than the practicalities, Lewin stresses the *emotional* impact of having official legal status granted by the state. She recounts her own experience going across the border into Canada to be married there when she could not do so in the United States. Her Canadian marriage was a matter of routine legal processing. Yet even from a routine civil ceremony in a foreign country, with no family or friends present, came a strong emotional sense of being truly "married." Even after returning to the United States, where her Canadian marriage did not affect any of her legal rights and obligations, that sense of being truly married persisted.

Lewin thus suggests from her own experience and that of the couples she studied that the approval of both religious and secular authority is important for same-sex couples. That combined approval attests to the authenticity of their relationship and permits them to emerge from concealment not only about sexual orientation per se but about the importance to them of a specific life partner—someone with whom they may already have been involved for years. That official certificate of authenticity may be especially important for same-sex couples who have children—or desire to have them. As always with kinship, the implications of state rules, religious practices, and cultural beliefs about how adults should come together as families plays out on and through the children.

Same-sex marriage also raises a continuing anthropological question about the degree of change and continuity in the contemporary world. If one considers the same-sex part of the issue, then there is clearly a change in social values that is still being contested by many people. On the other hand, if one considers the marriage part of the issue, then the degree of continuity is impressive. The fight for same-sex marriage has been a fight for a quite traditional notion of sexual and life partnership, and often for a traditional kind of ceremony that links two people together through secular and religious authority, and through individual vows, family inclusion, and community witness.

SOURCES

To expand the information on descent and marriage, some of the sources noted in the last chapter are also valuable, particularly Robin Fox's *Kinship and Marriage* (Penguin, 1967) and Linda Stone's *Kinship and Gender: An Introduction* (Westview Press, 2013; 5th ed.). The early social anthropological volume, A. R. Radcliffe-Brown and Daryll Forde (eds.), *African Systems of Kinship and Marriage* (Oxford University Press, 1950) remains a useful indicator of the sheer range of possibilities in descent systems as well as being a who's who of classic British social anthropology. Because these issues of marriage and descent can take some time to absorb, commercial film can be helpful. For example, the Chinese film *Red Firecracker, Green Firecracker* (1994) illustrates the tension in patrilineal systems when there are no sons. In the film that problem is resolved by designating a daughter as a son. As another example, the Dutch film *Antonia's Line* (1995) suggests how something like an informal matrilineage might develop in European society.

For the case examples a few sources that will help track the issue of son preference in China and Vietnam are Tine Gammeltoft's *Women's Bodies, Women's Worries* (Curzon Press, 1999); Dominique and Jonathan Haughton's "Son Preference in Vietnam," *Studies in Family Planning* 26 (1995): 325–37; Susan Short et al., "China's One-Child Policy and the Care of Children," *Social Forces* 79 (2001): 913–43; and Dudley Poston et al., "Son Preference and the Sex Ratio at Birth in China," *Social Biology* 44 (1997): 55–76,). The material on same-sex marriages is drawn largely from Ellen Lewin's comments in a special issue of the *Anthropology Newsletter* 45 (May 2004): 45–46. That special issue also includes other useful articles exploring family ties in the wake of then President Bush's call for a constitutional amendment barring homosexual marriage. See Lewin's *Recognizing Ourselves* (Columbia University Press, 1998) for more detail on her research, and Linda Stone and Nancy P. McKee's *Gender and Culture in America* (Prentice Hall, 2006; 2nd ed.) for a broader review of contemporary gender issues. With the issues of same-sex marriage resolved legally at the national level in both Canada and the United States and on the way in Mexico, other issues may move to the vanguard. Polygamy, for example, is quite common in the anthropological record. Other mixes of individuals in multiple, simultaneous relationships are also receiving increased attention; for example, see Deborah Anapol's *Polyamory in the 21st Century: Love and Intimacy with Multiple Partners* (Rowman and Littlefield, 2010).

11

Economics

Although kinship may be the area of human relationships toward which anthropologists have devoted the most attention, other ways in which human beings are linked together are also the focus of anthropological research. This and the next two chapters present three of those other frameworks for interaction: economics, politics, and religion. It is somewhat arbitrary to present these as separate topics since, in the reality of people's lives, they often intermingle. Events and actions that we label "economic" are often also political; those we call "political" are often also economic. The topic of religion, in turn, includes a variety of spiritual and practical issues that permeate all aspects of people's lives—and thus remerge in the flows of kinship, economics, and politics.

Despite such overlap, the conventional categories of economics, politics, and religion provide a useful framework for considering different aspects of social structure and interaction. This chapter begins by looking at the general topic of economics from an anthropological perspective and then continues with separate discussions of production, circulation, and consumption. The first of the case examples concerns gift giving in Japan and the complex web of social relations created through those gifts. The second case example concerns firefighters and how, in a contemporary society that often seems intent on hollowing out the personal meaning of work, they nevertheless find great fulfillment in their job.

THE NATURE OF ECONOMICS

Economics is a vast field in its own right. There are many potential ways to approach the subject. Often people are most interested in the particular economic arrangements found in industrial societies or in how the economic systems of industrial societies have affected nonindustrial societies. Often people are interested in specific aspects of economic systems. The nature of money, for example, is itself a fascinating topic. In pursuing such topics one can study economics as a large-scale system in which individual people are almost invisible, or one can focus on individual people, their day-to-day economic activities, and how they relate to broader economic systems. Furthermore, one might look at economics as a specific, narrowly defined academic field or more broadly as the basis on which all human life rests. In that broader sense much of the discussion of adaptations in part I of this book might be viewed as primarily about economics.

In this chapter the discussion of economics focuses on three issues that are important in anthropological analysis: first, the *production* of goods and services; second, the *circulation* of those goods and services; and, third, the *consumption* of those goods and services. These issues are not unique to anthropology, but there is a distinctive flavor to anthropological work on them that reflects the discipline's broad cross-cultural approach. Thus the consideration of production is not limited to our own industrial society but includes the full range of how things are produced—and have been produced—in all human societies. The anthropological consideration of circulation requires attention to a far broader range of goods and services exchanged than would occur in a more formal study of economics. Finally, the examination of consumption requires consideration of how people's consumption of goods relates to the totality of their lives. The anthropological approach to economic issues thus reflects anthropology's continuing emphasis on the diversity of the human experience and the need to study all aspects of all people's lives as an integrated whole.

PRODUCTION

RESOURCES, TECHNOLOGY, AND LABOR

In the earlier chapter on industrialism (chapter 7), a simple graphic model for production, figure 7.1, was presented (and is repeated in modified form in figure 11.1). The model suggests that combinations of resources, technology, and labor together create products of different kinds. In the case of agriculture, the product is a crop: rice, for example. The production of rice yields a harvest that can be used in a variety of ways: consumed, saved for later consumption, traded, converted into a more durable commodity (such as money), stolen, taxed, and so on. Likewise,

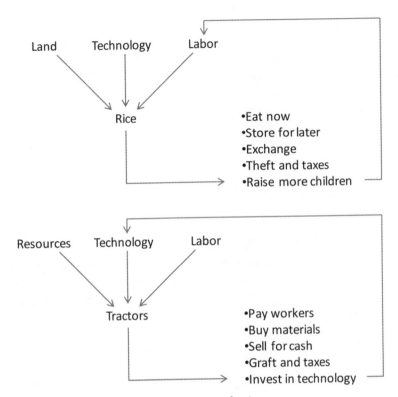

FIGURE 11.1. Models of rice and tractor production

in industrialism a broad range of products is created through a combination of resources, technology, and labor. Here, however, the products are rarely directly used by the producer. Instead they are converted into cash, which is used increasingly more for resources and technology than for labor—though the proportions vary greatly by industry. The worlds of production and consumption are thus largely separated: things are produced in one place and consumed somewhere else. Furthermore, as trade expands, the logistics of both production and consumption become ever more complex: more *resources* from more places used in more complex production processes, more *products* going to more places in more complex distribution networks.

There are many implications of this new kind of economic system. One is that as production, distribution, and consumption spill across national boundaries, there is an uneasy tension between transnational corporations, which function across those national boundaries, and nation-states, which are intent on maintaining those boundaries. In terms of people, the two most important implications are the shift in production from labor to technology and the continuing problem of labor being in the wrong place. The former has left many workers in already industrialized societies at risk; the latter has put pressure on workers to uproot themselves, often from family and community, in order to be where work opportunities exist. Among other things, the unpredictability of what kind of labor will be needed and where it will be needed places educational systems in jeopardy: what exactly is it that they are educating people for? The problem is compounded because while there are overall changes in how goods are produced, there is still enormous variation in production processes depending on the particular product.

GRAPE PRODUCTION IN THE UNITED STATES

As an example of the production process outlined in figure 11.1, consider the resources, technology, and labor going into the production of grapes in the United States.[1] The United States is the world's third-largest producer of grapes (after China and Italy), and nearly nine-tenths of that production is in California.[2] Those grapes are used for several different grape-based products. Well over half of the grapes (58 percent) are used for wine, about a fifth (20 percent) are used for raisins, and about a seventh (19 percent) are used for fresh table grapes—with the remainder mostly for grape juice.

Consider first the difference between producing table grapes and wine. For *table grapes*, it is absolutely essential that the grapes be ripe yet not too ripe, that the bunches be evenly ripe, and that there be no evident damage to any of the grapes. The product needs to taste good, but it also needs to look good. Although the actual growing of the grapes can be technologically complex—including irrigation systems—the harvesting will have to be done by hand. Harvesting is thus labor intensive, and, predictably, the price that is charged for table grapes ($1,520 per ton) is the highest for any category of grape product. The harvesting of *wine grapes* is different. Although the grapes also need to taste good, they do not have to look good since consumers will never see the grapes in their unprocessed form. Automation

---

1   For a good, comparative introduction to the implications of grape production, see Philip L. Martin, "Unauthorized Workers in US Agriculture," in *Illegal Immigration in America*, eds. David W. Haines and Karen E. Rosenblum (Westport, CT: Greenwood Press, 1999). Excellent updates on such agricultural issues and their labor implications appear in *Rural Migration News* (see website at U.C. Davis: http://migration.ucdavis.edu). The data here are from 2014 (latest available at time of writing) from the USDA National Agricultural Statistics Service. Note also that the United States now imports some grapes as well.

2   Canada has also increased its vineyards in recent years (particularly in Ontario), but the value of the wine produced is more than matched by imports of table grapes and grapes for home wine-making.

in harvesting makes sense because bruising the grapes is not a problem—they are going to be crushed anyway. Tractors go down the rows of grape vines shaking the ripe grapes loose. Those grapes fall onto belts or carts that carry the grapes down to the ends of the rows. At the end of the rows, the grapes go onto large gondolas, which are then hauled off to grape-processing areas. Good wine grapes receive a lower price than do table grapes. At $767 per ton, however, there is still adequate income to offset the costs of automation.

Wine grapes and table grapes thus represent two different production processes: one highly automated and one highly manual. The differences between the two make sense in terms of what technology is available and whether that technology is appropriate to the specific product—in this case wine versus table grapes. The situation of *raisin grapes*, however, is less clear cut. On the one hand, raisin grapes need to be relatively complete and treated with some care. People do not want raisin paste; they want recognizably individual raisins. That argues for a manual harvesting of the grapes. On the other hand, much of the surface of the raisins is so transformed by drying that less care is needed to make sure they are not bruised in harvesting. That would be an argument for automated harvesting. An automated system for harvesting raisins has long been available. The dried-on-the-vine (*DOV*) system requires growing grapes on pergolas, which support the vines. The vines are cut when the grapes are ripe, and the grapes then dry on the cut vines (which are held up by the pergolas). When the grapes are dry—and thus more resistant to damage in handling—they are shaken loose by a machine, and then hauled off for cleaning and packaging.[3]

Despite that option for automation, raisin harvesting has tended to remain a manual process. After nearly twenty years of development of the DOV process, only a quarter of the raisin acreage actually used it or some other automated process.[4] Part of the reason is that the DOV method requires significant investment up front. The machinery is expensive, and the fields need to be reconstructed with the pergolas. Just that reconstruction can run $10,000 per acre. With the size of holdings being relatively small and the price for raisin grapes far lower ($387 per ton) than for table or wine grapes, the arguments for automation are more tenuous. Finally, the cost of manual harvesting has not been very high. The reason for that has been the ready availability of immigrant labor, much of which is undocumented. Undocumented workers are willing to work for lower wages and in kinds of work

---

3   This could change again if new grape varieties that dry on the vine without being cut gain acceptability—the taste is a bit different. This is another case in which the logic of production may shift again: don't engineer the process; engineer the resources. Note also that there is yet another process, which allows the grapes to dry on the ground (on trays).

4   *Rural Migration News*, July 2015.

that are largely unacceptable to the native-born population. Thus, even in a highly industrialized country, the "old-fashioned" way of manual labor continues to win out over advanced technology.[5]

This single example of grape production illustrates the broader need for detailed attention to specific production processes. Even though there is much argument about North America being fully industrialized and even entering a "postindustrial" period, much of the actual production continues to be manual. This is a warning that assumptions about advanced industrial (or postindustrial) economies may get in the way of understanding how things are actually produced. The example also provides useful reminders of the social and political aspects of economic production. In particular, the size of landholdings and the dynamics of US immigration policy tilt the decision about production toward manual rather than automated processing. Economic decisions have social and cultural underpinnings.

CIRCULATION

Although anthropologists have always been interested in how things are produced, it is probably fair to say that the way goods move among people has been their stronger interest. Indeed, some anthropologists have argued that the circulation of goods among people is the very framework of a society. When you watch goods moving from person to person, you are watching the society's internal movements and witnessing the processes that make and remake its social structure.

Anthropologists distinguish three general ways in which goods circulate in a society: reciprocity, redistribution, and exchange. *Reciprocity* invokes a give and take between people that is more than simply economic. It is often phrased in terms of gift giving rather than economic exchange per se. *Redistribution* invokes a more centralized, ordered, and controlled circulation of items from where they are produced to where they will be used. Finally, *exchange* invokes a circulation of goods that is based more strictly and narrowly on our customary notions of "economic" factors. One item (or service) is given in exchange for another or, more conveniently, sold for a sum of money and another item (or service) is bought with that currency. For each of these kinds of circulation of goods, anthropologists are concerned not only with the circulation itself but also with the relationships among the people involved.

5　This example also illustrates why agricultural producers—who might be assumed to be relatively "conservative"—are usually a major force in efforts to protect undocumented migrants and even to provide legalization for them.

RECIPROCITY

One way to circulate goods is to give them away. Gifts are important in all human societies, and in almost all cases a gift given implies that there will also be a return gift. This give-and-take of gifts, the anthropological record tells us, is sometimes simple and at other times complex. At its simplest, gift giving occurs between individual people. Thus, as during the end-of-year Christmas period in North America, people give gifts to family members and friends. There is an expectation that if you give people such gifts, they will also give gifts to you. There is also an expectation that the value of the gifts will be roughly equivalent. An expensive gift should not be reciprocated with a cheap one—nor a thoughtful gift with a perfunctory one. Balance is needed. This kind of reciprocity between individuals is called *balanced reciprocity*.

Yet even a simple, simultaneous exchange—as at Christmas—can be complex. Some people (like parents) are much richer than others (like children), so the equivalency cannot be in cash value. But if equivalency is not in cash value, then what is the measure of equivalency? Attempts to assess the equivalent thoughtfulness of, for example, gifts between lovers can be excruciating. Achieving balance in reciprocal gift-giving is even more fraught when the return gift is later (for example, birthday gifts) or when the value of the gifts is high in either financial or emotional terms. To give somebody a valuable gift that has no possible immediate return gift requires a considerable amount of *trust*. I remembered your birthday with an expensive and thoughtful gift; will you remember mine?

Reciprocity also occurs between groups. Consider a North American wedding. The bride's family is likely to pay much of the cost of the event, for which they will themselves get little return. Various members of the family may also make contributions for specific parts of the overall ceremony: for food or drink at the reception, for example. Those attending will give gifts to the new couple and receive only token gifts in return. In some cases a gift may be returned at a subsequent wedding, but in many cases there will be no direct return at all. The older generation, after all, is generally already married, so this cannot be a system of exact balance among all those involved. This is *generalized reciprocity*. In the long run there will be return gifts to other people, and these generalized distributions may eventually even out: those who receive more at one wedding may, over time, contribute roughly equivalent gifts in return at other weddings. But it is not balanced exchange between individuals.

In both forms of reciprocity, goods are circulated in a way that is not "economic" in our usual sense of the term. Instead, the circulation is based on personal, social relationships that require some measure of trust between and among the people involved. One implication is that the relative value of these gifts must be determined by the parties themselves. If people see the return gifts as not balancing the original gifts, then their social relationships are likely to be damaged. That is one reason why return gifts are often somewhat more valuable than the original gift. If the return gift is "cheaper" in any way than the original gift, the return gift may well be seen as insulting. Probably better to err on the high side in the value of the return gift—but not so high as to create a ruinous escalation of costs.

REDISTRIBUTION

A different kind of circulation occurs when someone has the authority—or simply the raw power—to determine that certain goods should be moved from one place to another and from one person to another. This often occurs on a small scale in households. Sometimes it is the father, sometimes the mother, sometimes a grandparent who collects money or other goods from the family members and then redistributes them to meet everybody's needs. Redistribution also occurs on a large scale when governments tax people and use those taxes to support public activities. Those activities may not even benefit the people who paid the taxes—both nonparents and parents, after all, pay the taxes that support public schools. Redistribution may also occur at intermediate levels of society. Thus in societies with strong lineages, lineage organizations may have required contributions that move wealth from the more affluent members toward those with fewer resources.

As with reciprocity, the circulation of goods through redistribution is not exactly "economic" in the usual sense of the word. Instead, there is some person or set of people who have the authority to decide how goods will be circulated. This redistribution looks rather more political than economic. Several implications of this kind of circulation are especially important for the relationships among the people involved in the circulation. One is that the circulation can become rather impersonal compared to the direct, highly personal nature of reciprocity. Another is that the people providing the goods (or money) do not necessarily agree that the redistribution is fair. If people do agree that the redistribution is fair, that is certainly better, but not necessary. Nevertheless, if people do not agree that the redistribution is fair, they may try to oppose it by refusing to turn over wages to their family, neglecting to pay appropriate amounts to their lineage, contesting their tax bill on an individual basis, or taking political action to have taxes reduced.

EXCHANGE

Finally, goods may be exchanged based on more direct economic value. Barter is one possibility: exchanging something you do not need for something you need, or perhaps just need more. If there are many goods to be circulated, an actual physical marketplace provides advantages. Instead of going to different people in different places for different commodities, all goods can be brought together at one time. Weekly or monthly markets may suffice—and are common in agricultural societies. With sufficient volume, as in cities, continuing marketplaces develop. Such marketplaces may have buildings or only be sets of stalls in an open area or along the sides of a road. As these markets become more formal and institutionalized, they tend to become more impersonal. Nevertheless, some elements of personal interaction tend to creep back into even such explicitly economic transactions. After all, doing business with people on a regular basis requires something of the same trust seen in balanced reciprocity. As the markets cease to be actual stores and become online businesses, however, impersonality increases exponentially. There is almost no personal, human contact.

This kind of circulation is thus primarily economic. It benefits from the use of a standard currency so that all goods are automatically priced in terms of a single standard. The increasing use of money, in turn, itself changes social relationships. Money, unlike perishable products and single-use items, can be accrued indefinitely. That tends to undermine the logic of giving things away rather than hoarding them, of investing in social relationships rather than investing in investing. As exchanges become more mercenary and impersonal, formal legal structures may be needed to regulate them since people are no longer dealing with each other on the basis of personal connections, reputations, and trust. On the other hand, the increasingly broad world of online product reviews has created a new kind of metatrust based not on individual relationships but summed group experiences.

CONSUMPTION

Except in industrial societies, human beings have by and large consumed most of what they have produced, whether their "production" was by hunting or fishing, cultivating crops, or taking care of animals. Consider, for example, how pigs have been used as a food source in foraging societies compared to how they are used in industrial societies. In foraging societies pigs would be hunted in the wild. If multiple people are in on the hunt, those people would likely be kin or close friends. Those people would usually be using tools (bows and arrows, spears) that they themselves had made. When the pig was killed, it would be shared among the hunters who would, in turn, share it with their kin and friends. It is nice to share and, besides, hoarding is not going to work well without some way of preserving the meat. That is the practical logic of reciprocity: give your excess now and receive someone else's excess in the future. In industrial societies, by contrast, pigs are, for the most part, commercially raised. Those who raise the pigs sell them for cash. Those who kill the pigs do so in a disassembly line setting using tools that are provided to them. They do the killing and the carving when and how they are told to do so by people who are their bosses. Those bosses are generally trying to maximize the money they are making, rather than proving their social status by giving away the profits to the workers. On the work floor people are often strangers to each other and may not even have time to talk. From this job the workers take home not the pig but money, which they then share with a different set of people from those with whom they work.

The traditional link between production and consumption thus seems largely severed in industrial societies. Even growing crops is based on the new model; farmers may grow grain, but they still buy bread. Still, people in industrial societies often reestablish links between production and consumption in their lives. Hunting and fishing, for example, remain popular in North America, and here, as with foragers, what you get is what you eat. Cooking itself can provide a partial reunion of production and consumption with food "made from scratch" at home, especially if some of the food comes from one's own garden. Home improvement is similar: you may buy the overall product (the house), but you can still personalize it yourself. And, of course, human reproduction and child-rearing take place at home, and those are productive tasks, even though much of the raising of children has been taken over by formal educational systems. This new world of consumption, though largely cut off from the world of production and largely fed by impersonal forms of circulation, is still very much a human world.

The sheer scale of consumption in contemporary societies, and the degree to which the world is bound together by the production and circulation of all kinds of commodities, provide some intriguing options for considering the implications of how people decide what to consume, why they make the choices they do, and what kinds of human meaning they find and create in their consumption. People may no longer create the objects in their daily lives, but they do have options in choosing those objects and frequently customize them to make them more personal. Furthermore, the context in which products are used reflects and creates much social and cultural meaning. Televisions provide a good example. In North America they were originally for family viewing, one set to a household. In developing countries the first televisions are often for an even larger community, with neighbors and kin from outside the household joining in. Over time, however, watching television has become increasingly segmented and individualized, and indeed the basic product, the television, is now giving way to a variety of screens on which entertainment can be watched, including clips of it on social media. The range of choices in what to consume and how to consume it is vast indeed, and highly individualized.

The separation of the world of consumption from the world of production does, however, pose some problems for people. One is social. Human lives are divided in a fairly arbitrary way between work and home. Work provides the economic means to maintain people's families and homes, but it also requires their absence from those homes, usually for about half their waking hours.[6] Furthermore, if all household members are working (or going to school), much of the time at home is devoted to simple maintenance or some entertainment (especially television or equivalent), rather than with more elaborate social interaction. As different household members go off to different work, they are embedded in different environments that may pull them in different directions. Once back at home, they have little time to do the social repair work needed to reestablish their relationships and their solidarity against those outside influences. The fragmentation of families in contemporary society is one result. The more time people spend away from each other, the more time is needed for catching up with each other—but the less time there is for actually doing so.

There are also broader economic implications of the production/consumption divide for the society as a whole. If people have to buy the commodities they need to live, then they have to have money. Unless born wealthy, they have to work. If they do not have income and they cannot buy commodities, then there is less demand for goods. In a consumer-oriented economy, that is a big problem. Furthermore, if there are fewer people in a society, then there is also less demand for goods. In most industrialized societies fertility levels are falling and actual population declines will become more common. Sagging wages, increased unemployment, and fewer people is a recipe for disaster in capitalist-oriented economies. The Big Stall, which has followed the Great Recession, underlines this. Only the rapid development of China (the major engine of the last commodity supercycle) and the relatively large and stable economy of the United States kept the world system afloat. By 2017, with a cooling Chinese economy, a still slow North American economy, a virtual lack of growth in most other advanced economies, and the danger of full collapse in export-producing countries, the situation remained worrisome.

Anthropologists find themselves in a difficult situation in looking at economics in the contemporary world. Their research tends to focus on the human level and shows both how people manage to rehumanize increasingly dehumanized economic systems but also the way such systems do in fact damage people, undermining their current efforts and dooming their future ones. That helps explain the recent surge in anthropological concern with public policy: how can the broader economic and political system be reconstructed in ways that benefit all people in material terms and that also bring back into economic life the human rewards of social interaction and

---

6   US data from the Bureau of Labor Statistics, for example, show an average day for employed persons of roughly eight hours at work, eight hours sleeping, and eight hours for the rest (US DOL, *American Time Use Survey*, www.bls.gov/tus/).

free individual expression? Here, then, anthropologists must often turn from their innate appreciation of human adaptability and diversity to critique of the structures of power that constrain human adaptability and reshape diversity as inequality.

CASE EXAMPLE—GIFT GIVING IN JAPAN

In Japan, gift giving is an elaborate, well-developed social art. Gifts are given for many reasons, and return gifts for them are expected. Those return gifts then create an expectation of their own return gifts. The balancing of gift and return gift (and return gift for the return gift and so on) is a difficult one. A common warning to newcomers to Japan is that it is easy for the process to get out of control. With a tendency for the return gift to be more elaborate than the initial gift, this "balanced" reciprocity may turn out to be unbalanced and lead into an escalating and financially ruinous relationship.

One especially interesting aspect of Japanese gifts is the packaging. Even such token gifts as *omiyage*—gifts brought back from trips for friends, families, and coworkers—are elaborately wrapped. Indeed the wrapping and presentation are so extensive that it is sometimes hard for foreigners to tell what the object is and even whether it is something durable (a set of napkins) or something edible (a set of rolled sweets). More elaborate gifts are packaged in multiple layers. A black lacquer box with the imperial design that came to my family when I was young (and sits in my dining room today), for example, came inside a carefully crafted paulownia wooden box, which was wrapped in silk, and then placed within another carefully crafted regular wood box. One result of this packaging is that it is hard to forget that an object is indeed a gift. The packaging is itself so intricate that it is likely to be kept rather than discarded. The object itself can thus never be extracted from its social context. Indeed, such gifts are often kept in their original packaging and brought out only occasionally. That helps explain the clean interiors of Japanese houses. There is little clutter, since many possessions are only displayed when it is actually time to appreciate them.

This packaging has implications for actual gifts but also implications for things that we might not consider gifts at all. For example, if one purchases a service from somebody outside an actual store, it can be inappropriate to pay for it by counting out currency. That would imply that this is an economic transaction devoid of any human respect. Instead, money is placed in an envelope and presented more as a gift than a payment. It is better yet to wrap the money in some special paper, place that in a nice envelope, and perhaps also give a small token gift at the same time—which would, of course, also be wrapped. What would seem to be simple economic transactions are thus packaged as personal social relationships.

A market in Morocco. This one is in a town designated as a UNESCO heritage site. (Credit: D. Haines)

All this packaging does well in underlining the social aspects of reciprocity in Japanese society. Even economic exchanges can be packaged as gifts and return gifts, thus bringing the cold world of cold cash back into the warm glow of human reciprocity. There are, however, some potential negative implications as well. It can

Reciprocity can be as simple as two people paying attention to each other. (Credit: Garnet Photo / Shutterstock)

become difficult, for example, to distinguish a gift from a bribe. Was that elegant Satsuma pottery that now sits on my bureau simply a gift to acknowledge a neighbor or was it intended (as my father feared when he received it many years ago) to "buy" favorable action on a property dispute? Is the "gift" of a rather large sum of money for a modest New Year's door decoration in Japan anything other than extortion when the people providing the decorations are from the local underworld?

CASE EXAMPLE—THE LAST BEST WORK: FIREFIGHTERS IN NEW YORK CITY

Miriam Lee Kaprow was a native New Yorker and spent much of her adulthood in ballet and modern dance. An injury pushed her career interests in new directions, and she obtained a degree in anthropology when she was in her early forties. Her dissertation research was on Gypsies in Spain, and she continued that interest as a founding member of the American chapter of the Gypsy Lore society.[7] She was fascinated, among other things, by the ways Gypsies resisted the values and

---

7   The preferred term is now usually "Roma," since "Gypsy" is often viewed as pejorative. Nevertheless, I retain her original usage of the term here.

organizational structures of the wider society. They contested the identity that the wider and stronger society wished to impose on them. They were and continued to be their own people. She admired that.

Miriam Kaprow's friends suggest that she—always known as Mimi—was a particularly engaging person, professionally active, and with two twin devotions: her family and anthropology. She was, as anthropologists should be (and as few of us manage to be as often as we should), filled with energy, innately sociable and attentive to her friends, fully engaged with the people she studied, and a dutiful ethnographer of them. Like many other anthropologists, Mimi also developed new interests over the course of her life. One was firefighters. Firefighters were, she believed, resisters like the Gypsies. What they were resisting was people telling them how to do their job. That job was an extraordinarily hazardous one. The accounts she collected from firefighters suggest not only the general danger but the unpredictability of the danger. It was not so much the fire itself, but what different air flows could do to a fire. Simply opening the door to a smoldering room might introduce enough air to turn it into an inferno. A shift in wind might change a fire's direction. Firefighters had to consider not only what a fire was at the moment but all the different things it could become. Their lives hung in the balance.

To do their job—and to stay alive—required teamwork, but also great independent judgment. Firefighters had little patience with bureaucrats sitting in offices who tried to tell them how to do their job. That horrible risk of the job bought freedom from very much supervision. You were on your own to do your job because in saving lives, you were risking your own. For Mimi that was heroism, and it was also what made firefighting "the last best work." She noted the dying words of a New York fireman: "It's still the best job in the world." But firefighting was not only dangerous and heroic; it was also fun. Mimi recounted with relish the extent of jokes, pranks, and games among the firefighters: the way firefighters might wake to find themselves tied to their beds or their genitals painted (especially appropriate for men getting married) or the masked, naked firefighter who would appear from time to time at fires and—true to legend—remain anonymous despite numerous attempts to unmask him. We don't "go to work," firefighters would say to her; we "go to play."

Here then was that unusual job in the modern, bureaucratic world: a job that you performed independently using your own judgment and for your own satisfaction. The price paid for that freedom—and that satisfaction—was risk. It was the "red devil." But in that fight with the devil, you at least did not have a supervisor looking over your shoulder reciting what the manual said you were supposed to do. Your job was your job, and you did it. It might save other lives or cost you yours. But it was still the last best work in a society that created ever more restrictive, supervised, and dehumanized work environments.

SOURCES

For the (vast) subject of economics, four sets of work merit particular attention. One involves actual markets, for which Clifford Geertz's *Peddlers and Princes* (University of Chicago Press, 1968) still serves as a good example. Another is the early work in industrial anthropology, which is covered well in Elizabeth M. Eddy and William L. Partridge (eds.), *Applied Anthropology in America* (Columbia University Press, 1987). The third is the more recent analysis of contemporary work, for which a good source is the *Anthropology of Work Review*, a publication of the Society for the Anthropology of Work (itself a section of the American Anthropological Association). The fourth is the extensive work on reciprocity, for which Marcel Mauss's *The Gift* (various versions available) and Roger Sansi's *Art, Anthropology, and the Gift* (Bloomsbury, 2014) might provide useful brackets. Three more general overviews may also be useful: Chris Hann and Keith Hart's *Economic Anthropology* (Polity, 2011); Richard Wilk and Lisa Cliggett's *Economies and Cultures: Foundations of Economic Anthropology* (Westview Press, 2007; 2nd ed.); and James G. Carrier's *A Handbook of Economic Anthropology* (Elgar Original Reference, 2014; 2nd ed.). On the issue of slaughterhouses, there is an extensive literature, but I would single out the classic article by Mark Grey: "Immigrants, Migration, and Worker Turnover at the Hog Pride Pork Packing Plant," *Human Organization* 58 (1999): 16–27.

For the topic of gift giving in Japan, a good starting point is provided by Joy Hendry. She has written on the subject in various books, but the best introduction is her *An Anthropologist in Japan* (Routledge, 1999). Almost any book on Japanese culture—indeed almost any travel guide about Japan—will provide the basics not only of gift giving but of some of the interpersonal styles that also make sense in terms of reciprocity. For the example of firefighters, see the warm tribute to Miriam Kaprow in the Winter 1999 special issue of the *Anthropology of Work Review*, in which her colleagues carefully reconstructed her last work after her death from cancer. Firefighting continues to be one of the occupations with the highest personal satisfaction, and her work does exceptionally well in terms of capturing the spirit of independence in that work.

12

Politics

Politics is often defined in terms of formal government and sometimes conveys an implication of shrewd maneuvering to gain desired ends. For anthropologists, however, the term is far more general in meaning and covers a wide range of political forms, processes, and functions. One of the main concerns of anthropologists in studying these issues is to examine their variability from small societies of a few hundred people to countries such as India and China with populations of over a billion. For anthropologists, as well, politics is not just about personal maneuvering for power but also about the tasks that societies must accomplish to maintain themselves.

The discussion begins with a brief overall introduction and then focuses on three major concerns that anthropologists have in looking at politics: first, the different kinds of political systems that have been found throughout the world; second, the basic functions of politics (*external relations*, *internal order*, and *infrastructure*); and third, the nature of politics and governance in contemporary societies. The chapter's two case examples describe *"headless" government* among the pastoral Nuer in the Sudan and the situation of indigenous minorities (specifically the Yanomami of Brazil) within modern state systems.

THE NATURE OF POLITICS

Politics in its broadest sense is about social organization. The term assumes a social entity of some kind beyond the immediate family that has its own interests, options, obligations, and characteristics. In the contemporary world politics is usually seen in terms of nation-states that are geographically based, have clear borders, and a formal political apparatus. This need not always be the case. Social groups can be based on factors other than fixed territory, can move across boundaries, and often have no formal political roles. Yet such groups still have political systems and functions. They also usually have a sense of a definable people, a "we," who are bound together in a common destiny. The nature of that common destiny depends on who the "we" are and what other people are the "they." People living in relative isolation may well have a very different political system from a similar set of people living in close contact with others.

The nature of the common political destiny also hinges on the sheer mass of the society. In discussing the different adaptations in part I of this book, for example, the four recurring themes were control over the environment, density of settlement, complexity of social organization, and mobility. Nowhere are the implications of these themes clearer than in politics. The more *control* there is over nature, the more essential common responsibilities will be to maintain and monitor that control. For example, the more extensive the irrigation, drainage, and flood control structures of an agricultural society, the more vital will be the public task of maintaining that infrastructure over time. The greater the *complexity* in social organization, the greater the need for oversight and harmonization. The greater the population and *density* of settlement, the more likely that there will be disputes and that those disputes will be among strangers. Simple dispute resolution becomes a more extensive, more difficult, and more public task. Finally, *mobility* is crucial. The greater the mobility of the people, generally the more difficulty there will be in tracking them and ensuring that people are in the "right" place, especially that they are not moving at will across the borders of political systems or evading their public responsibilities.

These issues of control, density, complexity, and mobility underlie the initial two topics to be discussed below: first, the *different kinds of political systems* and, second, the *basic functions of political systems*. As political systems become more complex and more formal, however, a third issue arises. If there is to be a stable and effective political system that meets common needs, then there must be people to do that work. Those people must work toward the public good rather than toward their own personal interest. This problem of finding competent people who will work for the public good has been one of the most intractable problems of government. No sooner do people gain political power, it seems, than corruption begins. Those in politics thus become all too "political." That is the third of the topics addressed below: the distinction between *politics and governance*.

FOUR KINDS OF POLITICAL SYSTEMS

The different kinds of political systems that anthropologists have found correlate closely with the different adaptations described in part I of this book. The kind of political system found among foragers is called the *band*. Among horticulturalists are generally found *tribes*, which are, in technical anthropological terms, political systems based explicitly on kinship. Among some agriculturalists and pastoralists, there are more formal political systems that transcend kinship, which are called *chiefdoms*. Finally, in larger agricultural and industrial societies are found *states*— the form of government with which we have the most experience. These four types of political systems are outlined below in terms of (a) their essential characteristics, (b) the kinds of special political roles that exist in them, (c) the kinds of external and internal conflict to which they must respond, and (d) the way in which effective organization is achieved by that particular type of political system.

BANDS

Bands are small, loosely organized groups with informal leadership.

a. Band societies are found among foraging societies and are characterized by small, mobile, and flexible social groups. For most band societies it is difficult to even distinguish a separate political system. Politics, economics, and kinship overlay each other.

b. In band societies there are few, if any, formal political roles. There may be leaders, but their roles are informal and task limited. They are *primus inter pares* (first among equals) rather than having a formal status that distinguishes them from other people.

c. Band societies are subject to both internal and external conflict but usually have the option of resolving such conflict informally. Since ties to particular pieces of territory are not strong, external conflict can be avoided simply by moving away—and perhaps returning later. Internal conflict can be resolved through discussions among the relatively few members of the group.

d. The relatively small size of bands is crucial to how they work. The people have usually lived and worked together for many years and are usually related by ties of blood or marriage. They thus know with whom they are dealing, and they know from experience that they need to be on good relations with these people for their own future survival. The key to band societies is thus that *everybody knows everybody else*.

TRIBES

Tribes are well-defined groups structured along the lines of kinship.

a. Tribal systems are common among larger groups—usually horticultural or pastoralist—that have more complicated organizational needs. Here there is indeed a separate political system, but that system is grafted onto a kinship structure. In many cases that kinship structure is based on a careful accounting of blood relations; more often it is a combination of careful accounting of some blood relations and the assumption of prior blood relationships with other people. That means, in the kinship terms already described, that tribes will include both lineages and clans, and probably some assumed relationship among clans.

b. There are some formal political roles in tribal societies, but these are largely based on status in kinship groups. A tribal council, for example, is likely to be a council of the heads of kin groups. A tribal leader may well be the head of the most important lineage or clan, though sometimes other persons are chosen because of their capabilities.

c. Tribes may have both internal and external conflict. External conflict is hard to avoid. Among pastoralists, for example, reliance on resources even at one time of year—water in the dry season, for example—requires the certainty of access to that area, even though it is only needed during part of the year. Internal conflict is likely to be more common and more complicated simply because of the greater value of property and the increased number of people.

d. Perhaps the most important characteristic of tribal societies is that everybody is part of the kinship structure on which the political system is based. People may not necessarily know all the people with whom they deal, but they know the kinship group to which they belong, know the other kinship groups in the society, and know what the proper relation is between them. The key to tribal societies is thus that *everybody knows everybody else's group*.

CHIEFDOMS

Chiefdoms are centralized political entities with special, usually inherited, political offices.

a. In chiefdoms, political systems are separate and distinct from the kinship system. In agricultural or horticultural societies, with their storable and transportable surpluses, different groups of people become united under a chief, who may be outside their immediate kinship group or their local territory. Chiefdoms unite people from different groups—even groups that are antagonistic to each other.

b. Chiefdoms have special political positions. Above all, they have a ruler to whom special obligations are owed and from whom special services may be received. For example, the chief frequently decides disputes and determines how external conflicts will be resolved. Chiefs have their own resources and their own power.

c. Chiefdoms, are likely to have frequent internal and external conflict. The complexity of the society, which may include groups with diverging cultures and interests, provides the likelihood of internal friction and dispute. Externally, those outside the chiefdom may envy its resources, especially since they are conveniently gathered together by the chief. The more opulent the chief's lifestyle, the more clear it will be to others that there is indeed something worth taking.

d. Chiefdoms cannot be organized on the same basis as band societies, in which the small scale of the society permits a very personalized social interaction. Nor can they be organized like tribal societies, where everybody knows the kin groups of everybody else and what the mutual obligations are. In chiefdoms people may not know each other personally or understand how to interact with them according to rules of kinship. They do, however, know that they are all subject to the chief. The key to chiefdoms is thus that *everybody knows the chief.*

STATES

States are complex, centralized political entities with defined borders and formal officials.

a. State societies are generally based on intensive agriculture or industrialization. They are thus larger, far denser in population, and linked strongly to territory. The combination of valuable resources, transportable commodities, and people who often do not know each other well is both productive and volatile.

b. In state societies the political system is highly developed and based largely on territorial, rather than personal or kinship, bases. The political system includes formal organizations and defined tasks, whether these involve dispute resolution, irrigation systems, tax collection, transportation networks, or military action. Because much of this government work requires commitment and technical competence, one major state task is training and recruiting dependable, competent, honest state officials.

c. Because state systems are comparatively rich both in their resources (such as well-developed agricultural fields) and in their surplus (often concentrated in a capital city), they are natural targets for neighboring states and tribes who might like to claim those resources. Most state societies are also diverse in their population, so many ordinary day-to-day conflicts (over who inherits land, for example) are not easily resolved on a personal level and require state intervention.

d. State systems are run neither on the basis of individual personal interactions nor on the basis of kin groups. Nor can everyone possibly have direct access to the chief. Although many local matters may be resolved informally, in state systems there will generally be recourse to a wide range of formal government agencies. Indeed, there are likely to be several layers of government from the head of government (president, emperor, queen, commander) through a midlevel division (states, provinces) to the local level (appointed village head, district judge). What makes the system work is not that people know who is in each of these positions, but that they know the positions exist. The key to state societies is thus that *everybody knows the system*.

CORE POLITICAL FUNCTIONS

The different kinds of political systems can largely be understood in terms of the variation in societal size, complexity, and density. But whatever the specific political system, there are core political functions that have to be met. These functions may be performed informally by kin and neighbors or formally by designated bureaucrats. They may be decided at the whim of a chief or according to the formal written laws of a state. The three crucial functions are external relations, internal order, and infrastructure.

EXTERNAL RELATIONS

Few societies are so isolated that they do not have any neighbors. Those neighbors may be similar to them or different in terms of their general adaptation to the environment, their customs, their language, their beliefs, or their economic practices. Yet it is a rare neighbor—no matter how similar and apparently peaceful—who does not pose at least some potential threat. That threat may be unintended or intended, small or great, immediate or long term, but that potential threat cannot be ignored. It may be possible to form alliances, but alliances may dissolve, and, in any case, they simply spread the responsibility for risk rather than resolving it. Furthermore, alliances may raise the stakes of any potential conflict, making it wider and more destructive than it would otherwise be.

External relations can be handled in a variety of ways. If neighbors are potential problems, why not engage them in mutually beneficial trade or give them occasional gifts? If they show tendencies to attack, why not put up a wall to keep them out? The problem is that such inherently defensive approaches generally also require some offensive capability. A wall itself, for example, will not solve problems. It can only slow down an attack. A seemingly impregnable citadel may not be sufficient. While you wait out the enemy, they pillage the countryside that you depend on for food. The cost of victory may be famine. Perhaps offensive action is the best defense. If your neighbors have resources you desire, why not simply take them? If they pose a threat, why not take them over so that they will pose a reduced risk?

The nature of external relations depends greatly on the type of political system and the basic adaptational strategy of the society. Band societies, for example, have significant advantages on both offensive and defensive levels. In defensive terms, they are relatively mobile and can move away from danger. In offensive terms, if they have access to a fast means of movement, such as horses, they can be effective raiders. Tribal societies, because they are based on clear organizational principles of blood, are often capable of rapid mobilization. If they are pastoralists rather than horticulturalists, they may have the option of moving away from danger without losing their resources, since they can drive their animals with them. As with band societies, a fast means of transport will also make them effective raiders and their larger political systems—based on kinship—will make their impact greater. Thus the Mongols under Genghis Khan were able to sweep out of their ancestral lands and take over much of both Asia and Europe.

Agriculturally based chiefdoms and states, because they are more thoroughly sedentary, face somewhat different problems. They cannot afford to let an enemy run loose on their territory, since the destruction of the agricultural fields would be the destruction of the very foundations of the society. Conflict must thus be kept outside the society's agricultural land. Thus clear borders must be established and some kind of army created to defend those borders. Diplomatic strategies may help. A big state (for example, China) might create client states beyond those borders that could lessen the chance of attack; a smaller state (for example, Vietnam) might decide to send tribute to a larger state (China) in the hopes that this might lessen the danger of attack. The issue of borders becomes increasingly problematic in contemporary societies that are simultaneously committed to fortifying borders as a matter of national sovereignty and minimizing borders as a matter of economic development, which is increasingly based on transnational linkages.

INTERNAL ORDER

The second crucial political function is maintaining internal order. Again, the nature of that function varies among the different kinds of political systems, the nature of the basic environmental adaptation, and the society's size and density. In band societies, with relatively little property to argue about and with long-term personal relationships, order is maintained by informal means. In large state societies, with a great deal of property to argue about and relationships that are often between strangers, more formal means will be needed. Thus in band societies the resolution of disputes is on a personal basis and assessed in terms of the relationships among the people in dispute. In state societies the resolution is likely to be more impersonal based on the application of standardized rules and laws.

This distinction between informal and formal mechanisms for maintaining order can be seen in the different way disputes are resolved. Comparing band societies and state societies, for example, yields the distinctions below. Tribes and chiefdoms range in between these extremes, although tribes are a bit more like bands, and chiefdoms are a bit more like states. It is also the case that some of the mechanisms used in band societies are still used in state societies; they soften some of the rigidity of bureaucratic forms of dispute resolution.

Negotiation, mediation, and adjudication. In band societies, resolution of disputes is through *negotiation* between the parties since there are no formal authorities. If that negotiation does not work, there will likely be *mediation* by friends and relatives who want the dispute resolved for their own reasons. In state societies, on the other hand, the dispute is likely to be *adjudicated* by such formal authorities as judges.

Custom and law. In band societies the resolution is likely to be based on *custom* that reflects the common experience of all those involved. In state societies the resolution is likely to be in terms of formal written *law*. Those laws may have developed from customary practices but supersede them.

Compensation and punishment. In band societies the goal is usually *compensation*. The purpose is to return relationships to their prior balance so that people can again cooperate with each other. In state societies, on the other hand, the goal is more often *punishment* (being put in jail, for example).

Sanctions. In band societies the *sanctions* used against people are usually social. *Gossip* and *ridicule* are often enough to bring somebody back in line. If those measures do not work, there is always the threat of *ostracism*. Being cast out from society is a strong sanction. In state societies, on the other hand, sanctions are more formal and physical: people can be fined, they can have their property seized, and they can be put in jail or prison.

Death. Death is a particular kind of sanction used in all kinds of societies, but the way it is used as a sanction varies greatly. In band societies, though rarely used, it occurs as a kind of compensation imposed by the parties themselves. In state societies, however, death is a formal punishment that can only be imposed by the state. Many states today, it should be noted, no longer use the death penalty at all since they consider it inherently inhumane.

INFRASTRUCTURE

In addition to the responsibilities in external relations and internal order, most political systems—though particularly chiefdoms and states—have responsibilities for some aspects of the infrastructure of the society. The extent of this responsibility varies widely. Even among contemporary state societies, for example, some see a stronger government role than others. Communist governments, for example, have tended to see an absolutely central role for government in economic planning, while capitalist-oriented governments see a lesser role. Such variation aside, there are three major kinds of infrastructure in which most political systems take an active role.

The first is *economic development*. In early agricultural state societies, this responsibility is especially strong in terms of irrigation, drainage, and flood control. These are typically governmental responsibilities because of their scope and their centrality to the whole society. The interest of the government is not entirely selfless. A breakdown in the basic economic infrastructure, after all, would mean not only problems for the people but a decline in the tax base.

The second is *transportation*. Again this is partly a matter of supporting economic activity for the sake of the entire society, especially since central planning is likely to improve the overall transportation framework. In agriculturally based societies, for example, it does little good to have an agricultural surplus at the local level if this cannot be transported to the cities and to the other places where it is needed: for example, to armies at the borders. Roads and canals become essential to the society and to the government.

The third is *communications*. The bigger the political system, the more likely that there will be different regions, different languages, and different customs. Yet if there is to be standardization, there will need to be laws in a language that everybody understands. If there is even to be a standard tax levy, there will need to be standard measurements. It is not enough, for example, that people understand that they must provide three bags of rice as taxes if they do not also know exactly how

172   PART II: STRUCTURES

much a bag is supposed to be. That too is an issue of communication. The larger and more complicated the political system is, the more carefully communication will have to be standardized across regional, linguistic, and cultural divides.

POLITICS AND GOVERNANCE

Whatever the kind of political system or the basic function to be performed, practical problems remain. These problems become increasingly difficult as the scale of the political system grows. Four of these problems deserve particular note: rationality, mobilization, recruitment, and inclusion. These are discussed below, largely in terms of contemporary state societies for which these issues are most acute.

RATIONALITY

Although the general responsibilities of the political system may be clear—flood control, for example—the way to accomplish specific tasks in support of those functions is not always clear. If the effects of decisions are high, there must be careful, rational assessment of options and how to implement those options. The public good is at stake, and possibly the survival of the society. For that reason many of the functions of government must be separated from ongoing political debates and contests. *Governance*, the system of getting things done, must be separated from *politics*, the system of determining allocation of resources, specific tasks to be done, and who is to do those tasks. The rationality of governance operations must somehow counterbalance the frequent irrationality of politics.[1]

MOBILIZATION

Another challenge is how to *mobilize* people to get the work done. Why do people follow their government and leaders? At one extreme, they may do so because of governmental *power*. Those governing the society may use raw force to make people do things. That is coercion. At the other extreme, the political system may rely on its *authority*. Here people follow leaders, since those leaders are believed to have the right to provide direction. Most political systems have some measure of both of these. Governments based solely on power are subject to rebellion or less formal resistance such as sabotage. Yet even governments acknowledged to have the right to govern will require occasional use of force—against recalcitrant taxpayers, for example.

---

1   This situation might also be approached—and perhaps more anthropologically—as a contest between two different kinds of rationality: one form anchored in the effective use of resources for the overall society and the other anchored in either individual or group self-interest.

RECRUITMENT

As government takes on common tasks and responsibilities, its effectiveness depends on the individual people who work for it. Those workers must balance the demands of their work for the public, their own personal self-interest, and the demands placed on them by family and friends. It is not an easy task to balance those, and the *recruitment* of people for public service can thus be difficult. Even if recruitment is effective, and complemented by education and training, there is no guarantee that personal self-interest will not intervene. Governments thus face periodic problems of *corruption*. One solution—as the Chinese decided very early—is to have officials whose job it is to monitor other officials. The early Chinese version of this is usually translated as the *censorate*. In the contemporary United States, that function is met by such government agencies as the General Accountability Office or departmental internal audit agencies. It is also met increasingly by nonprofit "watchdog" groups. Indeed, the existence of an independent *civil society* is considered one of the best ways to maintain government accountability.[2]

INCLUSION

A final problem is inclusion. Although band and tribal societies may be composed of similar people with similar characteristics, chiefdoms and states inevitably consist of different kinds of people. Those people may be different in language, religion, marriage patterns, or other fundamental issues that make them who they are as a people. Race and ethnicity provide one example. Although issues of race and ethnicity are important (and complicated) in all areas of life, it is in the political arena that the overall problem of how to establish solidarity across such differences must be confronted. The contemporary world is filled with examples of political states that have fractured because of racial and ethnic differences, and often fractured with enormous bloodshed. Balancing such groups is particularly difficult when there are language differences. Even Canada's much admired bridging of the Anglo-Francophone divide, for example, has not gone unchallenged, and it is only a rare Canadian province (New Brunswick) or US state (New Mexico) that has been willing to take on the practical requirements of bilingualism. Coping with the vast range of languages and cultural traditions of recent immigrants to North America has also helped place these issues of inclusion at the center of political debates.

---

2   There are many different definitions of civil society, but the term in all its usages emphasizes private citizens, groups, and organizations that provide a kind of parallel private sector structure to the formal political and policy structures of government. Whether the relation between civil society and formal government is cooperative, coordinative, or oppositional depends on the particular situation.

The people within a political system may also be diverse in more strictly economic terms. They may, for example, have different kinds of jobs. If those jobs are very different, and particularly if those jobs pay very differently (the multimillion dollar salaries of CEOs, for example), such differences can also create social divisions. People are not just different, but richer or poorer, of higher or lower status. This is what is meant by *stratification* (a system that organizes people hierarchically) or *class* (a particular level in such a stratification system). Class can sometimes be sharply defined and maintained over generations. In many premodern complex political systems (such as India), differences in occupation were inherited and thus occupational divisions hardened into what are called *castes*. You inherited your identity from your parents, were restricted to marrying people within your own caste, and were subject to serious punishment if you acted in ways inappropriate for that group. In many other societies, class differences are inherited only in a general sense. In premodern China, for example, if you came from a wealthy family, you would have far better access to education and thus a far better opportunity for social advancement. Yet it was also possible for the less wealthy to improve their position and that of their families. There was the possibility of *class mobility*. Finally, as in contemporary North America, there are people who have more wealth than others, yet there are opportunities for the less wealthy to carve out new wealth for themselves. We may argue about the extent of equal opportunity in North America, but we agree that it should exist. This issue too is now at the center of political debates.[3]

Going Global

These issues of governance take on a somewhat different shape in the contemporary world as the nation-state—while remaining the central axis of political organization—is challenged on a number of fronts. There are, after all, a variety of organizations at the supranational level. Many came out of the experience of World War II and a desire to avoid further regional and global conflicts. Some of these were military (NATO, for example), some were political in general form (the UN, in

---

3   This issue of inclusion also applies to basic kinds of differences that exist in all societies but take on different meanings within complex political systems. Age differences are one example. In a modern industrial democracy, the "old" are no longer simply somebody's grandparents but an extremely potent bloc of voters. Turning eighteen and twenty-one are no longer just regular birthdays but convey the rights to vote and to drink. The changes in the implications of sex are also significant. In contemporary North American society, men and women are less frequently defined in terms of their personal relationships to each other (as fathers, mothers, sisters, uncles, etc.) and more often as individual human beings with—on paper at least—equal political and economic rights. In modern industrial democracies, men and women function in a wide range of situations in which their sex has become largely irrelevant (voting rights) or should be (equal pay for equal work). While the United States has been slower than many European countries to have women in political leadership, that too is changing.

particular), and some were economic (both such institutions at the World Bank and the International Monetary Fund and the rounds of negotiation that have led to the current World Trade Organization). Although such organizations may constrain the actions of nation-states, none is a serious challenge to national sovereignty—indeed, many of them are designed specifically to protect national sovereignty.

However, there are some shifts in recent years that do introduce direct challenges to the authority of nation-states. One is the European Union. Although it started as a limited economic project to rationalize the coal industry, it has expanded to be a distinct level of governance in its own right. It is by far the boldest experiment in true regional political integration. Another challenge to the nation-state is the increasing growth of civil society, particularly as links between civil society organizations are formed across national borders. While civil society has long been an important factor in public involvement with, and oversight of, national and local governments, it has the potential to serve that same role on a global level. Yet another challenge to the nation-state is the increasing strength and pervasiveness of transnational economic forces. In recent decades these have moved from relatively simple economic exchanges (a country produces a product for export and then exports it) to complicated transnational production circuits in which both the production of the product and the companies producing it span national borders. The effects in particular industries are often more regional than fully global, but the net effect overall is to create a new kind of nongovernmental governance that is in tension with the nation-state. Such transnational companies can evade much governmental oversight by moving resources, production facilities, and sometimes labor to different countries based on their own strategic interests. One result, to the great annoyance of national governments, is that they can control where and how and even if their profits are taxed.

Whether these changes signal an entirely new form of global political system is too early to tell. In some ways, new developments look much like traditional patterns. The European Union, for example, mirrors many of the structures and processes of regular state governance. Some of the transnational corporate entities themselves mirror state structure and processes, with formal organizational charts and their own rules that function much as laws. Other corporate processes are more unstructured and often based on personal relationships. In such cases corporate politics may look a bit like band society: people working together who have known each other personally and professionally for a long period of time recognize each other's strengths and weaknesses, and can trust each other. But one troubling aspect of these new forms of governance is that, unlike the political systems discussed earlier, there is often a sharp lack of understanding about how these new forms actually work. That is a change: political systems that do not have a transparent logic to

In medieval Florence, walls might protect a town but a tower was needed to protect the ruler. (Credit: D. Haines)

those who are often directly affected by them—whether they might like that logic or not. In a world of increased information flow, diminishing privacy, and seeming transparency, it is at times unclear *how* the world is being governed, whether from the shadows or through mechanisms too arcane for easy understanding.[4]

CASE EXAMPLE—"HEADLESS GOVERNMENT" AMONG THE NUER

The Nuer are pastoralists who have long lived along the upper reaches of the Nile River in the Sudan. They were discussed previously as one of the examples in the chapter on pastoralism (chapter 6). Like other pastoralists, their lives revolve around animals, in this case cattle. Cattle are central not only to their livelihood but to their very conception of life. They are valuable as images of beauty and as the currency through with social interactions are conducted. Exchanges of cattle, for example, are essential to

---

4   Anthropologists are increasingly paying attention to these problems, particularly through an analysis of the ways public policy is developed and implemented and what exact effects it has. As they have found, it is very difficult to follow policy processes all the way through since they are complex, sometimes disappear from view, and often cross institutional and national boundaries.

Yanomami on the move in Venezuela—motors are fine. (Credit: Alfredo Allais/iStock)

marriage negotiations. The Nuer also grow crops, particularly maize. The Nuer, their cattle, and their crops are governed by the seasons, which for them are a wet and dry season. As the rainy season begins, the Nuer move to higher ground, planting fields and moving their cattle into corrals. After the rains end and the waters start to subside, the Nuer begin moving into the lower land, letting their cattle graze over the new vegetation. As conditions become dryer, there are increasingly large concentrations of Nuer among the fewer available sources of water for the cattle.

In political terms the Nuer face several challenges. One is that since they move often during the course of the year, the political system must be *mobile*. It cannot be based on territory. The alternative, and a good one, is to base the political system on kinship. Kinship travels well. One's neighbors may change when one moves, but one's relatives do not. Furthermore, the Nuer kinship system, like that of most other pastoral groups, is patrilineal and quite extensive. Since it extends back to distant ancestors, it also extends laterally to distant relatives. This is a *tribal* political system in the technical anthropological sense. Another challenge is that the size of groups varies during the course of the year, so the political system must be *flexible* enough to adapt to such different groupings. The result is a combination of extended lineal descent groups and smaller more ad hoc groups, including nuclear families and relationships by marriage.

Another challenge is that the Nuer are not a small group overall; they numbered in the hundreds of thousands, even before recent population expansion. This increases the requirements on the system to be inclusive and detailed. It must be sufficiently large to include everybody and sufficiently detailed so that all people know how to relate to all these other people. Thus not only must the lineages go back far in time, but there must also be a way to account for the relationships among all the Nuer lineages. For the Nuer, this means that people must know the details of their own lineages but must also know how their lineage relates to all the other lineages. For the Nuer, lineages are grouped into clans, and the clans themselves are known to have some original connection of some kind with each other. Thus *all* Nuer can be placed within a single kinship system.

The result is a political structure that accounts for hundreds of thousands of people, is mobile and flexible, is without any formal political authorities (that is, "headless"), and is sufficiently detailed to provide an indication of how to relate to strangers. In meeting strangers one must first determine whether they are Nuer or not, and then compare ancestors to provide a basis for a relationship. A shared grandfather would yield a close *lineage* relationship; different lineage backgrounds might yield a shared *clan* membership. That assessment of relationship then can be applied to the current situation. If a dispute arises with somebody outside your lineage, you can probably count on the assistance of someone from within your lineage. In an outbreak of raiding between clans, shared clan membership is adequate to knowing which side you are on. Finally, if there is a threat from the outside—from non-Nuer—clan hostilities can be put aside to face a common enemy. That is precisely what the Nuer have done both against the British in the colonial period and against the northern part of the former Sudan in a civil war that lasted through a quarter century. Even in the postindependence period of the new Republic of South Sudan, those same linkage and cleavage lines have put the Nuer in sharp opposition to the neighboring Dinka.

For anthropologists, the Nuer case is intriguing for many of the details regarding how the Nuer call on different kin in different situations and how their kinship system is both extremely detailed as a patrilineal framework but also flexible through the course of seasonal changes. The more general point, however, is simply that the work of politics does not always require a separate political system. If a society is inherently well organized on some other basis, there may be little need to add a political superstructure to it, even if—as with the Nuer—the society is quite large.

CASE EXAMPLE—INDIGENOUS MINORITIES AND STATE SYSTEMS: THE YANOMAMI

State systems are rarely homogenous in their composition. Indeed, they are often extremely diverse. A state may include different kinds of territory with different environmental adaptations and ways of life: horticulturalists and foragers in the hills; agriculturalists in the valleys and on the plains. A state may include different languages that limit communication or merely regional dialects that fuel mutual suspicion. There may be different religions, some coexisting relatively harmoniously and others subject to violent outbreaks of mutual hostility. Sometimes different groups within the state will have relatively similar resources and power; sometimes they will differ greatly in numbers and resources, perhaps with a single majority and several minority groups.

Among those minorities are many indigenous groups who have been politically, economically, and demographically overwhelmed by newer arrivals on their land. Indigenous minorities exist in most parts of the world—the United Nations estimate is 300 million worldwide. With the growth of agricultural systems, industrialism, and the strength of central state power, they are usually pushed to the margins, either up further into the hills or back into wilderness areas that have limited agricultural or industrial use. The increasing reach of global economic systems (anxious to use any possible natural resource) and border-conscious political states (anxious to assert their control over even the most remote parts of their territory) make such refuges increasingly scarce.

Brazil's Amazon basin provides an example. Among the many peoples living along the Amazon basin are the Yanomami. Their territory stretches north from the Amazon and across the border into Venezuela. They number some 10,000 and represent the largest of the Amazon indigenous groups that have maintained their lives in relative isolation. That isolation disappeared in the 1970s. A road project that began in 1974 headed north of the Amazon through Yanomami territory. Although it was not finished, it still brought destruction to the southern part of Yanomami territory, and, perhaps worse, the workers on the road brought disease, particularly influenza and measles, that were often deadly to the Yanomami.

At the same time, a survey of the Amazon's mineral wealth was published. That survey indicated the presence of significant amounts of uranium, tin, diamonds, and gold on Yanomami territory. The regional government itself pursued the mining of tin and titanium, but it was the invasion of small-time miners searching for gold (the *garimpeiros*) who created the greatest problems. It was a gold rush. Miners invaded by the thousands, bringing further disease and destruction. They killed Yanomami, including several massacres, and even took over a Brazilian military outpost when it appeared the military would enforce the laws that limited mining operations. The miners were far better armed than the Yanomami and their supporters—and far better connected to the government. When protests from anthropologists, missionaries, and others escalated, the Brazilian government responded by requiring that the interlopers leave the region. When people were allowed to return some two years later, they found a population reduced by perhaps a fourth, with the remainder sick and often starving.

Ultimately a Yanomami reserve was set up by the Brazilian government in 1992. It was far smaller than the one originally envisioned by Yanomami advocates but still far better than the series of small, separated reserves originally suggested by the Brazilian government. Yet even this formal reserve remains vulnerable. It has been subject to periodic reinvasion by the garimpeiros. It is also now home to Brazilian army bases from which emanate further diseases and accusations of sexual abuse of Yanomami women. The mining industry has continued to press for opening up the reserve for mining, and the Brazilian military has continued to stress that, since the reserve is within sixty kilometers of the border, it is necessarily subject to national security oversight. The Yanomami thus confront perhaps the two strongest forces in the contemporary world: the economic desire for profit and the political desire for control over borders.

SOURCES

For classic reviews of the development of political systems, see Ronald Cohen and Elman Service's *Origins of the State* (Institute for the Study of Human Issues, 1978), and for a review of the anthropological engagement with political issues, see Joan Vincent's *Anthropology and Politics* (University of Arizona Press, 1990). *Ongka's Big Moka* (1976) about the Kawelka in New Guinea provides an engaging glimpse into the difficulties faced by a Big Man as he attempts to solidify his authority through a feast for an allied village. Note that much of the anthropological concern with politics has expanded into law, public anthropology, and the anthropology of policy. Browsing the websites of key anthropological organizations in these areas may be useful: Association for Political and Legal Anthropology (https://political andlegalanthro.org/), Association for the Anthropology of Policy (http://anthof policy.org/), and the Center for a Public Anthropology (http://www.public anthropology.org/).

Regarding the case examples, see E. E. Evans-Pritchard's *The Nuer* (Oxford University Press, 1969) for the classic discussion that is rather dangerously abridged here. As noted in the prior discussion of the Nuer in part I of this book, Sharon Hutchinson's *Nuer Dilemmas* (University of California Press, 1996) provides a more recent view of the Nuer. The situation of the Nuer in the new country of South Sudan remains difficult with, at press time, continuing internal fighting. Two books on the trials and tribulations of Nuer coming to the United States as refugees are Jon Holtzman's *Nuer Journeys, Nuer Lives* (Allyn and Bacon, 1999) and Dianna Shandy's *Nuer-American Passages: Globalizing Sudanese Migration*

(University of Florida Press, 2009). The Yanomami still living in relative isolation are well known through the writing and film of Napoleon Chagnon. For a
somewhat more recent account of the Yanomami, see Alcida Rita Ramos's *Sanumá
Memories: Yanomami Ethnography in Times of Crisis* (University of Wisconsin
Press, 1995). A short discussion of the Yanomami (from which I have drawn here)
is included in David Maybury-Lewis's *Indigenous Peoples, Ethnic Groups, and the
States* (Allyn and Bacon, 2002; 2nd ed.). The *Washington Post* published a useful
update on the Yanomami, with photographs by Sebastião Salgado, in 2014 (http://
www.washingtonpost.com/wp-srv/special/world/yanomami/). For updates on
Yanomami political action, see http://www.survivalinternational.org/news/tribes
/yanomami. I have not included the work of Napoleon Chagnon here, but the films
are worth watching, and the debate about his work provides an interesting test case
of anthropological field ethics.

13

Religion

Religion provides one of the most important structures within which people operate. Since religion is a framework for behavior, relationships, and institutions, and also a framework of meaning, it is an appropriate bridge to the more extended discussion of meaning that is provided in part III. Note that for anthropologists the topic of religion is not only about formally organized religions but about the entire spectrum of spiritual beliefs and practices that may, or may not, be manifested in formal religions with official representatives, scriptures, and places of worship.

The discussion begins by noting the many different vantage points that people take on religion and then focuses on three central dimensions of religion: the general understanding of how the world works, specific explanations people have of why particular things happen at particular times, and the search for assistance and guidance from the spiritual domain. Short discussions of ritual and of religiosity in contemporary North America round out the discussion. The first case example at the end of the chapter concerns the acquisition of "power" among the Cibecue Apache; the second introduces the range of Islamic experience in Indonesia, focusing on the matrilineal Minangkabau of Sumatra.

THE NATURE OF RELIGION

Religion is a complex and contentious subject. One indication of that complexity and contentiousness is the range of ways people attempt to explain religious beliefs, activities, and institutions. Consider some common issues raised about religion from psychological, sociological, political, and economic perspectives:

Psychological. There are several varieties of psychological explanation of religion. Many people, for example, note how representations of the Christian God look very much like a typical, bearded male patriarch. The implication is that people portray divinities in a way that matches their childhood images of authority figures. Another common strand of psychologizing about religion involves noting how religious beliefs and activities serve to ease people's tensions and uncertainties about their lives. Some people argue that religion is an "opiate" that masks the true realities of their lives—a sort of backhanded compliment about how effective religion can be.[1]

Sociological. Many sociological discussions of religion stress the positive functions that shared religious beliefs and activities have. It is valuable for people to have a shared framework of meaning and activities that honor that framework of meaning. It is not uncommon for fellow believers to see themselves as kin, people who have become bound to one another not by their shared blood or their shared territory, but by their shared beliefs. Religion is indeed an effective social glue, producing strong solidarity among believers. One problem is that religion is so good at gluing some sets of people together that it increases their hostility toward other people who do not share the same beliefs.

Political. The effectiveness of religion as a social glue underlies its political importance. If people share the same beliefs and belong to the same organizations, then religion can become the basis for political action. Religion can be an effective form of social control within a society. If a political leader or political system can claim a religious mantle, then political authority is enhanced. On the other hand, if those without power find a religious mandate for their opposition to authority, then their efforts are greatly strengthened. Religion is thus a potent political force whether for alliance or conflict, oppression or resistance.

Economic. The effectiveness of religion as a social glue is mirrored in economic areas. Most economic transactions, ranging from personal reciprocity to impersonal forms of market exchange, require some measure of trust. Who better to trust—aside from kin perhaps—than people who are bound to you by ties of

---

1 The "opiate" reference is often attributed to Karl Marx, who decidedly believed that religion was a matter of illusion and should be replaced by a more objective understanding of the dynamics of historical development. But the actual quote, originally published in 1844, is "Religion is the sigh of the oppressed creature, the heart of a heartless world, and the soul of soulless conditions. It is the opium of the people." An interesting discussion on the issue can be found at http://homelesspatriot.blogspot.com/2012/02/did-marx-really-call-religion-opiate-of.html.

shared belief? Another economic aspect of religion is that some religions are more supportive of particular kinds of economic activity—for example, engaging in trade, accumulating money, or collecting interest on loans.

These psychological, sociological, political, and economic considerations suggest the extent to which religion cuts across other areas of human life. To understand the pervasive effects of religion, however, it is essential to understand religion on its own terms. On its own terms, religion addresses three distinct issues: first, a *general framework* through which to understand how different aspects of the world and human life fit together; second, *specific explanations* of why particular things happen at particular times; and third, assistance and guidance in both the practical and spiritual aspects of life—the search for *solutions*. Details follow.

A GENERAL FRAMEWORK

Religion provides a framework for understanding the world—or, perhaps more accurately, the universe. That framework of understanding helps situate the individual and the society in a meaningful context for belief and action. Above all, to be effective, that framework must bind together both place and time, both the animate and the inanimate.

BINDING PLACE AND TIME

To be effective, a religion must somehow integrate the different physical places in the world. An example from Colin Turnbull's *The Forest People* helps illustrate this point. When Turnbull's assistant, Kenge, first comes out onto the plains east of the forest in which he lives, he has some difficulty coming to terms with this new world of wide-open vistas. For him, it was "the forest" that was alive and good, and this was certainly not forest. It does not take him long, however, to expand his notion of forest to include this new place. He soon realizes that "this God must be the same as our God in the forest. It must be one God."[2] As Kenge's epiphany suggests, a belief system is not very effective if it cannot account for all the places in the world with which people have some contact or interaction. Religion as a framework of meaning thus binds together *place*. Religions do this in many ways. Sometimes all places are seen as equally alive in spirituality. In other cases some places or objects are seen as having more spiritual power than others, so you go to those places when you need spiritual replenishment.

To be effective, a religion must also bind together *time*. It must tie together events that have already happened, those that are in process now, and those that will come

---

2   Colin Turnbull, *The Forest People* (New York: Simon and Schuster, 1961), 258.

to be in the future. The actual ways that past, present, and future are bound together vary. For societies in which ancestors are important, the line that runs through the present from the past to the future is the line of blood. In that sense no one fully dies since they live on in their descendants. Alternatively, many believe there is rebirth in this world after death. Those beliefs about rebirth take many forms. Hindu and Buddhist notions of *karma*, for example, explain how one's current life is a result of actions in past lives and how one's future lives will be the result of this one. For yet other people, the future lies not in death or rebirth in this world but a passage to a better place—some kind of "heaven" that offers an eternal reward for a life well spent. What all these beliefs provide is a mechanism to link one's current life back to the past and forward to the future.

Binding the Animate and the Inanimate

Religion also binds together all the animate and inanimate things in those different times and places. Since religion includes all places (whether seen or unseen, known or unknown) at all times (places that now exist, may once have existed, or may someday exist), the inventory of those animate and inanimate entities is often long and complex. Many, many people believe in a variety of "spirits." Some may be the "ghosts" of people who once lived; others are spirits of animals, of natural forces, or of natural objects. Some of those spirits are so sufficiently developed that they are called "gods." Spirits and gods may be good or bad, helpful or indifferent. Those spirits and gods, in turn, may be seen as subordinate to a higher, more inclusive "God" or as the manifestation of a more impersonal, pervasive force underlying the material world—such as the *mana* of Polynesia—roughly equivalent to "the force" of the Star Wars saga.

In order to come to terms with this complexity, those studying religion often try to impose some structure on these beliefs about the spiritual world. Thus Christianity is usually called "monotheistic" because there is a single God. However, it is also the case that many Christians acknowledge a wide range of spiritual forces (for example, saints and angels), and the emphasis on a triune God (Father, Son, and Holy Spirit) is an acknowledgment not only of unity but of diversity. Tylor's original ideas about beliefs in a "Supreme Being" may provide a better label than the "monotheistic" one.[3]

---

3   The conventional categories used to discuss religion may be worth noting, though attempting to force people's complex religious views into these conventional boxes is dangerous—an orthodoxy of analysis rather than an orthodoxy of the believers. With that caveat: *monotheism* is used to note a religion in which there is one god or at least one who has overriding authority and power, *polytheism* refers to the presence of multiple gods (who are not simply different versions of each other), *animism* refers to belief in spirits, and *animatism* refers to more general beliefs that what we would call supernatural power is an animate force underlying and pervading the natural world. By these definitions, "ancestor worship" is a kind of animism.

Such arguments about how to label religious beliefs may seem quibbling, but they often have serious consequences. If religion is to be a framework for how people understand their world, then there are likely to be efforts to control that framework: to decide what exactly are the proper beliefs and the proper behavior. The religious quest for a framework of meaning may thus have important social consequences that are divisive (expelling the unbeliever and wrong believer) while uniting the true believers.[4] Here "religion" in the broad sense of a framework of understanding yields to "religion" as a fully defined and formalized social organization with official texts and leaders.

AN EXPLANATION FOR EVENTS

Understanding the general nature of the world (and universe) is helpful. However, that general understanding does not always provide an answer to more specific questions about why particular things happen to particular people at particular times. In everyday life, for example, people know that death occurs from a variety of causes such as traffic accidents, cancer, homicide, and terrorist attacks. The statistical probabilities for many of these kinds of death are well known. The probabilities can even be adjusted for people's specific age, gender, race, ethnicity, occupation, and location. Yet that does not fully explain why particular people die at particular times. After all, many of the people who die from different causes are not even in high-risk groups. Many people in high-risk groups for one kind of death actually die from a different cause. There is still a mystery, then, in why a particular person dies at a particular time. In times of catastrophic loss, the reverse question also arises. Why was one person spared when so many others perished? People escaping danger often find their personal relief turns into guilt because of this nagging question of why others did not survive. Thus although people have a general framework for understanding why events take place—whether "scientific" or "religious"—the specifics of loss or survival still require attention.

One classic example of this problem of specific explanations was provided by E. E. Evans-Pritchard. His discussion of the Nuer was noted earlier, but this case derives from his work among the Azande, who live somewhat to the west of the Nuer in central Africa. The Azande believe in witchcraft. As a good social anthropologist, Evans-Pritchard was not content to simply note their belief in witchcraft as part of

---

4   Sometimes this effort may be *ecumenical*, meaning that it seeks the common ground among different beliefs and practices. On the other hand, the effort may be to define *orthodoxy* ("straight" or correct beliefs) and *orthopraxy* ("straight" or correct practices). In such cases, *heterodoxy* ("other" beliefs) and *heteropraxy* ("other" practices) may then be the grounds for persecution—even unto death.

their traditions, but he wanted to understand the logic of their belief in witchcraft. His explanation was as follows.

The Azande construct huts to provide protection from the elements. The huts are built from long poles on the tops of which are constructed pyramidal roofs. The huts are simple wooden structures. The Azande know well that termites eat wood and that, with the number of termites they have, the pillars that support the roof will eventually be eaten away and the hut will collapse. The Azande, like us, have a clear and "scientific" explanation of why huts collapse. When a hut collapses, they are not surprised and have no need for "supernatural" explanations. The termites did it.

However, if someone is under the roof when it collapses, Azande analysis becomes very different. They are not satisfied with a probabilistic explanation. They—like us in many ways—are inclined to believe there might have been foul play. They—like us again—are likely to investigate. However, their suspicions run deep, and their explanation of how the foul play occurred extends beyond our customary explanations. We might suspect that somebody caused the collapse by hollowing out the wood to make it weaker. They suspect that someone used *sorcery* to make the hut collapse at the specific time the victim was under it. How else, they would argue, could this particular hut have collapsed at this particular time when this particular person was under it? That this is just a coincidence is, from their point of view, rather sloppy thinking. The Azande are thus likely to conclude that sorcery is involved. That conclusion, of course, draws from their more general framework for understanding how the world works, which includes the notion of witches. Yet the example suggests they have two distinct ways of explaining things: one is a general framework, which is largely "scientific" in our terms, and the other is a more specific explanation that invokes witchcraft and that we might tend to classify as "supernatural." For the Azande, however, there is no inconsistency between the two; they are just being logical and practical.

There can, however, be tension between general explanations and specific ones. Cambodian holocaust survivors, for example, have a general Buddhist framework for understanding the world, which includes notions of karma. They also acknowledge Buddhist scriptures that suggest an apocalypse that is to come. Yet on the personal level, these frameworks are inadequate for explaining the holocaust that occurred in their country in the late 1970s. It does not explain why they survived and so many others, including other members of their families, died. The general framework of Buddhism, which explains why there is suffering in the world, cannot explain why so much suffering was visited on Cambodia, by Cambodians, at this particular point in time. Their reactions to this rupture in the meaning of the world have varied. Many have moved on through the experience; others have not. Some have simply gone blind, disavowing the eyes that saw the holocaust.[5]

SEEKING HELP

Both the general framework and the specific explanation provide help in understanding how and why things happen. It is useful to have an understanding of the general structure of the world and explanations for why specific things happen to specific people. However, such understanding does not necessarily resolve problems. Diagnosis is not a cure, and much of religion is about the cure: how to fix things. To fix things, assistance may be needed. Obtaining such assistance hinges on what resources are available, whether you yourself can obtain or connect with those resources, and, if not, whether there is someone else who can connect to those resources for you. These two issues of "what is available" and "how to connect" deserve additional comment.

KNOWING WHAT HELP IS AVAILABLE

In most societies people believe in a broad range of what we would call spiritual forces. There may be a general force or power that resides within, below, or above the world of everyday life. Sometimes that power has concrete manifestations; for example, great serpents twining beneath the surface of the world. Sometimes the forces are less concrete; for example, an energy that you absorb with your very breathing. There may also be spiritual forces within particular objects, associated with particular animals, or freely moving on their own. There may be spirits of parts of the land (sacred mountains, for example) or of animals (reflecting the strength of eagle, whale, or bear). If one's ancestors remain nearby as spirits, they may be a useful source of assistance. Finally, there are gods sometimes visualized as a vast pantheon, sometimes as a single entity with many manifestations. Of all these options, some spiritual forces may be more easily accessed and more inclined to help than others.

KNOWING HOW TO CONNECT

But how do you connect to these potential sources of assistance? The anthropological record is rich on the different ways in which human beings make such connections. Those connections fall into two general categories: direct or mediated.

---

5   For a recent, integrated review of the Cambodian case, including the diaspora, see Khatharya Um, *From the Land of Shadows: War, Revolution, and the Making of the Cambodian Diaspora* (New York: New York University Press, 2015).

A *direct connection* with a particular spiritual force may be the result of a planned attempt at contact (a vision quest, for example) or as a result of an illness that brings you close to death and thus, inevitably, closer to the spirit world. Sometimes the connection is made through your own control over the spirits, sometimes it is made through supplication to the spirits, and sometimes it is made through the spirit's control over you. A sorcerer might thus "command" a spirit to work for good or ill, while an ordinary person might beseech a god to mercifully grant some benefit.

If you yourself do not have the ability (or opportunity) for such direct contact, an intermediary is needed. Some people have greater familiarity with the spirit world and can help others make contact with it. Anthropologists usually make a general distinction between *shamans* (individuals who have established some direct personal contact with the spirit world and thus can more easily do so again) and *priests* (who represent an established religious organization).[6] There are, however, many options in between. Even objects can become intermediaries to the spirit world. Bones cracking in a fire or teas leaves in a bowl may bring a message. Spiritual forces themselves can also be intermediaries: your personal guardian spirit may intercede with other spirits, the Virgin Mary may intercede with God, or the Buddhist Goddess of Mercy (*Guanyin / Quan Am / Kannon*) may be a more approachable figure than Buddha himself.

RITUAL

In making a connection to spiritual forces, people are dealing with a domain that is special, difficult to reach, and sometimes dangerous. If you do achieve some kind of connection, you would probably want a way to continue that connection or recreate it. Such connections and reconnections are often conducted through *ritual*. You can think of ritual as a sort of package deal for connecting to the spiritual domain.[7] There are three distinctive features of ritual.

First, ritual is *structured and repetitive*. Rituals are structured roughly the same each time, and there is often effort to do *exactly* the same things each time. Sometimes that repetitiveness is based solely on people's memories; sometimes the ritual is written down in painstaking detail.

Second, ritual involves separation from the everyday world in terms of *location*. A sacred mountain, a mosque, a grove of ancient trees, a sylvan glade . . . all of those

---

6   A distinction is often made between shamans as part-time religious practitioners and priests as full-time ones. That is probably accurate as a rough generalization but is, it seems to me, a secondary consideration.

7   The word "ritual" in North America has two contrasting usages. One refers to a meaningful set of repeated activities such as "the ritual of first communion was very important in our church" or "having dinner together on Sunday was an important ritual in our family." The other refers to a repetitive and meaningless set of activities ("what a ritual!").

will do well. If the more poetic options are not available, at least some marking of space is needed. An altar on a family's living room wall might provide a space for the ancestors; lighting incense will help transform that space into something special and more appropriate for prayer.

Third, ritual is also separated from the everyday world in terms of *time*. That issue of time has to do with the actual time of the ritual (dawn, the equinox, the new moon, a death anniversary) as well as the marking of ritual time with beginning and ending events. Just as taking off one's shoes entering a Buddhist temple or Islamic mosque helps mark the edge of a special space, a call to worship marks the beginning of a special time. Putting one's shoes back on marks the return to the regular world, and a benediction or final prayer marks a return to normal time.

If all this works and people are brought closer to the spiritual world, then ritual is a positive thing indeed: it is a "real ritual." If the effort yields only the mindless repetition of meaningless activities, then the effort may seem wasted and the ritual becomes "just a ritual." Even under the best conditions, things may go awry as the spirit fails to move into the special place and time at the heart of the ritual. Yet whether successful or not, elaborate or minimalist, heavily spiritual or merely social among close family, rituals provide a useful guide to what people consider worthy of the effort needed to prepare a special time and place for some greater communion.

RELIGION IN CONTEMPORARY NORTH AMERICA

The issue of religion in contemporary North America deserves some comment. There are, of course, great variations in indigenous religious beliefs across Canada, Mexico, and the United States. In addition, the colonizing of North America often had religious underpinnings, particularly the search for freedom by oppressed religious minorities. Even many of those we think of as regular immigrants fit into that category: Catholics from an Ireland dominated by Protestants—in that case an oppressed majority—or the Jews who fled from Russia and Eastern Europe and were such a major component of immigration to North America at the turn of the twentieth century. In more recent years the many streams of Christianity and Judaism have been joined by the broad range of religions among, especially, refugees and immigrants from non-European sources. So Canada, Mexico, and the United States are places of great religious diversity. For anthropologists this provides a wonderful opportunity for understanding how religious beliefs and behaviors with very different origins both endure and change when they meet in a common place.

But do people take their religion seriously? Is it just nominal membership, the use of religion as a cultural marker? Or is it something more profound that touches on the full range of spiritual beliefs and connections? From ethnographic material we know that the answer is that religion is quite nominal for some people and quite fervent for others. Survey data are helpful in drawing a more general portrait. But—and this is an important lesson about survey research—the findings can be summarized in quite different ways. Consider the different headlines that could be generated from the Pew Research Center's major survey on religion in the United States.[8]

One headline might be "Religion Declining in America!" The survey data support this in showing that (a) membership is down and (b) people are praying less. That suggests that both the formal organizational part of religion (the churches, mosques, synagogues, and temples) and the major personal aspect of religion (prayer) are losing ground. But another headline might be "Religion Still Strong in America!" While it is true that there are statistical declines, still the level of religiosity in the United States remains far higher than in Europe—or in the rest of North America for that matter. Perhaps the most compelling statistic is that over half of those in the United States pray on a daily basis, and that number has declined only a small amount.

Yet another headline might be "Americans Becoming More Spiritual!" That headline is justified by survey findings of an increase in general spiritual reflections and feelings. The percentage of people who had "wondered about the universe" or "had a deep sense of spiritual peace and well-being" actually rose. The findings thus suggest that while those in the United States are (modestly) less religious *if* the word "religion" is in the question, they are actually more *spiritual* if the word "religion" is avoided—presumably because the word "religion" evokes formal organized religions rather than more general spiritual issues.[9]

Given that overall religiosity (and the variation in it), it is not surprising that religion spills over into other areas of life. Politics is one example. Although there is formal separation of church and state in the United States, it would be a very unwise US political candidate who did not occasionally throw in a "God bless America." Furthermore, the 2016 US election showed the vital importance of evangelicals to the Republican Party and included a broad attack on Islam from that party's presidential candidate and ultimate election victor. That attack, in turn, horrified other people who see inclusion of religious minorities as absolutely central to the history and core values of the United States.

---

8   The data here come from the Pew Research Center's "US Public Becoming Less Religious." See http://www.pewforum.org/2015/11/03/u-s-public-becoming-less-religious/. This is a large survey (about 35,000 respondents) that follows up on a similar 2007 survey.

9   The survey also has useful findings on degrees of religiosity by religious affiliations. For example, evangelicals are indeed far more religious and far more conservative in social values than mainstream Protestants. Muslims are also varied internally but, as a group, fall in between evangelicals and mainstream Protestants.

Contrary to many expectations, religion has not disappeared from the contemporary world, and its effects continue to flow widely through people's personal lives and through their social and political institutions. The range of religious beliefs and practices remains wide. Furthermore, the increasing mobility of people across national borders and across regional, religious, and ethnic divisions is bringing that range of beliefs and practices into ever closer contact. For the United States, a razor thin election in 2016 that often focused on both migration and religion suggests that the people are quite evenly split on whether the range of people and the range of beliefs is good in creating a more diverse, inclusive, and syncretic society or whether it is bad in undermining traditional American institutions. There is also a broader question of whether the different structures of kinship, economics, politics, and religion, as we know them from the anthropological record, are adequate to the challenges of the contemporary world, which elements of them may have renewed relevance today, and in what areas we may truly need to look for change.

CASE EXAMPLE—FINDING AND LIVING WITH POWER AMONG THE CIBECUE APACHE

The Cibecue Apache—the matrilineal Arizona people discussed earlier—live lives in which things can go wrong. Some of those problems are relatively minor (losing your truck keys), and some are major (serious disease); some are short-term and some long-term. There are also things that can go right: getting some money, finding a good spouse, or just finding those truck keys. In all these aspects of life, it is good to have some help. It is good to have help from your friends and family and also good to have help from the spirit world. For the Apache that means it is good to have *diyi*, which can be loosely translated as a "power."

There are many different kinds of diyi. Some match basic elements of nature. There are powers of wind, rain, lightning, thunder, water, moon, and sun. Some match animals (bear, eagle, snake, wolf, coyote), and at least one matches flora (the root of the manzanita). Some are more like deities: the *gan* (male deities who appear in masked dances) and Changing Woman (who appears during girls' puberty ceremonies). The Apache thus have—as most people do—a broad range of spiritual forces that they recognize. Furthermore, the Apache believe that there are vast supplies of each of these powers and that some portion of that power can be gained by human beings. That raises two practical questions: first, how do you get a power and, second, what can you do with it?

The Apache distinguish two ways of connecting to a power. One way is for *you to find it*. For the Apache, that means choosing the desired power and then learning the chants that are associated with that power. Learning the chants is time consuming

A winged Virgin Mary stands guard over Quito in Ecuador. (Credit: D. Haines)

and expensive. You have to find somebody who knows the proper chants and convince them to teach the chants to you, including what they are and how they should be performed. You then have to memorize them: perhaps fifty or sixty chants, some of which require a half hour to complete. That will get you a connection to the spirit, and, probably, the spirit will then act on your behalf—though it may take some time for the spirit to accept you as worthy of its help. The second way to connect to a power is for *it to find you*. Sometimes a power may find you to be so worthy that it will manifest itself to you. That may be in a dream, or it may be in waking life. A dream of lightning, or a lightning bolt striking close to you during waking hours, might mean that lightning power is making itself available to you. After that initial contact, however, you will also need to learn the chants associated with that power in order to continue the connection.

Getting a power is not an easy process, but, then again, it is not prohibitively difficult considering the potential advantages. Sometimes, what the power can do is clear and predictable. Thus when Changing Woman temporarily enters a girl during the puberty ceremony, the implication is of health and long life—for Changing Woman is herself forever changing and living. For most powers, however, what the power can do is less predictable. Rain power might help with rain but might not; instead it might help with something that has no relation to rain, like finding lost objects. Deer power might actually help one man in hunting but might aid another in gambling. For an Apache, living with a power is a trial-and-error process. Over

Old and new versions of a Minangkabau mosque in Sumatra. (Credit: D. Haines)

time you find out what the power is capable of and what it is willing to do for you. Power may also leave you, especially if you become old and weak (without enough power for the power), if you treat it with disrespect, or if you become unworthy of it. While you have it, however, you will have some good practical assistance. You are also likely to be respected by other people—unless they come to believe you are using your power to their disadvantage.

CASE EXAMPLE—MATRILINEAL MUSLIMS IN INDONESIA

The image of Islam and Christianity in conflict has become commonplace in recent decades. But both religions are themselves highly variable. The differences between Islam and Christianity, for example, often pale in comparison to the internal differences within the two religions. Given the recent emphasis on Islam in the Middle East, for example, it is helpful to consider Islam in its most populous nation, Indonesia. There, the range in Islam is enormous from the northern tip of Sumatra, where Sharia law prevails, to the major cities of Java, with a more moderate Islam. Furthermore, Islam is not the only religion. There is formal legal acceptance of all major world religions. In that sense Islam is on equal footing with Buddhism, Christianity, Hinduism, and Confucianism.

In this rich mix of different religions and different varieties of Islamic life, one of the most intriguing societies is that of the Minangkabau of central Sumatra. They are reckoned as the world's largest matrilineal society, with around five million people. Property is generally in the hands of women, and when couples marry, the husband goes to live with his wife's family. The traditional housing pattern was a longhouse with an open area to the front of the house, where children and unmarried adults would sleep, and separate private rooms along the back of the house, where married women would live with their husbands. As a woman grew up, she would first be sleeping with her mother as an infant in one of those back rooms, but would then be living for her childhood and early adolescence in the front of the house with her brothers and sisters, graduating to a private room in the back when she married, moving perhaps into a bigger room as she became more senior, and possibly circulating out to the front of the house in later life, a grandmother sleeping with her grandchildren.

For men, life was different. As children, they would be part of their mother's group. But when they became young adults, it was expected that they would go off on their own to make their fortune. This might be in another area of Sumatra or farther off in business and trade. The men might well be gone for long periods of time and have long-term residence somewhere else, for example, in Jakarta with all its economic and political opportunities. Because of this, Minangkabau men were often quite cosmopolitan. Their work moved them along the trade routes with exposure to other peoples of neighboring islands and to Europeans. During the Indonesian struggle for independence, these Minangkabau men were disproportionately among the most influential of the leaders of the movement. They were people of the world. Matrilineality thus gave women stability of property and of residence while it gave men the freedom to pursue their fortunes elsewhere and, indeed, virtually required them to do so to meet social expectations. When men and women married, they brought to their union different experiences. Not surprisingly, marriages often did not last as men exercised their freedom of movement to go off again on business or to marry another woman. Those break-ups might well be painful for both the women and their children. The autonomy of women in matrilineal societies does not preclude pain or loss.

Islam among the Minangkabau developed in this context of dual autonomy for men and women. Both men and women had their own spheres of experience and their own access to resources. It was, perhaps inevitably, the men who studied the Koran, the men who most closely conformed to Islamic patterns, and the men who went on *haj* (pilgrimage to Mecca). But that did not give men dominion over women. They could have multiple wives and could divorce those wives, but the wives retained their property and they retained their children. The men were obliged to support the overall matrilineal structure of their society. They were thus obligated to read the Koran thoroughly to explain how Islam can coexist with matrilineality.

While some people in the West have been prone to focus on strains of violence in societies that are largely Islamic, observations from these matrilineal Minangkabau suggest the need to equally consider the strains of violence in societies that are largely Christian. Anthropologist Peggy Reeves Sanday, for example, spent much time among the Minangkabau but also conducted research in her native United

States. She has noted the somewhat disorienting experience of living among the Islamic Minangkabau in an environment of great respect and safety for women, while also developing her research on fraternity gang rape in the largely Christian United States.

SOURCES

The debt to Evans-Pritchard for appreciating the logic of religious belief will be clear; see his *Witchcraft, Oracles and Magic among the Azande* (Clarendon Press, 1992; abridged). For three recent textbook approaches to religion from an anthropological perspective, see Rebecca L. Stein and Philip Stein's *Anthropology of Religion, Magic, and Witchcraft* (Routledge 2015; 3rd ed.); Robert L. Winzeler's *Anthropology and Religion: What We Know, Think, and Question* (Altamira, 2012; 2nd ed.); and John R. Bowen's *Religions in Practice: An Approach to the Anthropology of Religion* (Routledge, 2013; 6th ed.). The film *Kataragama* (1973), though dated, remains an excellent review of the different functions of religion as discussed in the text (framework of meaning, explanation of specific events, actual assistance).

The first case example is drawn—as was the previous discussion of the Apache—from the work of Keith Basso, specifically his early general monograph *The Cibecue Apache* (Waveland, 1986). For a contrasting view of a situation in which it is the women who are shamans, see Laurel Kendall's research from Korea in *Shamans, Housewives, and Restless Spirits* (University of Hawaii Press, 1985). For the situation of the Minangkabau in Indonesia, see Peggy Reeves Sanday's *Women at the Center: Life in a Modern Matriarchy* (Cornell University Press, 2002) and Jeffrey Hadler's *Muslims and Matriarchs: Cultural Resilience in Indonesia through Jihad and Colonialism* (Cornell University Press, 2008).

Part III
MEANINGS

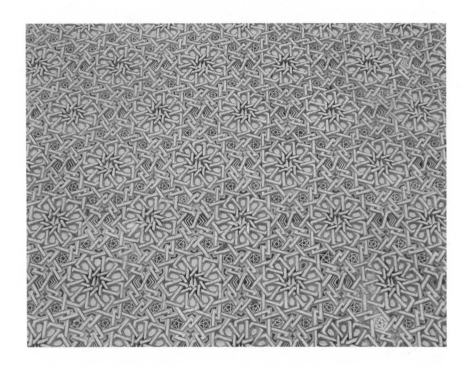

14

Introduction to Part III

As parts I and II have indicated, anthropologists are interested in understanding people in the specific environments in which they live and through the structures that organize their lives. These are, in many ways, relatively objective concerns. Although anthropologists may be close to the people and involved in their lives, much of what they describe is how life might look from the outside: people have visible characteristics, perform real actions, and relate to each other in observable ways. Yet anthropologists are also keenly interested in the meaning of human life. To attain that more subjective understanding of life, they must grapple with the same issues that confront others in both the humanities and social sciences: How do people experience life, and how do they themselves make sense of it? Since anthropologists themselves are also trying to make sense of their own lives, this quest for meaning is thus a two-channeled story that involves both the anthropologists and the people they study.

This quest to understand the meaning of life from the inside is the focus of part III. The emphasis is on the frameworks and mechanisms through which people find life intelligible, including cognition, language, expression, and action. As a beginning point, this chapter outlines three general ways in which the lived experience of people takes on meaning. People may find meaning in their lives through reference to a *set of core values*, through interaction with others in an *arena of negotiation* (and sometimes conflict), and through individual or group *acts of creation*. As an example of these three, *identity* will then be discussed, since it is a frequently used framework within which people try to make sense of their lives. The chapter concludes with a brief introduction to the structure of part III and some key themes that will emerge in it.

THREE APPROACHES TO MEANING

Anthropologists have taken a wide range of approaches to looking at the lived experience of human life. Such an inquiry is a kind of cross-cultural philosophy that attempts to go beyond the European tradition to include the many kinds of cultural reasoning that exist in the world. For introductory purposes, three general approaches to understanding the meaning of lived experience are outlined below—though they are far from being the only alternatives.

CORE VALUES

The first way of looking at meaning involves a set of core values.[1] Thus—as in the previous discussions of religion—we might say that people have a general framework for understanding their lives and that the framework is based on a core set of values. Those values provide a guide for understanding the world and for action in it. This emphasis—whatever its philosophical strengths and weaknesses—has some practical advantages in forcing inquiry toward the most crucial of people's beliefs, the one that may be most vital to their self-identity and most important for preserving for future generations. Much of the continuing turmoil in Afghanistan, for example, can be explained in terms of the *puktunwali* code of the Pashtun, the majority ethnic group in Afghanistan. The two central elements of that code are hospitality and revenge. This framework of two key values (hospitality and revenge) provides a powerful tool for understanding and simplifying the complexity of Afghan social and political life. Such a reduction of meaning to core values can be an effective means of understanding a people and their enduring society and culture.

There are dangers, however, in such an emphasis on a core set of values. One danger is oversimplification. The neater and more satisfying explanations—both for the outsider and the insider—are likely to be the ones that boil everything down to a single issue or two. That will tend to eliminate other issues that are more minor

---

1   The discussion here might be better framed as "belief and values" rather than simply "values." There are long debates about the meanings and relative importance of the two, and about how they interrelate. Simply put, you do not have to value all the things you believe, and you do not have to believe in all the things you value. You might, for example, believe in the existence of evil but value the fight against it (even if you do not actually believe that resistance will be successful). In any case, here I have stuck with "values" for simplicity in presentation.

or perhaps contradictory to the core principles. Furthermore, a consideration of meaning as a core set of values runs the danger of ignoring the diversity in values that exists even among well-integrated communities. Values among men and women—or among old and young—are likely to be rather different even in the same society. One might ask, for example, whether puktunwali is a Pashtun code or simply a code for a certain set of Pashtun adult males.[2] Despite such problems, an emphasis on meaning as a core set of values is common in anthropology since it matches so well the anthropological impulse to find out who other people really are, how they live their lives, how their traditions endure, and how understanding their lives can enrich our own.

AN ARENA OF NEGOTIATION

It is also possible to look at meaning in other ways. One problem with the core values approach is that values are neither universally shared nor necessarily enduring over time. Instead, one might consider how meaning develops in interaction with other people. Meaning is not simply established tradition but subject to change. Values may even be in conflict: for example, mercy versus vengeance. Nor are values necessarily equally shared by all people in a society. This suggests the need to look at the diversity and possible inconsistency in human meanings. If meanings are variable and in flux, then there must be some dynamic by which one interpretation is accepted rather than another. Rather than looking at core values, then, we might look at the different values that exist in a particular society and how those different values are applied, not applied, or modified to suit the situation. Sometimes one value may win over the other. Sometimes there may be an attempt to seek a broader framework that can incorporate a variety of diverging values. Much of the recent North American interest in multiculturalism has precisely this purpose: to create a new overarching value of diversity within which a broad range of different cultural values can coexist. Such an overarching value requires a great deal of negotiation.

The emphasis on how meaning develops through a process of negotiation also has its problems. Since anthropologists often work with people who have borne the brunt of colonialism or other external control, they are sensitive to situations in which there are differences in relative power. Such differences in power greatly affect the outcome of any conflict about meaning. The dominating society may even take action to completely eradicate "old" ways and beliefs. One mechanism used for that purpose with indigenous peoples in both North America and Australia was to put the children in boarding schools, thus ensuring there would be limited opportunity

---

2   A useful, if now somewhat dated, film portrayal is *The Pathan* (David Ash and Andre Singer, 1980) from the *Disappearing World* series.

for the transmission of core values from the older to younger generations. Thus while it is possible to see an arena of negotiation between different values that is relatively sportive with teams that are fairly matched, anthropologists are likely to see the darker side of a contest between strong and weak, where there are no rules of fair play and no incorporation of diversity. Instead, there may be an attempted obliteration of the smaller or less powerful group's beliefs and values—a sort of *cultural genocide* that is sometimes called ethnocide.

ACTS OF CREATION

A third option is to see meaning as an act of creation. After all, even a well-established set of core values requires some mechanism to transmit it to future generations. Furthermore, meaning is not simply about beliefs and values that exist; it must be about actively applying those to new situations that arise and adapting them if needed. If circumstances change, core beliefs and values will need to be re-created, reworked, recalibrated, reinvented, or simply reremembered. This active aspect of meaning making is seen in many areas, from assessing how people integrate new technology and media, to considering the roles of play, art, and performance in human life. What matters, then, is what is important enough to people that they create and re-create it.

The emphasis on meaning as creation has its own problems as well. The emphasis on creativity may preclude a recognition of how limited people's options sometimes are. Even in the explicitly creative areas of the arts, much that is produced and performed is conventional, and those who seek the unconventional are often punished for it or simply ignored. Creativity is thus thwarted. Nevertheless, an emphasis on meaning as creation encourages appreciation of how inventive human beings can be under even very limiting circumstances.

IDENTITY AS CORE, NEGOTIATED, AND CREATED MEANING

An example concerning identities may help illuminate how these three frameworks work. Identities are important. It is difficult to make much sense of your life if you do not have some idea of who you are. It is also hard to make sense of other people if you do not know who they are. Finally, it is hard to interact with people unless both you and they have some sense of your identities and how they interact. In some languages you cannot even begin a sentence without figuring out who you are, whom you are talking with, and who else may be listening. Predictably, gender and generation are the most essential characteristics for those linguistic situations, but general social status and kin relationships may also be important. There are many other aspects of personal identity that are also crucial. Some are fleeting (being a freshman) and some durable (being a college graduate). Some are wide-ranging in their implications (race and nationality, for example) and some more narrow in their consequences (hair color—well, usually).

Some of these characteristics are about you as an individual. But many are about the set of people to whom you belong. These are "your people." Such group identity may be on the basis of kinship or something broader, such as nationality or ethnicity. Consider "being Japanese" as an example of such a group identity. "Japanese" is the common designation for people who live in Japan. The people who live in Japan are diverse in many ways (by class and region, for example) and include some people who may not even consider themselves Japanese or be considered by other Japanese to be so. There are, for example, people of Chinese and Korean ancestry in Japan and some indigenous people on the country's northern island of Hokkaido. Nevertheless, there is a tendency by Japanese and non-Japanese alike to view the Japanese as a relatively coherent set of people about whom there is something distinctively Japanese. They are not just a random set of people who happen to live on the islands that are called Japan. They are presumed to be bound together by social ties of kinship and shared location, by a shared language, and by shared values that enable them to live together in an orderly way. Some anthropologists have attempted to look at what that core of shared values might be, what is essential to their culture as Japanese. The results have included emphasis on such values as hard work, self-discipline, "saving face," and loyalty to the group.

The nature of Japanese identity changes, however, when you take the Japanese out of Japan.[3] For example, many Japanese emigrated in the latter part of the nineteenth century and early part of the twentieth. Many came to North America, but some went to South America. Of those going to South America, the largest group went to Brazil. Once they were in Brazil, there were some identity options. They could still consider themselves Japanese, they could consider themselves Brazilian, or they could pick something in between. Over the generations—as you would expect—they came to rely more on Portuguese than Japanese as a language and were at least somewhat "Brazilian" in that sense. However, they tended to marry among themselves and to consider themselves as distinct from the rest of the Brazilian population. Thus "being Japanese" continued to be an important part of their identity.

---

3   This discussion is drawn particularly from the pioneering work of Keiko Yamanaka and Takeyuki Tsuda, but see the work of Ayumi Takenaka for useful comparative information on Japanese in Peru. Articles by all of these appear in *Beyond Boundaries: Selected Papers on Refugees and Immigrants,* vol. 5, ed. Ruth Krulfeld and Diane Baxter (American Anthropological Association, 1997). For a more recent consideration of the topic, see Koji Sasaki, "To Return or Not to Return," in *Return: Nationalizing Transnational Mobility in Asia,* ed. Xiang Biao, Brenda Yeoh, and Mika Toyota (Durham, NC: Duke University Press, 2013).

By the latter part of the twentieth century, there were some 1.3 million people in Brazil who were of Japanese origin and did not speak Japanese (or at least did not speak it well), but who nevertheless considered themselves Japanese. At the same time in Japan, employers were having difficulty finding enough employees and were thus looking abroad for alternate sources of labor. They saw these Japanese in Brazil and decided they would be excellent candidates for working in Japan. They were, after all, Japanese. Since these two groups recognized each other as Japanese— and thus as basically the same kind of people—recruiting for workers from Brazil emerged as an explicit economic policy, including special visa considerations for them. Ultimately, several hundred thousand workers came from Brazil to Japan.

Since the Japanese in Japan and the returning Japanese from Brazil shared a common Japanese identity, the assumption was that they could communicate and get along. However, problems quickly emerged. The Japanese from Brazil had limited Japanese-language skills, so there was a language problem. Furthermore, the returning workers had absorbed much of Brazilian culture and often acted in ways that did not seem "Japanese" to the Japanese. To those from Brazil, in turn, the Japanese of Japan seemed unpredictable and rather cold. The assumption that being Japanese involved a core set of beliefs, values, and skills was thus challenged. Instead, the situation of these people required some negotiation. What, after all, did it mean to "be Japanese?" Since the Brazilians were very much the newcomers and very much the minority, this was not a negotiation among equals.

Those from Brazil now faced an identity dilemma. Were they to redouble their efforts to become fully Japanese in the eyes of their hosts? Were they to return to Brazil? Or were they to stay in Japan but create some new hybrid identity? They were not the same as their hosts in terms of core values and behaviors, and they were unlikely to force their hosts into some broader and more inclusive definition of what "Japanese" might mean. So, instead, they would be Japanese Brazilian. To create that identity, one mechanism was to reach back into their Brazilian heritage for an activity that would demonstrate in a positive way their semi-Japaneseness and semi-Brazilianness. It was time for the samba. Soon there were samba parades in various Japanese cities, fortifying a new hybrid identity of Japanese Brazilian. The Brazilian part of their identity had a nice boost in 2002 as they watched Brazil win the final game of the 2002 World Cup that was jointly held in Japan and Korea.

The example shows the three different ways of looking at the meaning of identity. The *core-values* approach looks toward what helps bind together a set of people with a single identity—in this case, being Japanese. This example is helpful in showing the extent to which such assumptions of shared values may be just that: assumptions. Yet it also shows how important such assumptions can be to people. The *arena-of-negotiation* approach is especially appropriate to the returned Japanese from Brazil in their interaction with their hosts. Its strengths as an approach lie in indicating the fluidity of meaning and the way that power affects its negotiation. Finally, the *act-of-creation* approach is effective in indicating how the returned workers themselves helped create a new hybrid identity. The example also illustrates some other aspects of meaning that will reappear in the coming chapters: for example, the importance of language in creating a shared identity and the way events—such as a samba parade—can be used both to indicate meaning and to simultaneously create it.

SO WHAT IS HUMAN MEANING?

This example of returned Japanese suggests that even for a relatively familiar area of human meaning—figuring out who you are—the nature, construction, and implications of human meaning are complex. The investigation of human meaning can become murky, frustrating, and annoying. That being the case, a few general comments may be helpful as a rough guide. While the many meanings of different parts of life may be complex, multiple, and ever shifting with circumstances, there are some themes that will appear through part III of this book.[4] One is that human meaning is *open*. There can be new values, or beliefs, or creative acts, or interpretations, or combinations of any of those. Meaning is not closed; there can always be something new and fresh. People often enjoy that freedom, creativity, and freshness, whether in work or play, routine daily life, or the many special events that mark the human calendar. Meaning is also *context driven*. As will be especially clear in terms of cognition and language, people cannot ignore context even when they want to—or even when they might be better off if they could. Context may not be everything, but human beings have great difficulty ignoring it. It is hard to talk about what anything means, including your own identity, without considering the context. Human meaning is also *order seeking*. Our brains seek simple guidelines for managing complexity. However, that can result in simplifications that obstruct further thought. People from the Euro-American tradition, for example, are prone to thinking in terms of dichotomies ("well, you're either with us or against us") and often like to further reduce everything to a single factor ("well, it all boils down to . . ."). Finally, human meaning usually includes some form of *marking* for both practical and expressive reasons. If you figure something out, after all, you do not want to have to figure it out again tomorrow. If you figure out something really important, you might want to create some lasting tribute to it. The specific ways

---

4   These four can be in conflict. The search for order, for example, may well have the result of closing down systems of meaning rather than opening them up. The marking of meaning, as another example, may serve either as a means for creativity and openness or as a mechanism to close down options and create the kind of orthodoxy and orthopraxy noted for religion in chapter 13.

that meaning is marked are numerous, ranging from verbal stories and written texts, to ritual and ceremony, to the linguistic labels we use, to the way we mark our own bodies, to the specific ways we engage with the world around us.

STRUCTURE OF THE CHAPTERS IN PART III

Part III has four chapters that examine the construction of human meaning from different angles. The first of these, chapter 15, looks at cognition. The purpose of that chapter is to reconsider how biology, culture, and environment all affect the way we think about ourselves and the world in which we live. Much of what we think is "out there," for example, is greatly influenced by what's going on inside us as biological entities. Chapter 16 considers language. Topics include the nature of human language, how languages are structured, and how they affect the way people understand their world. There is considerable irony in any consideration of language, since the capacity for language is something all humans share even though the diversity of languages often keeps people apart. Chapter 17 considers how human expression both represents the meanings of people's lives and creates new ones. Whether in work or play, creative processes reshape human meaning in reciprocal processes between peoples, their bodies, and their environments. Finally, chapter 18 explores the world of anthropological action. Anthropologists are people and themselves attempt to create a world of meaning. Much of that attempt—clear in the formative years of anthropology—involves applying the anthropological understanding of human society toward maintaining the world and improving the condition of people in it. The meaning of anthropology, after all, lies both with understanding the world and immersing ourselves in it.

15

Cognition

In considering the frameworks and mechanisms through which people make sense of the world and their lives in it, one place to start is with the basic question of how humans think. That is a two-part, intertwined story of cognition and language. Language reflects human mental abilities, and human mental abilities are reflected in language. Even in evolutionary terms, the development of the brain and the speech centers are intertwined. Nevertheless, this chapter attempts to address cognition while keeping language largely in the background. Language, in turn, will be in the foreground in the next chapter.

This chapter has four main sections. The first is a review of what is known about the brain based on the rapid expansion of research during the last few decades. This quick tour of the brain is hardly definitive but provides a reminder of the need to include biology, along with culture and environment, in any anthropological analysis of human thinking. The second section addresses the distinction between *perception* (what our senses tell us about what is "out there") and *conception* (how we structure that information more abstractly). A few visual illusions will be provided to indicate how our minds mingle issues of perception and conception. The third section addresses the contrast between *thought* and *emotion*. Both are fundamental ways in which humans interact with their environment, and both have their advantages and disadvantages. Finally, the fourth section of the chapter focuses on the use of *symbols* and *routines*. Symbols highlight the structure and durability of human meaning, and routines capture something of the processes through which life is experienced on a daily basis. The case examples at the end of the chapter concern machine intelligence (especially the final computer triumph in the game of *go*) and the way simple cognitive categories can end up at the core of genocide (in this case, the Rwandan genocide of 1994).

THE HUMAN BRAIN

Much of what humans are derives directly from a biological foundation. Upright posture, for example, frees the hands for other work; the precision grip between thumb and fingers provides the potential for extraordinarily detailed work. Other animals may use tools, but they do not polish projectile points, attach them to pieces of wood, and shoot them from a bow as they are running across a field. The finely developed human vocal apparatus—including the ability for minute, carefully controlled movements of the throat, mouth, and lungs (to produce air for speech)—is also unique. Other animals can vocalize, but they cannot produce the flow of varied-yet-regulated sound required for all but the simplest human communication. The human brain is also an impressive element of human biology. It is not an abstract thinking machine. Rather, it is living tissue with complex connections that run throughout the body. Research in the last few decades has greatly expanded the understanding of exactly which parts of the brain are related to which activities and how the brain does its many jobs.

Consider the development of the brain. As the fetus develops, a neural tube is created with a new kind of cell: the neuron. During late pregnancy, estimates are that over 250,000 neurons may be created every minute. During that same period, the neural tube develops a somewhat bulbous projection on one end that will eventually be the brain. Since the neurons are not being created in the same place where they will be needed, thousands and thousands of neurons must migrate along a trail marked out by *glial* cells. The trail is established by sniffing out trace chemicals. The neurons then clamber along the trail of glial cells. Predictably, some of the neurons get lost along the way. There is some debate about it, but it seems that many of them can fit in even if they go to the wrong place: the auditory neurons, for example, just start acting like visual neurons. Neurons thus show the same ability to adapt to their environment that is characteristic of humans in their environment.

Once all these neurons are in the right place—or have decided to fake it—the real work begins. The neurons begin to develop extensions, projections, and just plain bumps that will enable them to communicate with other neurons. That communication requires that the neuron do two things. One involves sending out a single tentacle (an *axon*) that may terminate at the next cell or may weave its way through the brain and even halfway through the body. The other involves a larger number of smaller tentacles (*dendrites*) that will receive messages sent from the axons of other neurons. Once all the neurons are in place *and* have traced out the routes by which to connect to each other, the brain is in business. The neural networks provide information from the senses and can direct the body to respond to that information. Much, but not all, of that routing occurs through that bulbous region that developed at the end of the prenatal neural tube. Like all mammalian brains, the human brain has three general parts. The first is a *forebrain*, which is the seat of higher and more abstract functions. The second is a *midbrain*, which is the seat of more routine functioning. The third is the *hindbrain*, which is essential to the most basic biological processes. Each of these areas has subareas that deal with particular tasks: whether it is the visual cortex for watching things or the amygdala that that can respond to danger by putting the entire body on high alert.

This abbreviated review of the biological context for human thought suggests three key points. The first is the *complexity* of the brain. Research on the brain, after all, is not demonstrating that the brain is somehow simpler than we thought it was now that we can see its operations more clearly. Instead, we are finding ever greater complexities. Remember that you have billions of neurons. The greatest number are in your brain, but others are snaking around throughout your body. They have trillions of connections. The second point is the *flexibility* of the brain. The notion that there is a place in the brain for each activity would seem sensible, yet the brain in many cases does not act that way. Research on people who have suffered damage to parts of the brain suggests that other parts of the brain can take over the functions of the damaged parts even if it is not normally their job. Furthermore, not everything is routed through the brain and, of that, not all routed through conscious thought. A great deal is on automatic pilot. The third point is the *processual nature* of the brain. What we think of as the brain is not so much a specific structure in a specific place as a set of connections that extend throughout the body. Those connections are, in part, chemical and, in part, electrical.

These points about complexity, flexibility, and process reflect the fact that the brain is alive. It is not just a machine programmed to do particular kinds of tasks. It not only absorbs information but develops new ways of organizing that information. Some of that matches our usual notions of conscious thought, yet much of it is unconscious, automatic, and more emotional than conceptual. Discussions of machine "intelligence" must thus confront human thought processes that are not simply logical but also biologically embodied with multiple pathways for reacting to the environment, including emotional responses that may override the brain's more conscious and rationalistic efforts.

PERCEPTION AND CONCEPTION

The great advances in research on the human brain are interesting but do not resolve the more subjective issue of how people understand their worlds. Here, more traditional research is still helpful. That research is usually phrased in terms of a distinction between *perception* (the recognition of things "out there") and *conception* (the organization of those perceptions). That distinction follows common usage of the root words *perceive* (which implies you are sensing something that is out there) and *conceive* (which implies a more abstract—and creative—kind of mental activity). Another way to put it is that perception has more to do with the senses themselves (sight, touch, smell, etc.) while conception has more to do with the integration of information from the senses and the assessment of its implications. As an example, you might perceive a set of long, narrow, yellowish things halfway tucked into a colorful package. Your brain identifies these as french fries and considers how these might relate to what your senses are telling you of your hunger (integrating different sensory stimuli). Your brain might also ponder the effect of fast food on global nutrition (a higher-level integration of a broad range of information).[1]

If we compare conception and perception, there are some key differences. Although conception might be rather free floating, perception is grounded more closely in an objective external reality. It is easy, for example, to conceive of things that do not exist, but you should not be perceiving things that do not exist. The former is creativity, but the latter is hallucination. Thus, perceptions ought to be relatively accurate. Sometimes, however, they are not. Consider some simple illusions. For both the Müller-Lyer (figure 15.1) and Ponzo (figure 15.2) illusions, there are two straight parallel lines of equal length. However, they do not look the same length. We perceive these lines as being of different lengths even though we have seen these illusions before and know that we are being fooled. Here, our higher, more abstract thinking is more realistic. But why—at the perceptual level—are we fooled by these simple illusions? Some people have suggested that the Ponzo illusion works because it looks like train tracks and thus makes us see these two horizontal lines as at different distances.[2] That would suggest cultural and environmental explanations: our brains have rewired the way we see things because of our previous experiences.

---

1   It is probably better to consider perception and conception as on a continuum rather than as an either-or issue. After all, often when you are simply perceiving something you still integrate it with other thoughts and emotions.

2   There has been some cross-cultural work on these illusions. To summarize a long series of arguments, there appear to be some differences between people exposed to urban life versus those from more rural or undeveloped areas, but also some differences between people exposed to open horizons rather than enclosed environments like dense forests. Those with urban, open-horizon experience tend to be more swayed by the illusions. That would suggest, as would be expected, that there are both cultural and biological factors at work.

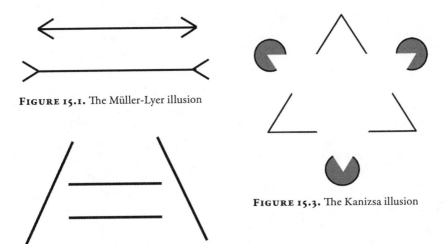

FIGURE 15.1. The Müller-Lyer illusion

FIGURE 15.3. The Kanizsa illusion

FIGURE 15.2. The Ponzo illusion

However, there is an even simpler point to be made. The lines are not presented alone but with a broader visual context. It would seem that we are incapable of removing unnecessary context even when we ought to. There is an indication here that the importance of context applies even to our most basic physical perceptions. In many, many situations, that attention to context will give us a broader and richer understanding of what is actually out there. In cases like these, however, the automatic incorporation of context stands in the way of solving a simple problem about the length of two lines.

Consider also the Kanizsa illusion in figure 15.3. Here, the traditional interpretation was that people tend to see two overlapping triangles and that those triangles, in turn, overlay the small circles. The explanation is that the mind tends to simplify a large number of independent lines into a smaller number of basic geometric shapes. The mind is seeking order: searching for a simple structure in a complex pattern. These days, however, it is hard to find anyone who does not see Pac-Men munching their way in from the periphery of the figure.[3] That explanation emphasizes the influences of experience and culture on visual perception.[4]

---

3   Although the discussion of perception here is of things "out there," perception is very much within the body and conditioned by the senses themselves. Thus, in some reports from people who have gone into trance, people "see" certain kinds of images: dots and jagged lines to start, whorls and tunnels soon after, and eventually usually some distorted images against that whorled background.

4   Illusions that involve a time dimension can also be very interesting. Just as your brain includes spatial context, it also includes temporal context. Some extremely entertaining examples come from an annual contest on illusions: see www.illusionoftheyear.com.

The mixed influence of biology, culture, and environment on perception is also reflected in real-world situations. Colin Turnbull's discussion of his guide Kenge's first encounter with the open savannah is a good example. Kenge's experience had been in the forest, and he had never seen wide-open plains. Initially, he saw buffalo far in the distance as insects; he saw a boat on the lake in the distance as a tiny piece of wood. He had no prior experience judging objects at great distances. He was correct in *perceiving* that the buffalo and boat were "small," but he did not automatically adjust that perceived size for distance. That was both a perceptual problem (how to accurately judge size at a distance) and a conceptual one (how small could a buffalo actually be). But Kenge quickly learned. That perceptual adjustment also had conceptual implications. Kenge had conceived of the world itself as being the forest. The forest was a living presence and generally a positive one. Yet here was a place that was not forest. His solution—as described in the chapter on religion—was to reframe his notion of the forest into something broader that could encompass both forest and savannah. His solution shows how perception and conception are linked, how new conceptions change perceptions, and how new perceptions modify conceptions or even create entirely new ones.

THOUGHT AND EMOTION

The discussion of cognition so far has focused on what, at least from a Western perspective, is the "cooler" mind versus the "warmer" heart. But what is the role of emotion in how humans relate to their world? This has long been a topic in philosophy and now is increasingly so in psychology and biology. There have been two main formulations of the issue. One is that reason and emotion are different but *complementary* ways of interacting with one's environment. Reason is a slower, more purposeful approach while emotion is a quicker more instinctive approach. The other formulation is that reason and emotion are often (if not always) *oppositional* and that people must choose between them: to break free from the shackles of emotion toward the light of reason or to break free from the shackles of reason to embrace the heart's true desires.

The burgeoning field of neuroscience is providing important clues about how emotion and thought fit together. The weight of the evidence supports the biological differences between thought and emotion, but it also tends to indicate complementary roles between the two. In terms of difference, the separation of cognitive and affective parts of the brain remains largely substantiated by the research. Emotionally we still share many of the same brain features relating to emotion that other animals have (the so-called limbic system), and our brains wrap around that a vastly expanded cortical area, which is the seat of "higher" thinking. Clearly as well, emotions have a far higher correspondence with actual bodily sensations than do more abstract thoughts. The basic emotions, like fear, have clear physical correlates.

The way thought and emotion complement each other may be the most important point from the new research. Evolutionary biologists, for example, have emphasized certain emotions as hardwired ways to respond to crucial situations. *Fear*, for example, focuses the entire body on a danger and energizes it for action. A rapidly beating heart elevates oxygen in the blood for muscles as cascades of hormones are released. *Anger* also energizes, this time for attack rather than flight. *Surprise* alerts all the senses that something is different and needs attention. *Disgust* ensures avoidance of something that the body senses may be damaging. Overall, then, emotion takes you back to basics; it interrupts your regular routine and focuses you back to more elemental issues. But that emotional response may also occur simultaneously with a more reasoned approach. The cortical brain does not stop working just because of an emotional override through the limbic system. Perhaps the best illustration of this is the classic tracing of fear by Joseph LeDoux. He found, exactly as discussed above, that the emotion of fear induced rapid changes in the body by going directly through the limbic system, specifically the amygdala, the area of the brain coordinating emotions. But, at the same time, messages were also sent to the cortical area of the brain, which then made its own determination of the danger and sent a separate set of instructions, slower but more reasoned, to the amygdala.

Human emotions are not always so basic and physical. Emotions may be more general and longer lasting (often called "moods"), and thoughts may themselves blend from quite abstract to fully emotional. For example, social justice for some is an abstract thought; for others it is a driving commitment of a deeply emotional nature. So it is important to remember that emotion is a way of interacting with the environment that is sometimes crucial in a primal survival sense and sometimes simply an alternative way of being in the world. Emotion is also a reminder of what is most important in life. One recent line of inquiry in neuroscience and anthropology has been how emotion helps organize memory by providing an index for what is really worth remembering. If you are emotional about something, that means you care, you need to pay attention, and you need to remember.

SYMBOLS AND ROUTINES

A consideration of symbols and routines rounds out this chapter's discussion of cognition. A *symbol* is something that stands for something else. Symbols range from specific and action oriented to abstract and meaning oriented. At the more specific end of the continuum are things like a red light, which means to stop. There is no complex web of meaning here; this is a simple practical instruction. Symbols like these are sometimes called *signs*—or sometimes simply *signals*. At the other end of the continuum are more complex symbols that may invoke strong feelings but are less clear about precisely what action is required. A national flag, for example, invokes a range of feelings and thoughts, but it is not necessarily clear what you are supposed to do when you see it.[5]

Symbols vary in their complexity and profundity, but all symbols work in much the same way. Something relatively simple—a flag, a Valentine heart, a smile, or even a color—stands for something else. Symbols can be highly individual, but they are most effective when they are shared. That sharing occurs on two levels. First, the literal aspect of the symbol itself is shared. For example, a sun, a moon, a flag, or an eagle is a familiar sight. Thus the symbol itself is familiar. A symbol will not be as effective if people have to ask what the symbol itself is; so symbols tend to be relatively common objects or representations of them. Second, the meaning of the symbol is also generally shared. If we both recognize a picture of an eagle—on a T-shirt perhaps—but you think the eagle is a vicious raptor and I think of it as a soaring, fearless flyer, our uses of the symbol will be different. We share the symbol, but not the meaning of it. Symbols are thus a mechanism to test whether our views are similar and whether we are together. If the symbol is not shared, then we are not fully together in our understanding of the world. We can stray apart either if one of us does not know what an eagle is or if we disagree on the meaning of the symbol ("they may fly high but they kill"). On the other hand, if we both recognize the symbol and the meaning of it, we are fully together. Even if we only think we share the meaning, we can still be together. Symbols can give a sense of unity by covering up differences.

Symbols help show what is common to people, and their use demonstrates social solidarity. Rally round the flag. When those symbols *and* their meaning are not shared, however, there is a lack of solidarity. Both those who salute and those who burn a national flag, after all, recognize that the flag is a potent symbol of a country. They just differ on what that means. Such agreement and disagreement is achieved quickly through symbols without requiring much discussion. They pack in much meaning and often with much verve. For example, would a Gadsden flag with its coiled rattlesnake and "don't tread on me" phrase, for example, work as well if it pictured a rabbit rather than a rattlesnake? Symbols are appealing because they are compacted pieces of meaning in well-known form. An analysis of symbols is a good research strategy in identifying the central values and points of tension within human societies.

---

5   Some people restrict the word "symbol" for this more complex situation, but it is probably best to think of symbols as a continuum running from relatively simple practical instructions to abstract and compli-cated invocations of meaning with many variations in between.

While symbols convey meaning encapsulated in familiar and concrete forms, *routines* are processes that get us through the day without an explicit consideration of the meaning of what we do. Daily life is often rather messy. On any given day, things will vary somewhat, so no master plan is likely to work well without revision. To refigure the master plan for each new set of events each new day would be forbidding. In order to avoid that constant refiguring, people rely on routines. Something worked last time, it seemed to work okay, so you do it again. You get up and have a cup of coffee, then take a run, clean up and read your e-mail after you check the latest online news. If those things do not work, you may try to think through a new routine, or, more likely, you find that you have already launched one. The cup of coffee becomes two cups of coffee; the morning run disappears. No more Twitter; just check humansofny, the *Guardian*, and NASA on Instagram. If you tried to figure all these things out consciously, you probably couldn't make it through the day. Yet people do make it through the day. Their routines often work pretty well—thus requiring little conscious thought. Your active mind, the part that does all that conceptual work, may be largely absent as you go about your day. You may function rather well without it.

The net implication is that human thinking is not always very rational or even explicit. People perceive things in the environment, react to them, and sometimes alter their routines without much of what we normally regard as "thinking." This issue of routines is a useful reminder that people are not always acting out a script, or performing their expected roles, or implementing a predesigned project. They are interacting with their world, repeating established routines, and creating new ones. They are making sense of things on the run. As they do so, however, they will have some clear reference points in the symbols that they recognize and share with those around them. Those symbols may sometimes tell them what to do (stop! go!) or sometimes simply reassure them that there is some general sense and order to the world, that it all does mean something.

CASE EXAMPLE—*GO!* THE TRIUMPH OF MACHINE INTELLIGENCE

Much of the discussion of artificial intelligence is framed as if thought were a mechanical, logical process. Machines are given a set of directions to follow and—because their memory is vast and their computational speed great—they can follow those directions accurately and quickly. But that is not thought in the way it has been described in this chapter. For example, much human "thought" is just a set of reactions to the environment at a low level of cognitive complexity. We do not always think about things; we often just react. Sometimes that is our "emotional" system racing ahead of our more cerebral one. Sometimes life involves routinized

The Statue of Liberty is a powerful symbol of the United States, but it is from the French and whether it welcomes or excludes is currently in debate. (Credit: D. Haines)

behavior, not a formal plan of action. As a practical matter, after all, we do not have time to rethink everything we do every day.

There have been some examinations of that kind of more ad hoc response in virtual environments. Philip Agre,[6] for example, once gave a computer the task of placing a set of virtual blocks on top of each other. Rather than writing a step-by-step plan, he instead gave a long list of rules to which the computer could refer. The implications of doing it that way were interesting. Agre measured the actual computer activity required at different stages of the process and found that there was a general pattern of decreasing computer activity as the task progressed. There was initially a high level of activity as the computer ran through the long list of rules

---

6   Philip Agre received his PhD from MIT and was later faculty at UCLA. His work noted here was—at least for an anthropological perspective—an appealing blend of philosophy (especially phenomenology) and information science. His personal story became a bit convoluted over time and is nicely conveyed in an appreciation that can be found at http://www.continentcontinent.cc/index.php/continent/article /view/177.

Go is far more difficult than chess. The number of possibilities exceeds the number of atoms in the universe. (Credit: Saran Paroong/iStock)

to find the ones that applied to the specific situation. But that activity decreased as the computer identified the most relevant rules. Effectively, the computer was establishing a routine based on which rules (of a large list) seemed to work in this particular virtual environment.

Something roughly similar emerged in Google's 2016 attempt to have a computer win at *go* against an acknowledged *go* master of the human variety. IBM's "Big Blue" had nearly two decades earlier bested chess champion Gary Kasparov in the game of chess. But *go* is a far more complex game based on a gridded playing board and piles of black and white tiles. The rules are intensely simple: on your turn, place one of your pieces anywhere, which will flip any of your opponent's pieces that lie between that new tile and any of your previous pieces. But the number of possibilities is huge, well beyond the number of atoms in the universe. So the Google team preparing the computer to play *go* had to think how the computer could do more actual "thinking" rather than simply memorizing sequences of moves from prior games. By the team's description, they used two deep neural networks that enabled AlphaGo to disregard huge numbers of poor play choices to focus on a smaller set of good options for a particular game situation. That, the team claimed, brought it far, far closer to what we know of human thought. And that spelled doom for Lee Sedol, the Korean grandmaster of the game who went down in a 4-to-1 defeat.

The *go* victory came at a crucial time in the evolution of computers. By 2016 the ability to create ever smaller circuits (the basis of "Moore's Law") was reaching its limit. So the possibility of endlessly increasing computer capabilities through more memory and more computational speed might finally have to yield to designing better ways to integrate memory and computation in ways more like human thought. Questions of artificial intelligence must always address these issues of whether mechanical intelligence can ever be the same as a human intelligence that is quite bound into biological beings. As computers also develop better interfaces with their environments (driverless cars, for example) and with people, they will also have to develop more subtle ways of social thinking and interaction. Unfortunately, there is some evidence now that learning from people may not be exactly what we want computers to do. The same month that saw machine victory in the game of *go* also saw the failure of an interactive virtual companion on social media. The Twitter-bot Tay had to be turned off since it had picked up some inappropriate ways of talking about sensitive issues, for example, defending white supremacy and genocide.

CASE EXAMPLE—HUTU AND TUTSI IN RWANDA: CREATING CATEGORIES FOR KILLING

Discussions of perception and conception, thought and emotion, symbols and routines, may seem abstract, but the practical implications can be enormous. Consider, for example, some of the ways that people think about who they are and who other people are. People frequently characterize themselves and others as belonging to clearly defined racial, ethnic, gender, and sexual orientation categories. Those categories certainly provide a simple way to organize human diversity and to routinize relations with other people. The problem with such categories is that actual human beings do not fit into them very precisely, and the reasons for putting people into those categories may not be benign.

As a particularly extreme example, consider the meaning of the terms *Hutu* and *Tutsi* in Rwanda. The people called Hutu and Tutsi lived together in relative peace, spoke the same language, generally followed the same religion, lived in the same neighborhoods, often worked side by side, and intermarried extensively. Hutu and Tutsi were thus often related to each other by blood and marriage and interacted with each other in the course of daily life. Yet the two categories were also considered different. Hutu were thought to be short; Tutsi were tall. Hutu were longer established in Rwanda and traditionally horticulturalist; Tutsi were thought to be later migrants into Rwanda and pastoralist. So there were similarities and differences between the two, but the line between them was not always clear.

Ultimately the differences overcame the similarities. In 100 days in 1994, Hutu massacred some 800,000 people, largely Tutsi but including some Hutu as well. It was arguably the most efficient killing the world had ever seen. It was also one of the most chilling, since the killing was largely done with machetes and often by people who knew the victims personally. The roots of the genocide were multiple, including the withdrawal of international forces from Rwanda at exactly the moment when they were most needed to forestall the killing. In longer historical terms, colonial policies had helped sharpen the divide between Hutu and Tutsi, and postindependence governments also exploited the Hutu/Tutsi divide for their own political purposes. By the time of the genocide, there was an active public relations campaign by a radical set of Hutu that fanned the flames and organized the killing. The Tutsi were "cockroaches," and they were to be exterminated.

"Hutu" and "Tutsi" thus came to be symbols of identities that were implacably opposed to each other. Those fanning the flames, however, had a practical problem. It was not always easy to tell if some actual person was Hutu or Tutsi, because of the extensive overlap of the two groups. One bureaucratic task was to issue identity cards that would officially establish whether a person was Hutu or Tutsi. Since many people had both Hutu and Tutsi relatives, that formal identity process was also arbitrary. During the course of the genocide, most accounts indicate that the killing was also often quite arbitrary. Many people were killed because they looked like stereotypical Tutsi. However, people were also killed because their identity cards indicated they were Tutsi—even though sometimes they did not look Tutsi. If the card said "Hutu" but people looked Tutsi, they might be killed anyway. People were also killed because they looked well off (rich people were assumed to be Tutsi), seemed well educated (good education was a sign of being Tutsi), acted strangely (they looked guilty or fearful), would not themselves kill others (they must be protecting their own kind), had been accused by somebody of being Tutsi (whether correctly or for spite), or simply had something that the killers wanted.

It is not easy to draw overall lessons from the Rwandan genocide because many of the factors were unique to the situation. Yet it is clear from human history that genocides occur. The underlying assumption is that some kind of difference between people is so strong, so clear, and so unchangeable that those on the other side of the divide deserve to be slaughtered. In the Rwandan case the divide was based on a notion of physical differences, yet those physical differences had to be organized both bureaucratically (identity cards) and socially (Hutu had to report which of their neighbors were Tutsi). There was also extensive propaganda asserting that Tutsi were a unitary force and that the continued existence of the Tutsi was dangerous to the survival of the Hutu. In this case we can see how human thought goes astray as people are re-created as symbols ("cockroaches") rather than people. We also see how people routinize even the most violent behavior, murdering their own neighbors. In Rwanda—as with race relations in the United States—not even shared Christianity was enough to soften the divide.

SOURCES

Cognition is often dealt with passingly in anthropology texts or as a brief aside to discussions of language or belief systems. Two texts that deal with it in more detail—and particularly well, I think—are Emily Shultz and Robert Lavenda's *Cultural Anthropology: A Perspective on the Human Condition* (Oxford University Press; various eds.) and Mari Womack's *Being Human: An Introduction to Cultural Anthropology* (Prentice-Hall, 2001), or see her *Symbols and Meaning: A Concise Introduction* (AltaMira, 2005). For discussions of the brain, Joseph LeDoux's books are well informed and quite readable: see *Synaptic Self: How Our Brains Become Who We Are* (Viking, 2002) and *Anxious: Using the Brain to Understand and Treat Fear and Anxiety* (Viking, 2015). Elizabeth Johnston and Leah Olson focus on the emotional side of the brain in *The Feeling Brain: The Biology and Psychology of Emotions* (W.W. Norton, 2015). Some earlier, more anthropological discussions are in Maurice Bloch's *How We Think They Think: Anthropological Approaches to Cognition, Memory, and Literacy* (Westview, 1998) and Michael Tomasello's *The Cultural Origins of Human Cognition* (Harvard University Press, 2001). The subject of symbols is a richly studied area in anthropology, and Victor Turner's *The Forest of Symbols* (Cornell University Press, 1970) and Mary Douglas's *Purity and Danger* (Routledge, 1984) remain solid places to begin an anthropological consideration of them. For routines, the classic phenomenological discussions of Martin Heidegger and Alfred Schütz are foundational, as is Hugh Mehan and Houston Wood's *The Reality of Ethnomethodology* (Krieger Publishing, 1975).

For the artificial intelligence example, see Philip E. Agre's *Computation and Human Experience* (Cambridge University Press, 1997). His example program is sensible, and he discusses his findings explicitly in terms of *sense making* as identified in phenomenology—so it is an interesting book on those grounds. For updates on the other developments in 2016, online media will provide the basic details, but particularly good reviews of technology for a lay audience are found periodically in the *Economist* and the *New York Times*. For Rwanda, a good place to start is Philip Gourevitch's *We Wish to Inform You That Tomorrow We Will Be Killed with Our Families* (Picador, 1999). There are a variety of good films on Rwanda, but the 1999 Frontline presentation (and accompanying background web materials) of *Triumph of Evil* is an especially good companion to Gourevitch's book. For a review of how the resolution of the Rwanda situation opened up even more deadly problems in the Congo, see Sadako Ogata's *The Turbulent Decade: Confronting the Refugee Crises of the 1990s* (W.W. Norton, 2005).

16

Language

This chapter continues the discussion in the last chapter by bringing in language. There is not much thought without language and not much language without thought. The same argument can probably be made about language and emotion. Words can sway, flay, blame, inflame. There might well be emotion without words, but it would be much harder to elaborate different kinds of emotion and certainly to communicate emotions. Yet there is a cruel irony. While language may be what makes us most fully human, we speak different languages. The result is that whether or not we have similar thoughts and emotions, the world is split between people we can understand and those we cannot. Thus language enables communication, but the multiplicity of languages limits it—and sometimes makes it impossible.

This chapter's discussion of language is in four sections. The first section addresses the general characteristics of human language, its overall potential, and how languages develop. The second section provides the details of how languages work: their sound systems, word constructions, phrase and sentence structures, and written forms. The third section considers the interaction of language and culture, particularly the way language shapes how we understand the world. Finally, the fourth section discusses the relationships among language, society, and politics. The case examples at the end of the chapter concern the way time is constructed in the Hopi language, and the difficulties in translating works of literature—specifically the thousand-year-old Japanese novel *The Tale of Genji*.

THE NATURE OF LANGUAGE AND LANGUAGES

CHARACTERISTICS OF LANGUAGE

There has been a long-running debate about human language and the extent to which it differs from communication among other animals. Research and experiments have shown that other animals—especially primates such as gorillas, chimpanzees, and bonobos—can do much of what we can: use arbitrary words to communicate, put those words into structured sentences, and even make up new words. Yet the breadth and depth of human language together are unique. In his classic discussion of human language compared to the communication systems of animals, Charles Hockett posited seven key characteristics of language. These continue to provide a good outline of what language enables us to do.

Openness. Languages are not limited in their elements or combinations. New elements can be added, and new combinations can be created. Languages are neither closed systems nor unchanging ones. We are limited only by the limits of our creativity: we can make up new words and new structures.

Displacement. Language does not require that the things being discussed be nearby or viewable. We can talk about the chair in the next room; the site of the first hockey game in Windsor, Nova Scotia; or the remains of a spacecraft on Mars. That ability to talk about things even in their absence is very useful.

Positionality. We can talk about these things (which may or may not be here) from any particular angle. We can talk about the chair or hockey pond or spacecraft from the front, side, top, from any distance, or under any light conditions. That is also very useful. Language enables us to create multidimensional virtual worlds through which we can move at will.

Arbitrariness. One of the features that makes language so open is the ability to use sounds and writing to convey meaning even though they have no intrinsic relationship to that meaning. Although in English cats do "meow" and in Vietnamese helicopters are described by their "wap-wap" sound, we do not have to match the sound of the object or action to the words we use. We can make up anything we want.

Multiplicity of patterning. One additional feature of this arbitrariness is that we do not have to use the same kind of approach for different parts of a language. We can have complex declensions for nouns but no conjugation for verbs; we can have complex words but simple grammatical structures, we can have a writing system that is phonetic or not, or even has both phonetic and nonphonetic components (as Chinese does). We can even have different sets of words for different situations: general versus technical, or polite versus informal versus just plain vulgar.

Semanticity. Language even permits us to talk about "things" that are not really "things" at all. We can thus talk about meaning itself. ("Semantics" is the study of meaning.) Such discussions can sometimes be difficult, since we are talking about what we cannot directly access with our senses, but it is possible.

Prevarication. Language also permits us to talk about things that are not only not "here" but do not exist at all. We can say it is raining when it is not, that something happened when it did not, or that something did not happen that did. This too is a very useful, if often destructive, feature of language.

Divergence and Durability

Hockett's seven criteria indicate the overall potential of human language. But how do individual languages develop? There are two general themes. One is *divergence*. Languages change quickly, and change in ways that lead to greater numbers of mutually unintelligible languages. As language speakers spread out from each other, with less frequent intercommunication, new *dialects* (variations of a language) develop. Initially, they are mutually intelligible, but changes in vocabulary, pronunciation, and grammar gradually render them so different that they become separate languages. This, then, is the first major theme in the history of languages: divergence and mutual unintelligibility. It resembles the biblical story of the Tower of Babel. Maintaining a common language in the face of such divergence has been—at least until the development of mass media—a difficult task.

There is another theme, however, and that is *durability*. Much of the argument about Ebonics (called African American Vernacular English or Black English, by linguists) is that though the words from the languages originally spoken by slaves brought to the Americas may have disappeared, the grammatical structures themselves have continued. That durability of grammatical structures is seen more generally in contacts between different languages. If two language groups meet and have some need for communication, a limited utilitarian language often develops, based on the more powerful group's language. Such a language is called a trade language or, more technically, a *pidgin*. Pidgins are grammatically simple languages that use limited vocabulary to enable basic communication. Such pidgins can continue for many generations. Yet when people start speaking these pidgins in their own community, fuller grammatical structures develop, often from the prior languages. The pidgins become full languages, what are called *creoles*. Creoles, unlike pidgins, are complete languages with full grammars. Haitian

Creole, for example, is a complete language in its own right, not simply a version of French.

KINESICS AND PARALANGUAGE

One further comment about languages is needed before considering their actual structure. The formal languages under discussion here are not the only form of human communication. Instead, they are part of a broader range of ways that people communicate. Much of that broader communication involves *kinesics* ("body language" and facial gestures); much involves how we are dressed and adorned; and, at close distances, some of it is olfactory. That broader communication can also be vocal. Laughing and belching convey messages, as does loudness. Yelling and whispering the same words send very different messages. These nonlinguistic vocalizations are called *paralanguage*. So stand tall (kinesics), clear your throat (paralanguage), and get on with what you have to say.

THE STRUCTURE OF LANGUAGES

There are, it is estimated, some 6,800 languages in the world today—many of which are nearing extinction as their last living speakers grow old. Each of these languages has a grammar with three main parts: *phonology*, *morphology*, and *syntax*. Many also have *writing* systems. Details follow below.

PHONOLOGY

Phonology refers to the sound system of a language (~*phon* means sound and ~*ology* means knowledge about something). The number of possible sounds humans can make is large, so there has to be a selection of a more limited number of recognizable sounds from the range of possibilities. One of the most difficult tasks in learning a new language is exactly this problem: how to recognize the distinct sounds before trying to understand the meanings of those sounds.

The smallest unit of sound that is recognized in a particular language is called a *phoneme*. The phonemes in languages vary. For example, in English "r" is one phoneme and "l" is a different phoneme. You know they are different phonemes because you cannot use them interchangeably without the danger of changing or losing a word's meaning. "Lung" is not "rung." Yet in Japanese, a sound somewhere between our "r" and our "l" is a single phoneme. For them, the sounds of an English speaker saying "lung" and "rung" would *not* sound different. As another example, "ah" (pronounced as in "ma") would be a single phoneme in English but in Vietnamese it is potentially six phonemes. Vietnamese is a tonal language and, in the northern dialect, there are: a neutral tone "ah"; a rising tone "ah"; a falling tone "ah"; a falling then rising tone "ah"; a sharp falling then rising tone "ah"; and a sinking, almost glottalized falling tone "ah."[1] English speakers hear these six distinct Vietnamese phonemes (each with a different meaning) as only a single phoneme.

Morphology

Morphology (~*morph* for shape or form) refers to the way meaning is constructed out of these units of sound. The smallest unit of meaning in a language is called a *morpheme*. Thus the English word "dog" includes three phonemes ("d" "aw" "g") but is a single morpheme.[2] (You can take the "g" away and still have the word "do," but it does not have anything to do with a dog.) Morphemes can be either bound or unbound. An *unbound morpheme*, like an unbound dog, can go where it wishes and stand on its own.[3] A *bound morpheme*, by contrast, only has meaning when attached to something else. Thus, in English the "z" sound indicates a plural: the single "dog" with the addition of the "z" sound becomes "dogs" which has four phonemes ("d" "aw" "g" "z") and two morphemes ("dog" and "multiple-of-them"). Likewise, the three phonemes and single morpheme of "kill" can be indicated as past action in English by adding the "d" sound and producing "killed" (four phonemes and two morphemes: "kill" and "did-it-already"). In the cases of "dogs" and "killed," these bound morphemes are called *suffixes* (because they come at the end). There are also *prefixes* ("re"-build, "pre"-cook) and, in some languages, *infixes* (bound morphemes that are inserted in the middle of words).

The results of these morphological constructions are what we call words. These words comprise the *lexicon* of a language. The style of the words constructed in different languages varies a great deal. Some languages tend toward relatively compact words with mostly unbound morphemes; others construct elaborate words by combining bound and unbound morphemes. Some places of honor for such elaboration

---

1   In English, to the despair of those trying to learn the language, the letter "a" actually represents several different phonemes, from the "a" in "ma" and "father" to that in "made." Even the "aw" of dog noted in the text is subject to regional variation.

2   To continue the English-Vietnamese comparison: In English "ma" has two phonemes that together constitute one morpheme. That morpheme is an informal reference to one's "mother." In Vietnamese, by contrast, the single phoneme "m" combines with all the different tones of "a" to create six different words depending on the tone. One of those words is also an informal reference to one's mother, but the others include "ghost," "horse," "grave," and "rice seedling"—which makes proper pronunciation of the tones essential.

3   In English the vast majority of morphemes are unbound, whether noun, pronoun, adjective, verb, adverb, proposition, conjunction, or interjection. This is not the case in all languages. In many languages, for example, there are verb stems that cannot be used independently without case endings.

go to German for long nouns and Japanese for long verbs. Vietnamese and Chinese, by contrast, use no endings (bound morphemes) for either nouns or verbs and, indeed, are based largely on monosyllabic unbound morphemes.[4] That makes for extraordinary conciseness and—many would argue—an intrinsically concise and poetic nature to those languages.

Syntax

Syntax refers to the way these words of various kinds are put together in phrases and sentences. Thus the standard format in English is subject-verb-object, as in "I kill the dog."[5] Many other languages use similar constructions: Vietnamese, for example, tends to organize that sentence in the same way. Other languages are different. Verbs, for example, can go at the end of the sentence. Thus the object of the action is known before the action itself. There are also more subtle issues of syntax than simple word order. English, for example, requires the use of articles. We cannot have a sentence simply with "dog." Instead it must be *a dog, the dog, this dog*, or *that dog*. Nor can we generally have a sentence without a subject. Those aspects of English often cause problems for nonnative speakers. On the other hand, the lack of such precision in other languages makes them difficult for English speakers. Any translation thus requires a full reenvisioning of the ambience of the literary scene rather than a simple translation of what the author put on the page in the original language.

Writing

Finally, languages often have written forms. Hockett's comment about "multiplicity of patterning" is particularly helpful in regard to written language, since it is *not* necessary that the written form of the language conform to the spoken form. English, for example, is written with an alphabet but is hardly rigorously phonetic—or at least the rules for pronunciation are exceedingly complex and often require you to know whether words have Germanic, Latin, or Greek roots. Other languages, Spanish and French for example, do a far better job of conformity between the spoken and written language. At the other end of the spectrum is Chinese, which is based on characters that originally represented the concept

---

4   As a technical clarification, the early monosyllabic nature of Chinese and Vietnamese has yielded to frequent use of two-syllable compound nouns even if the word has only a single meaning. That is accomplished either by pairing two words with similar meanings or a regular word with a repeating sound—a kind of "nonsense" word—that is itself without meaning.

5   It is, of course, possible to use other constructions in English, such as the passive tense. Yet any writing guide will remind you to use subject-verb-object as the stronger style.

of a word rather than the way it is spoken. The characters for tree, grove of trees, and forest visually convey their message by using representations of one tree, two trees, and three trees respectively. A human leaning against a tree means "to rest," and the combination of images of sun and moon means "clear and bright." One extraordinary advantage of this approach is that people can share an understanding of something in written form even though they may not speak the same language at all. Thus China could function as a single political entity despite the "Chinese" language being, in fact, a set of distinct (although related) languages. Even beyond China, others could use the Chinese writing system. The Japanese, Koreans, and Vietnamese all adopted Chinese characters even though they had their own spoken languages, which were quite different in origin and structure from Chinese.

LANGUAGE AND CULTURE

Any language thus includes phonology, morphology, syntax, and, in many cases, a writing system that has its own complexities. Language is an enormous human achievement that permits an impressive breadth and depth of communication, expression, and thought. One might well argue that it is language that makes people fully human. Yet if language is so important and people speak such different languages, is it even possible to communicate across linguistic differences? If people do so much of their thinking through language, and they have different languages, is there equivalence in their way of thinking?

In anthropology this relationship between language and thought is especially associated with the names of Edward Sapir and Benjamin Whorf. The former was one of Boas's early students, and the latter, in turn, was a student of Sapir. The central question Sapir and Whorf raised was about the relationship between language and thought. This has come to be known as the *Sapir-Whorf Hypothesis*.[6] The central idea is that the nature of any particular language affects, conditions, constrains, and channels the way people think. That may involve the words people use: some languages have more words for some things than other languages do (kin terms, for example), or the words they use may have different implications (thus "brown" in Chinese and Japanese means "tea color"). Differences in morphology and syntax may also be significant.

---

6   It is hardly a hypothesis in the normal social science sense, but more a simple observation that it would
     be difficult for people to understand their lives and to assess the meanings of their lives outside the
     conceptual context of their language.

ENGLISH

I	*killed*	*a dog*
(subject)	(verb / past tense)	(indefinite article / object)

The relationship between language and culture ranges from complex, philosophical considerations of how language shapes reality to the more practical mechanics of what words and structures are used in daily communication. As a simple, combined example, consider the English sentence "I killed a dog." This simple subject-verb-object sentence is not the only way to get this idea across in English, but it is certainly the standard way to do so. The sentence seems simple and straightforward, although it has an emotional element because of concern about the dog. The sentence begins with "I," so you know the person talking is the one who is doing something. "Kill" is a verb and, because this is English, there is a suffix (bound morpheme at the end of a word) that tells us the action has already taken place. Finally, due to the English use of articles, we know that this is simply "a" dog, not "the" dog, "this" dog, or "that" dog. So as this sentence unfolds in English, we know first that the speaker is the subject of the sentence; then that the action is a serious one (killing); then that the action has already taken place; and, finally, that the object of the killing was some undefined dog.

JAPANESE

watakushi wa	*inu o*	*koroshimashita*
(subject / particle)	(object / particle)	(verb in past tense)
(semiformal)		(semiformal)

Now consider the same sentence in Japanese. The sentence appears to start in the same way: with the subject. Indeed the subject is not only in the first place but has a special particle (*wa*) after it that indicates it is, indeed, the subject of the sentence.[7] However, *watakushi* is not the only way to say "I." *Watakushi* is a semiformal form, so we know (and the speaker must have determined) that this is *not* an informal setting.[8] Thus, as we launch into the sentence, we already have some information

---

7   *Wa* is a particle that indicates the topic of the sentence. If this sentence were part of an ongoing conversation, *wa* would probably be used, and, in fact, the subject/topic might also be omitted. See the case example at the end of the chapter for more discussion of indefiniteness in Japanese. The sentence might also start with *watakushi ga*. *Ga* would emphasize the subject and generally be used only if the subject were new to the discussion or particularly important.

8   *Watakushi* is technically gender neutral, but women might well use alternative forms such as *atakushi* or *atashi*, which cannot be used by men. Furthermore, there is the somewhat more informal *watashi*, which can be used by either men or women.

about the relative formality of the social setting and are in a more socially defined world than we would be in English. The second part of the sentence gives the object. As with the subject, there is a particle after the word (*o*) that tells us specifically that the dog is indeed the object of the action. So in Japanese, we now have the subject and the object, along with something of the social setting. But we do not yet know what the action is, whether it is good or bad, or whether it is past, present, or future. Finally, along comes the verb. The first part of the verb (*koro . . .*) suggests the sentence is about killing, and the rest of the verb (*. . . shimashita*) tells us that it happened in the past. The verb form also reiterates that this is a semiformal situation (just as *watakushi* at the beginning of the sentence did). Note that only *after* the verb is given do we know that the action was of killing rather than *not* killing. In Japanese you can usually bail out at the end of the sentence—something that it is harder to do but not impossible in English: "I killed the dog . . . Not!"

VIETNAMESE

toi	*giet*	*con cho*
(subject)	(verb)	(classifier / object)

Finally, consider the sentence in Vietnamese. The basic structure of the sentence is parallel to the English one. The structure is subject/verb/object, and there is even something like an article in front of the dog. In this case it is what is called a *classifier*. *Con* is a classifier for animals—there are others for books, people, flat objects, and so on. Classifiers aside, the sentence appears relatively straightforward. However, there are two hidden complications. One is that Vietnamese verbs do not indicate tense. Thus, unless we know the context, or someone clues us in with additional information, we could listen to this sentence and not know a critical piece of information: has this happened yet? The other complication is the word *toi*, which is not simply a translation for "I." In Vietnamese, the use of *toi* indicates that this is a relatively formal situation between people who have no close personal relationship. As with Japanese, then, the very start of the sentence requires an assessment of the overall social situation in which the sentence is being spoken. If the speaker is among known people, the *toi* would likely be replaced by *anh, chi, em, con, bac,* or something of the kind. These alternatives are largely kin terms, which helps explain much of the warmth that is possible in Vietnamese conversation—a constant reiteration of kin or kinlike reciprocal relations. The use of *toi* avoids all those familial implications, and thus a sentence that was neutral in English and formal in Japanese becomes a bit cold in Vietnamese.

In this example one can see how language channels communication and—as the Japanese and Vietnamese examples suggest—forces a recognition of the social context in which a sentence is used. It may be possible to translate the basic meaning of a sentence between languages, but it is extremely difficult—and perhaps impossible—to translate the full meaning of the sentence. This suggests (as the Hopi case example will illustrate) that people live in worlds that have different frameworks of meaning. It also suggests (as the Genji case example will illustrate after that) that the process of translation can be enormously complex.

LANGUAGE, SOCIETY, AND POLITICS

The discussion so far in this chapter suggests only the beginning of the complexities in how language interacts with culture. After all, any study of language includes not only the general structures that we refer to as *linguistics* but the actual use of language in daily life. Thus in any particular situation, people choose from among many options in what they say. Others then respond with their own choices. The result may be language that is elegant or crude, verbose or terse, cold or warm, creative or dull. Cumulatively those choices may mean that, by the end of the conversation, the social world has changed. Perhaps a relatively formal discussion about work that begins in English drifts into a more informal, friendly, or familial talk in Spanish. This interaction between the possibilities represented by the formal language and the social situations in which languages are used is generally called *sociolinguistics*, though analysis of the way language is used to shape systems of power and control often appears under the label of *discourse analysis*.

Language has a strong relationship to politics, both as a tool of political control and as a tool of political resistance. Since language affects the way people view the world, it inevitably affects how people view and discuss political issues and options. Furthermore, language itself also marks people socially and politically as the same as some other people (those who speak that language) and different from yet other people (those who speak some other language). That power of language as a social marker applies even to variations within a language. Few other social markers are so strong. Language, like religion, may even trump race. The African-looking person who speaks perfect Parisian French, the South Asian with a strong Australian accent, or the tanned California-looking person who speaks in clipped British tones, all mark themselves immediately and strongly as being not quite who they originally appeared to be.

Language is connected strongly to people's internal lives, to who they think they are, to what they think of other people, and to what other people think of them. A demonstration of linguistic competence may help someone fit into a social group to which they did not previously belong. That can be useful. By belonging in that new group, however, that same person may be cut off from the old group. That may seem like a reasonable and perhaps volitional trade-off when speaking about adults. If the topic is changed from adults to children, this issue of language competence takes on a different tone. Children's education is not the only issue that links language to politics, but it does serve to indicate how strong, volatile, and consequential that connection can be.

Controlling Children's Language

It is hard to teach adults a new language and virtually impossible to make them forget the language (or languages) they already know. Thus, for adults, language is largely a given. Children, however, learn language quickly, so, for them, adding a different language is relatively easy. In colonial situations, for example, it was usually not possible to do well in life without learning the colonizer's language. Thus to have a future meant to learn English, or French, or Spanish, or German, or Japanese. Parents who might themselves refuse to use the colonizer's language still had to consider the future of their children. Their decision was sometimes to enroll their children in schools using the colonial language. In some cases, learning the colonial language was not simply an option for children who wished to move ahead (and their parents who wished them to do so) but a requirement for everybody whatever their future goals. During the period of Japanese colonization of Korea, Korean children attended schools conducted entirely in Japanese. A child who spoke Korean at school would get a beating. As the ultimate linguistic insult, Korean children had to obtain and use Japanese, rather than Korean, names.

Such control of children's language is one of the most effective ways to rupture the ties between them, their parents, and their parents' culture. This was a common strategy not only of colonialism but in the control of indigenous groups— often referred to as internal colonialism. In both North America and Australia, for example, the government set up special English-language boarding schools for indigenous children. These schools removed children physically from their parents and also removed them from their parents' language. It was hoped that when they returned home from school, they would abide by the rules and attitudes of the dominant society. With lack of language competence in the "old" ways, there would be nothing left for them but the "new" ways of the dominant society. Rather than eradicating the people, the governments aimed to eradicate their culture by making sure it was not passed on to future generations.

Echoes of this kind of language policy—and resistance to it—can be seen in the fervor with which issues of language are pursued even today: why many in the United States (and some in Canada) demand a full English-only policy (so that newcomers *will* abide by the core rules and attitudes of the dominant society) and why most immigrant parents in North America agonize over the degree to which their children should learn English (or French in Quebec) and the degree to which they should become fully competent in their parents' language. Bilingualism is the dream for many—but it is a difficult process on the individual level and one with which the United States, unlike Canada, has little experience at the formal governmental level.

CONTROLLING WRITTEN LANGUAGE

One final example of this combination of language and politics may help to show both the importance of the subject and the different ways control can be exercised through language policy. When the French colonized Vietnam, they made no particular effort to abolish the Vietnamese language. Indeed, they often supported it as a cultural medium. Supporting Vietnamese culture was an attractive way to keep Vietnamese intellectuals out of politics. The colonizers did, of course, emphasize French as the language of the elite and the language necessary for any serious economic or political future. The crucial twist in the language issue in colonial Vietnam, however, lay in how Vietnamese was written. At the time of the French conquest, Vietnamese wrote both in Chinese and in a writing system that mixed different Chinese writing components to convey both the meaning *and* pronunciation of Vietnamese. It was a difficult system, and the French could claim practicality, science, and even Vietnamese nationalism on their side in abolishing it. Why should the Vietnamese continue to write their language in Chinese characters? Instead, surely they should use the modern, rational, romanized system formalized (predictably enough) by Western missionaries. This new romanized system even came to be called the "national language" (*quoc ngu*).

The Vietnamese language survived French colonialism intact, but its use of Chinese characters did not. That might not seem so bad except for two negative implications of the change. First, the built-in ability to communicate in writing (if not in speech) with Chinese, Japanese, and Koreans was undermined. What better way to control and isolate a colonial people than to cut them off from their region? Second, Vietnamese now found themselves cut off from their own history. The texts from that history now appeared in something that looked like a foreign language. What better way to control and isolate a colonial people than to cut them off from their history?

Language, it appears, is not simply a powerful tool for human communication, thought, and expression, but also an important element in political and social control. In the attempt to control what people think, language is easily adapted to different purposes and different media. The proliferation of false news on the Internet,

Since pictures cannot be used in decoration, Arabic itself becomes a decorative motif, here in a former school in Morocco. (Credit: D. Haines)

for example, is a reminder of Hockett's point that prevarication is a fundamental capability of human language. Language makes it possible to just make things up. Given the importance of language as both an object and tool of control, it is not surprising how often language emerges as a core political and social issue, whether in the Canadian commitment to bilingualism, the frequent call in the United States for a more definitive "English only" policy, or simply the concern of educators that students grasp the full potential of the spoken and written versions of their primary language and have at least some exposure to the different possibilities of other languages.

CASE EXAMPLE—LANGUAGE AND THE HOPI SENSE OF TIME

The Hopi currently inhabit an area encased within Navajo territory in Arizona and live mostly in a series of villages along three high mesas. In learning their language, Benjamin Whorf became intrigued by the grammatical structures of the language and how those structures affected the way the Hopi understood the universe. He was particularly interested in the way time was handled in the Hopi language and

A twelfth-century depiction of the early eleventh-century *Tale of Genji*. (Credit: Everett-Art/Shutterstock)

came to believe that the Hopi conception of time was fundamentally different than in European languages. His argument goes—with some simplification—as follows.

In English, and in European languages in general, time has three aspects: the past, the present, and the future. The past consists of events that have already happened and are removed in time from us; the present is this exact moment of time at which we currently exist; and the future consists of a limitless expanse of time where things that do not yet exist will come to be. That sense of time is built, Whorf argued, directly into the structure of English. Verbs, for example, have clear tenses: "I went to Boston" lies in the past; "I am in Montpelier" lies in the present; and "I will be in Montreal" lies in the future (God willing).

Whorf argued that this is only one grammatically constrained way of looking at time and contrasted it with the Hopi language. For the Hopi there are only two kinds of temporal arrangements: what has come to be and what has not yet come to be. For what has already come to be, Whorf used the term *manifested*—which means obvious or apparent. Thus for the Hopi, both the past and present have come to be. They are fully manifested. In terms of the future, the Hopi see events that have not yet come to be or, more accurately, have not yet *fully* come to be. For this, Whorf used the term *manifesting*. He argued that the Hopi did not see the future, as we often do, as some new unexplored and unpredictable territory but rather as a set of events that are already on their way. The future, for the Hopi, grows organically out of the present. The distinguishing feature of the future, one might say, is that it is not yet fully cooked.

Whorf's argument was not simply a philosophical one. He argued that the Hopi way of dealing with time was built into the grammatical structures of the Hopi language. Their language constrained them to view time in this manifested versus manifesting way. Likewise, the grammatical structures of English constrain us to view the past, present, and future as quite distinct domains. We must decide—just as in the "I killed a dog" sentence—which tense to use. Without that, we do not even have a grammatically correct sentence. What Whorf suggested, then, is that there are different realities embedded in different languages. That idea is a forbidding one in some ways. How can we ever think beyond the confines of our own language? In other ways, however, the idea is liberating. It suggests that in learning different languages, we do indeed have the opportunity to enter different realities—and thus consider the limitations of the reality in which our own language holds us.

CASE EXAMPLE—*THE TALE OF GENJI*: TRANSLATING A JAPANESE NOVEL

Japanese is very different from English in its phonology, morphology, syntax, and writing. Translating even a simple sentence from Japanese to English can be difficult. It becomes even more difficult when the writing seeks to use the full force of the language for literary purposes. Whether in prose or poetry, literary work thrives on the full range of nuance available in a language; writers may even create new words or grammatical structures. This is language at its most open and creative. Thus translating Japanese literature can be expected to be exceedingly difficult. It is actually worse than that, suggested Ivan Morris, one of the premier translators of Japanese literature. Looking at *The Tale of Genji*, the classic of Heian Japan written about a thousand years ago, he noted that what could reach "nightmare proportions" was the lack of specificity in the language. Proper names were avoided, the subject of the sentence was often omitted, and such elementary distinctions as past versus present tense, singular versus plural, and male versus female were absent. Sometimes, he noted with much frustration, it is "not even clear if the sentence is positive or negative."

Consider this fragment of a sentence in what Morris presents as a roughly literal translation: "Recalling all sorts of things what an underhand thing this is to the person/people who joining heart/hearts to a remarkable extent led me . . ."

There are problems. We do not know who is recalling what, what was underhanded to whom, and where the leading might be going. As it turns out from the context of the fragment, it is fairly clear that this is a man named Niou. He is on his way to a place called Uji for the purposes of seducing a woman in whom his close friend Kaoru is interested. Thus Morris provides what for us is a more conventional phrasing: "Various thoughts occurred to Niou. He recalled how remarkably helpful Kaoru had been in introducing him to Uji in the first place."

That is a clear translation, but it might be criticized for lacking the flair of what is an acknowledged literary masterpiece. Consider a more florid translation by the great Arthur Waley: "It all seemed strangely familiar. Who was he with that second time? Why, of course, with Kaoru; and he became slightly uncomfortable when he remembered all the trouble his friend had taken to bring him and Kozeri together. 'I am afraid he would think this rather an odd way of repaying his kindness,' Niou said to himself."[9]

Waley certainly wins the flair award for translating, but also the award for taking liberties. He has filled in all the gaps that a Western reader might find with the original and, in the process, has more than doubled the number of words from Morris's translation and turned a fragment of one sentence into four complete sentences.

Waley provides here, as in many of his classic translations, a very good read indeed. But does that reading convey the tone and sense of the original? There is no final answer to this dilemma of translation. The world that is created in one language according to its rules and opportunities must somehow be disassembled and then reassembled in another language according to that language's rules and opportunities. The translator must be adept in both languages and must have the literary skill to actively re-create the work in a new language. The task is parallel to that of the anthropologist: to try to understand the reality that is another people's existence and to find some way to convey that reality back to one's own culture, or perhaps on to another culture.

SOURCES

The general discussions of the nature and structure of language are fairly standard and can be supplemented with almost any general full-length anthropology text, though I have given more attention to written language than is probably customary in anthropology. There are several introductions to anthropological linguistics that may be helpful, including Harriet Joseph Ottenheimer's *The Anthropology of Language: An Introduction to Linguistic Anthropology* (Wadsworth, 2012; 3rd ed.);

---

9   The actual quotations in the text are from Ivan Morris, *The World of the Shining Prince* (New York: Kodansha, 1994), 280–83.

Laura M. Ahearn's *Living Language: An Introduction to Linguistic Anthropology* (Wiley Blackwell, 2011); and Zdenek Salzmann, James Stanlaw, and Nobuko Adachi's *Language, Culture, and Society: An Introduction to Linguistic Anthropology* (Westview, 2014; 6th ed.). A good volume for browsing issues in linguistic anthropology is Alessandro Duranti (ed.), *Linguistic Anthropology: A Reader* (Blackwell, 2009, 2nd ed.). For the issues of language extinction and language preservation, see Daniel Nettle and Suzanne Romaine's *Vanishing Voices: The Extinction of the World's Languages* (Oxford University Press, 2002) and Joshua Fishman (ed.), *Handbook of Language and Ethnic Identity* (Oxford University Press, 2001). For a broader view of Charles Hockett's views, on which I rely heavily, see his *Language, Mathematics, and Linguistics* (Walter de Gruyter, 1967). Language and communication are approached in an unusually thoughful way in the commercial film *Arrival* (2016), including explicit mention of the Sapir-Whorf hypothesis.

For the case examples, see Benjamin Whorf's *Language, Thought, and Reality: Selected Writings*, ed. John B. Carroll (MIT Press, 1964) and Emily Schultz's *Dialogue at the Margins: Whorf, Bakhtin, and Linguistic Relativity* (University of Wisconsin Press, 1990). For the translation example, see Ivan Morris's stellar description of translational problems in *The World of the Shining Prince* (Kodansha, 1964) and translations of *The Tale of Genji* by Edward Seidensticker (Alfred A. Knopf, 1976) and Royall Tyler (Viking, 2001).

17

Expression

Human beings have thoughts and feelings and ways to communicate them. The thoughts and feelings may be simple or complex, physical or cerebral. The means of communication may likewise be simple or complex, physical or cerebral. Language is certainly the most extensive, subtle, and durable of those means of thinking and communicating, but this chapter explores human expression more broadly. Such human expression may be new and creative or established and routine. It may also be individualistic or social. While most expressions of thought and feeling have some social component, it is still possible to express something for which there is no audience. Humans, after all, can be either social or solitary.

This chapter focuses first on play, a form of human expression that connotes spontaneity, freedom, and pleasure. The discussion then turns to the arts, which, like play, also have elements of spontaneity, freedom, and pleasure. With the arts, however, conscious human action is more central, and the demands of particular art forms often render it more like work than play. The final part of the chapter considers the expression of thought and feeling in more mundane daily life. The section emphasizes the way human expression varies depending on the medium of expression, particularly how expression involves an interaction between people, their bodies, the environments in which they live; the objects they find and create in those environments; and the events and performances in which they participate. The first case example at the end of the chapter considers a Yolngu art installation that demonstrates the intersection of old and new meanings through a collaborative artistic process; the second example examines Internet posting as a seemingly new kind of human expression.

PLAY

As a beginning to a consideration of play, an animal example may be helpful. Consider some recent research on beluga whales in captivity. Researchers started to notice that the whales occasionally blew bubbles. There were all different kinds of bubbles, some small, some large. Sometimes the whales would blow a bubble ring that they could then swim through. The creation of these bubbles had a clear social context. Bubbles were usually from a pair of whales swimming side by side and blowing similar kinds of bubbles. But what exactly were the whales expressing? What was the meaning behind the bubbles? The researchers were uncertain. The bubbles had a social meaning of being together in a friendly way. But an analysis of social bonding seemed inadequate to the complexity of the bubbles. Since this was an activity only observed among captive beluga whales, some of the researchers began to suspect that the whales might be bored and blowing bubbles to pass the time in captivity. They had found a way to entertain themselves in a limited environment. They were just passing the time and having some fun.[1]

The bubbles provide a good example of what anthropologists (and others) generally call play. Humans are not the only species that plays, but humans do seem to play more and for longer periods of their lives. Sometimes that play has practical utility.[2] For example, the play of children prepares them for adult life. Playing with a bow as a child yields better hunting skills as an adult; swinging on ropes yields better dexterity; playing with other children yields better social skills. But when we try to consider play from the inside (and wonder what the beluga whales are experiencing), play seems to be more than just training for life. In the human case, the continuing search for play throughout life also suggests it is something elemental to the human spirit: an expression of one's very self, whether physical (as in sports), mental (as in many games), or artistic (whether in producing objects or performing). Play, then, is an essential form of human expression. It can be structured or unstructured, interactive or solitary. At the structured and interactive end of the spectrum are games played with official rules. They may be for private enjoyment (a game of cards, a pick-up

---

1   Jennie Rothenberg Gritz, "Beluga Bubbles," *Smithsonian*, March 2016, 16. The main researcher is Michael Noonan of Canisius College. There are a variety of clips on line of the whales and the bubbles; just search for "beluga bubbles."

2   Animals, of course, do play, and other primates play in many of the same ways that humans do. Chimpanzees, for example, play as children and as adults. That adult play is often with children. So there are similarities.

game of basketball), or public spectacles with professional players, who "play" the game but for whom it is also a job with advantages (money and fame) and disadvantages (short careers and frequent physical damage). Those professional games sometimes look a great deal like work yet also sometimes like play (for example, low-scoring defensive games versus high-scoring offensive games).

In all these kinds of play, whether structured or unstructured, anthropologists have some interesting options for research. One is to consider the ways in which play reflects basic human biology and the ways in which it reflects culture. On the physical side, several anthropologists have been looking at how play reflects human physical movement. One example is running, the result of distinct evolutionary changes in human anatomy. To run is a common human activity. That so many physical games involve running links those games to what humans are on a biological basis. On the other hand, the variations in the way people play in different cultures are testament to the role of culture. In terms of formal games, for example, "football" is a very different game depending on the country: a rugby-derived game of carrying, throwing, and sometimes kicking a ball (as in North America football) and the far more popular global game of moving the ball with feet only, and an occasional header. Even if the rules of a game are shared across national borders, the style of play may be different. Japanese baseball, for example, focuses far more on the incremental goal of a single run, based on teamwork in advancing runners, rather than the American power version. It is even possible to end a Japanese baseball game with a tie score.[3] Such cultural differences are also seen in the more spontaneous play of children. Comparative studies of children playing in preschools in different countries, for example, show great differences in how much of children's play is spontaneous, how much is organized by the children themselves, and how much is organized by adults in terms of what they consider proper play.[4]

ART

Play may thus be spontaneous or structured, individualized or collective, for its own sake or for its benefits as a learning tool. Play may also become art. Musicians, after all, "play" their instruments even though it is hardly free, unstructured play. Even an improvisation, a jam, or an extended free-form solo is based on rigorous work.

---

3   See Charles W. Hayford, "Samurai Baseball vs. Baseball in Japan," *Japan Focus*, April 2007, for a useful review of the different views of Japanese versus US baseball.

4   See particularly Joseph J. Tobin, David Y.H. Wu, and Dana Davidson, *Preschool in Three Cultures: Japan, China and the United States* (New Haven, CT: Yale University Press, 1991); and Joseph Tobin, Yeh Hsueh, and Mayumi Karasawa, *Preschool in Three Cultures Revisited: China, Japan, and the United States* (Chicago: University of Chicago Press, 2009).

Musicians are not simply expressing themselves, but expressing themselves through a particular medium based on particular skills. Neither is a professional athlete merely "playing" a game. It is also a job and it is also work, and some suggest it is also an art. So there is a continuum in human expression from free-form spontaneity to more rigorous and structured effort and perhaps, after much effort and practice, again to a new kind of spontaneity when high technical competence is reached. As humans ply their crafts and create their art, there is both play and work in what they express. The result of that expression may be in various forms: objects that we classify as painting or sculpture, performances that are visual or auditory (or both), or expressions through language that we generally call literature.

These artistic expressions can be classified in various ways. One common distinction in Western society is between high culture (classics of literature, great paintings, symphonies) and more popular culture (detective stories, poster art, popular music). Another common distinction is between individualized creative art (the recent Western tradition) and more collective and traditional "folk" art. We might also distinguish art for art's sake from art that has a more religious structure and use, or perhaps arts (creative and individual) versus crafts (repetitive and traditional). From an anthropological point of view, most of these distinctions seem quite culture bound. The high art galleries in the West, for example, point directly to the way individual objects are owned, sold, and displayed in the West. They also point to the way creative expression is structured in the West, particularly with an individualized notion of talent that often puts artists outside "normal" society. By contrast, in more traditionalistic cultures, creative artists are at the center of the society maintaining its values and traditions.

Understanding art requires attention to two separate elements: the creative process and the appreciation process, the artist and the audience. The two may be bound together through a painting, a song, a dance. Sometimes the art, the audience, and the relationship between the two are similar across cultural and national lines. But sometimes the same artistic form shifts in meaning. Japanese woodblock prints, for example, were a popularized format in Japan but taken up as serious high art by the French impressionists. Likewise, "folk" art from non-Western countries, designed for both utilitarian and religious reasons, ends up in "art" galleries in the West or displayed on the walls of returning tourists. Over time, objects also move even in the same cultural context to take up new residences: medieval European altar pieces (designed for worship) end up as objects in art galleries (designed for viewing as cultural and artistic objects).

The implication is that "the arts" are not a fixed target that can be definitively classified either in terms of creation or appreciation. Even in the West this idea is now increasingly accepted. One interesting case involves the so-called ethnographic turn among some Western artists. In Barcelona, for example, artists began rethinking the standard, individualized model of art so common in the West. To break free from it, they opted for more collaborative projects that had multiple artists and that would also include the ultimate recipients. In one case they decided to create a garden in a museum terrace using plants that local residents were growing in vacant lots in the area. The garden was not just an artistic project (artists build, people view), but drew out of the community. In another Barcelona project a dozen years later, a similar theme was developed. People from the neighborhood brought in plants to help document the full range of plants in the neighborhood. In exchange for the plants they brought in, they received drawings of themselves and their plants from the resident artist.[5] Again, the artistic process was anchored in the community with involvement from both artist and audience—and interaction between the two in the form of gift exchanges. In both these Barcelona cases, the typical Western artistic creative process was changed to become more collaborative, more inclusive, and more reciprocal in that supremely human relationship of gift exchange.

MODES OF EXPRESSION

There are many other ways that people express themselves in daily and seasonal life. A consideration of these ways helps indicate how expressions of meaning interact with the world in which people live. Those expressions may be spontaneous and transient (as in play) or more carefully crafted and enduring (as in most of the arts). But they are also part of our daily lives as we interact with our environment and the people and objects in it.

BODIES

As a beginning, consider how human expression relates to what we are as biological entities. We frequently modify our bodies so that they reflect what we think is important about them and about us. This is a kind of expression in which the body is both the source of meaning and something on which we impose meaning. One crucial area is sex and gender. The division of society into "men" and "women" reflects basic biological differences. Yet human societies often go to great lengths to further accentuate the differences between men and women in terms of how they assess what behavior is appropriate for men and women. Part of that is how people look. Men and women generally dress differently, and the degree of difference in that gender-based clothing may be minimal or extensive. Furthermore, bodies may be modified by

---

5   Both these projects have web pages: https://www.fundaciotapies.org/site/spip.php?rubrique488 and https://todaslasplantasdelbarrio.wordpress.com/ (accessed May 9, 2017).

painting, piercing, tattooing, or surgical change. In contemporary North America the dynamics of sex and gender are shifting so that gender for some becomes the primal difference, and the physical body needs to be changed to match that primal gender. Instead of biological sex as the basis of gender, we now also have gender as the basis of biological sex.

This interaction between people and their bodies is seen in many ways in the anthropological record. Colin Turnbull describes the time when several Mbuti elders decided he really was, in some way, one of them. Their way of marking this was to cut lines across his forehead and insert dirt from the forest into those cuts. In that case, an elementary aspect of the environment (dirt) was permanently sealed within Turnbull's body. A military tattoo from duty overseas is a similar physical marking that you "were there" and that it was important enough to be permanently marked into your skin. Tattoos, however, have different meanings in different cultures at different times. In some cases the tattoo is an organizational marker that you belong to a particular group. That is the case for gang tattoos in North America and the extensive full body tattoos used by Japanese *yakuza*. Members of the yakuza (organized crime groups) may show nary a tattoo when in a business suit, but a rolled up cuff or loosened shirt collar will show the beginning of full body tattoos. Here there are two kinds of changes to the body that have different meanings, one of clothing and one of tattooing. The business suit signifies a businessman; the exposed tattoo signifies a specific kind of business.

PLACES

Another ready medium through which to express meaning is place. The environments in which people live are an important objective factor in their lives, and they are also a convenient place to store meaning. In many religious traditions there are specific places where spirits reside or where important people have died, and where they can be more easily reached in a spiritual sense. Pilgrimage is a classic feature of religious behavior. If you cannot go to that place, there are options. The mixture of dirt and blood in Turnbull's forehead is an example of one option: if you cannot be in a place, you can at least take something of that place in you. Alternatively, if you cannot take something of the place with you, then perhaps something of you can remain in the place. The sweat and blood may be figurative but can also be literal. Battlefields, for example, are consecrated by the actual blood that flowed there. A house you built yourself may indeed have your actual sweat in it. The importance of agricultural land to people whose ancestors have worked on that land for generations is another example. The sweat of the ancestors has poured into that place; their bones likely lie in graves and tombs nearby.

One of the great advantages of place as a medium of expression is that it endures. You can always return to visit it. The place will normally outlast the people and, in that sense, is much more durable. What that enduring place conveys includes the memory of events. Those events may be as common and personal as where one grew up. They may be more personal events of loss: flowers at a grave or a cross at the site of an automobile accident. The events may also be epic and widely shared, such as the Normandy shores where the Allies first landed in World War II or the two Japanese cities on which atomic bombs were dropped at the end of the war. Such places may be unmarked, marked by only a small sign (Washington slept here; Jacques Cartier landed here), or turned into full memorial parks.[6]

The specific meanings of places can be complex. One problem is the variation: places may have different meanings for different people. Battlefields from the US Civil War, for example, have a rather different meaning for northerners (who may think, "we won and they were wrong") and southerners (some of whom may think, "they won but we were right—and fought better"). Places may also have intrinsically mixed meanings: southern US plantations—including those of Washington and Jefferson—provide messages both of liberty and of slavery. One result is that the meaning of a place is often contested. For example, the Vietnam War Memorial in Washington, DC, is, all would agree, a place on the mall that concerns the US involvement in Vietnam. The original memorial—the Wall—invokes a meaning of the place as a memorial to Americans who died there. In a reaction to that notion of a death memorial, a more traditional statue of soldiers was erected to invoke the soldiers as alive, thus making it more a memorial to those who fought. That, in turn, annoyed many of those who had appreciated the Wall's somber implication of loss. Similar questions arose about the area of the former World Trade Center in New York City. The importance of the place was clear, but should the rebuilding be as a tribute to the American life force or as a more somber memorial for the dead?

OBJECTS

As media through which to express meaning, the great advantage of the body is its mobility, and the great advantage of place is its durability. Objects of various kinds provide an alternative to both. They can, unlike places, usually be moved,

---

6   These places may be relatively natural or clearly man-made. Carving huge statues out of bare rock has a certain appeal. The raw emergence of rock from the earth complements the size of the carving in showing the magnitude and durability of the people's influence—whether it be US presidents at Mount Rushmore, images of the Buddha in Afghanistan, or southern civil war leaders carved into the rock at Stone Mountain, Georgia. It is also possible to incorporate the actual body of somebody into the place. The power of mausoleums comes from this combination. Thus long lines of people queue up to see the actual bodies of Ho Chi Minh in Hanoi and of Mao Zedong in Beijing.

even if they are very large. They can also be created from scratch and duplicated as needed, even mass-produced. They can also do double duty, providing both practical utility and symbolic importance. Cars, for example, are a means of transportation and a symbol of status and identity. A car has utility as a more-or-less efficient, powerful means of getting from one place to another. On the symbolic level, a car generally indicates something about socioeconomic status and also something of a person's values and lifestyle: big trucks and small trucks, SUVs, sports cars, performance cars, or electrics to show you are green. Cars also provide a mobile personal billboard for smaller objects that advertise one's experiences and values, whether with license plates, bumper stickers, flag decals, or head-bobbing dogs in the back window. So a car is a practical everyday object that also does a good job expressing who a person is.

The *kula* valuables from the Trobriand Islands provide a more traditional anthropological example. The Trobriand system of exchange involves red shell necklaces (*soulava*), which are always exchanged for white shell arm bands (*mwali*). The exchange system follows a general pattern in which—looking from the air—the soulava are traded in a clockwise direction, and the mwali are traded in a counterclockwise direction. This is, in the terms of the chapter on economics, balanced reciprocity based on different items being exchanged, with an often long delay between the initial gift and the return gift. Furthermore, the necklaces and arm bands are quite valuable, even though their direct practical utility is limited. The value of these objects comes partly from their physical characteristics: some are bigger, more finely colored, or better shaped. Value also comes from their history as they have moved around this exchange network. A necklace may have come from a valued trading partner and have a well-known history—people may even remember when it last came around the full exchange circle. Value has been added to the necklace by the events in which it has participated. The value of each necklace and arm band is thus partly drawn from its physical nature, partly from the way those physical materials are made into a particular article (necklace or arm band), and partly from the meaning of this item as enmeshed within a comprehensive exchange network. Obtaining such an object demonstrates that you are part of this network and that this network has endured for a long time. In turn, giving it away to a trading partner is a perfect expression of your commitment to this overall exchange system.

Some objects in North American society also increase in value as they pass through different hands. Consider an old family Bible. The names of several generations are carefully written on the inside of the front cover. Like the kula valuables, this object has increased in value because of the many hands that have touched it and the events (births of children) of which it is an official record. For the family this is thus an invaluable heirloom. It is an object with a history and it is also an object that, because it lists the generations, is itself a history—though abridged—of the family. So this old book may be one of the most valuable items that the family possesses. If these people are immigrants or refugees, it may be one of the few objects they could bring with them that connect them to their former home. It is also, of course, a religious text. This one small object comes to incorporate family, homeland, and God. To touch it is to express your connection to all three.

EVENTS AND PERFORMANCES

Events and performances provide a different kind of medium for human expression. Both vary greatly in nature, in practical significance, and in symbolic importance. A simple daily routine such as eating dinner, for example, has practical aspects, but when people eat together it also creates a sense of being together. That meaning of "those who eat together" is a strong one; it is a primal expression of solidarity. If such an event has some spiritual content—such as a prayer before eating—the joint image of being together for nutritional and spiritual nourishment is stronger yet. More elaborate events take on all the aspects of ritual described in the chapter on religion. Such events usually draw on the expressive potential of bodies, places, and objects. A wedding, for example, is an event to which people attach great meaning and from which they also draw much meaning. The wedding dress itself is essential. It is a temporary modification of the bride's body and, if inherited from a mother or grandmother, is an object that brings the past into the present: it expresses family solidarity and durability. Place is important as well for weddings. For those who are even nominally religious, a church or some other religious setting is essential. Taking pictures captures something of the spirit of the event. Those pictures become objects that carry the meaning of the event through time and across place.

These various forms of human expression through bodies, places, objects, and events often provide good clues about people as individuals and about the social and cultural contexts in which they live. They are excellent topics for anthropological research. As with art and play, the nature of these human expressions may be structured or flexible, new or traditional, simple or complex, routine or heartfelt. Much like the beluga whales, humans create new elements in and out of their environment and then swim among and through them. Unlike the bubbles, however, much of human expression is embodied in forms that continue through time and extend across space to people who are not otherwise connected. Collectively all these human expressions create the social and cultural world in which we live. Those expressions may include changing the physical bodies we inhabit and the physical

Two Singapore buildings bridge the old and new with mirrored profiles. (Credit: D. Haines)

environments in which we live. The world becomes a physical reality of which we are simultaneously the artists, the players, the participants, and the audience. Our expressions become actions creating the future.

CASE EXAMPLE—A YOLNGU CHRISTMAS

The Yolngu live in the northeastern part of Australia. They are, in their origins, a foraging group located near the coast in an area with abundant resources, and they were a case example in the chapter on foragers (chapter 3). As discussed in that earlier chapter, some of their maritime resources were of great interest to outsiders. The Yolngu had thus been involved in trade and, as traders, had learned how to negotiate cultural divides. Their interaction with white Australian settlers (the *balanda*) was affected by that prior exposure, and, more effectively than most other aboriginal groups, they were able to cohabit with those new strangers. One of the elements brought to them by the white settlers was Christmas. Today, the Yolngu celebrate this holiday, but they do so with a strong emphasis on the ancestors. Their Christmas is a bit like the regular Christmas of the other Australians and a bit like the New Year veneration of ancestors in East Asia. It also incorporates the Yolngu emphasis on what is usually translated as the "Dreaming."

Human artistic expression is nothing new: here cave paintings from Thailand, roughly 4,000 years in age. (Credit: Pinkcandy/Shutterstock)

In 2011, three people came together to create an installation art exhibit based on this Yolngu Christmas. The three were a balanda PhD anthropologist, a balanda filmmaker working on his MA, and an elder of the local Yolngu group. The exhibit included a three-screen projection of a film of the local village. The exhibit room itself also had a series of wooden posts to indicate the ancestors. The purpose was to recreate the Yolngu sense of the ancestors at Christmas along with, through the film, an evocation of the village. Those who visited the exhibit included both Yolngu and balanda. By all accounts, the balanda found the installation interesting, and the Yolngu found it consistent with their own experience of Christmas.

But what was the meaning of the creative process to the three key people working together on the project? One part of the answer lay in how they had come together. It was not planned in the usual sense of the word. The anthropologist had come to the area, having worked there previously, and was at something of a gap in her professional career. She wanted to do something about this Yolngu Christmas but did not have a clear idea of how to create the spirit of the event in an exhibit. She also had little experience with film. The young filmmaker, in turn, had come to the area on an entirely different project and was at a loss about what to do for his MA project requirement. He too was at loose ends. Finally, the Yolngu elder was glad to work with the anthropologist (and the filmmaker when he finally met him) but had little idea of how this multimedia presentation could be organized. The three thus came together by chance, looking for something, but not this particular project.

The Yolngu elder, as you might expect from the earlier discussion of the Yolngu, did not consider this "chance." Instead, he saw it as a meeting that was meant to be but that had to wait until the proper people were revealed to each other at the proper time. From their own accounts, the two balanda were not as sure on this point, though they tended to defer to the Yolngu elder. The filmmaker did readily recognize, however, that this was a different kind of collaboration: "I knew right away that the project wasn't about me or what I wanted or what I saw. It was about how we would all work together to translate it into something else." Both balanda also had to concede that they did not really "find" each other through any kind of purposive search, but rather that the other team members were indeed revealed to them in the proper course of time. With due respect to the balanda, it was the Yolngu elder who was best able to articulate the way the artistic project emerged. From his perspective it was not a creation but rather helping something that already existed come alive. "That's the secret thing. The reality. Making the songs alive, the sacred places and connections between clans alive, the photos alive, the paintings alive, and the people, the audience, alive. So the spirits walk amongst us in that room." In this collaborative project, then, "art" was not a personal expression of a new meaning but a collective expression of a meaning that already existed and needed to be brought to life again in a different context.[7]

CASE EXAMPLE—WHY WE POST: CULTURAL VARIATION IN A VIRTUAL WORLD

Technological developments often have unexpected uses. When telephones were first introduced, for example, they were intended for serious uses in business. But, like many inventions, telephones escaped their original narrow use to become an almost universal medium of communication. People wanted them for their home lives, not just for formal, work-oriented goals.[8] Much the same has happened with computer-mediated communication. Active groups of technologically interested people have been communicating online for many decades. But something changed with simplified protocols for communication, the spread of both wired and wireless connectivity, and especially the Internet. The result is an explosion in what we generally call social media. Facebook users, for example, numbered nearly 2 billion by 2017, and several other platforms were around the 1 billion mark. The assumption has tended to be that the use of these media is changing human communication and human relationships around the world, and doing so in similar ways. But a group of

---

7   The quotations in the text are from Arnd Schneider and Christopher Wright, eds., *Anthropology and Art Practice* (New York: Bloomsbury, 2013), 110 and 112, respectively.

8   See, for example, Clive Thompson, "OMG! We've Been Here B4," *Smithsonian* (March 2016): 23–24.

anthropologists at University College London (UCL) decided they should take a closer look. They set up an ambitious project with anthropologists assigned to study social media usage for a full fifteen months in widely scattered parts of the world. The final list of nine sites included Chile, Brazil, Trinidad, England, Italy, Turkey, India, and two sites in China.

The research provided some big surprises at the individual site level. Team members had chosen sites for particular reasons but were often wildly off target in their expectations on social media usage at those sites. One anthropologist, for example, had done work in Lebanon on politics. She picked an area of Turkey as a research site that would provide useful comparative information on how politics is addressed through online media. But it turned out social media were rarely used in discussion of politics in Turkey, partly because explicit public political statements could be dangerous. So instead of politics, she focused on gender and family relationships. Another member of the team was interested in Chinese moving from the countryside to the city. She expected to see strong use of social media by the migrants to maintain contact with family at home in the countryside. But, no, that is not what these Chinese migrants valued about social media. Their online contacts were urban oriented and *away* from rural family contexts. Yet another of the anthropologists chose a site in India where he expected that sharp economic and caste differences would result in sharp differences in the use of social media. Wrong again. Instead he found that social media were used in similar ways by all groups to emphasize the priority of family ties and issues of traditional Indian identity.

Three of the project's overall findings are of special relevance to understanding human life in the twenty-first century. First, these anthropologists found that social media do not necessarily change human relationships. Sometimes they do, but sometimes they simply fortify previous ways of interacting. Facebook pages, for example, were used by some families as a new way to present the family to the public but to do so in exactly traditional ways: the family online should look exactly like the family in public. Second, the content of social media seemed to be more important than the actual social media platforms. People in different sites chose particular media for practical reasons (available, easy to use) but then adapted them for their own purposes. The media did not constrain people or push them in any particular direction; the media simply became another option for human expression and communication. Third, one way in which the media did provide new options for many people in different countries lay in how they could use these media to better control the degree of formality versus intimacy in their relationships with other people. Media were sometimes used for closed groups (whether of peers or of family) that walled people off from the outside world, much like a wall around a physical residence. On the other hand, the social media were also sometimes used to open up to other people, whether with a structured, airbrushed presentation of self or with a more transparent, exploratory reaching out.

Overall, then, this collaborative, comparative study suggests that the new virtual world often looks a great deal like the old regular world. Technology may change people's options, but it does not necessarily change who they are or how they interact. The title of the team's final overview volume is thus not "How Social Media Changed the World" but rather "How the World Changed Social Media."

SOURCES

For play (whether spontaneous or structured into formal games), see Thomas S. Henricks's *Play and the Human Condition* (University of Illinois Press, 2015) and Robert Sands and Linda Sands's *The Anthropology of Sport and Human Movement: A Biocultural Perspective* (Lexington Books, 2010), which includes extensive discussion of running from both a biological and cultural perspective. For the arts, see Arnd Schneider and Christopher Wright (eds.), *Anthropology and Art Practice* (Bloomsbury, 2013) and Roger Sansi's *Art, Anthropology and the Gift* (Bloomsbury, 2015), from which the Barcelona examples are drawn. For an engaging discussion of the interactive nature of human creativity, see Tim Ingold's *Making: Anthropology, Archaeology, Art and Architecture* (Routledge, 2013). There is a wide and scattered literature on the other issues covered in this chapter. I have aimed to provide a relatively stabilized view, but just as human beings in general can draw meaning from, and write meaning onto, bodies, places, objects, and events, so too can academics.

The discussion of posting comes from a cooperative anthropology project anchored at University College London (UCL). From the project home page at https://www.ucl.ac.uk/why-we-post you can access numerous online resources, including e-classes on social media, a series of online books on the project overall, and on the individual case examples. The project is an exemplary use of collective research in a discipline that tends otherwise to be rather individualistic. For the telephone parallel, see Clive Thompson's "OMG! We've Been Here B4," *Smithsonian*, March 2016, 23–28. For the discussion of the Yolngu, see Jennifer Deger's "In-Between," in *Anthropology and Art Practice*, ed. Arnd Schneider and Christopher Wright (Bloomsbury, 2013). You can also view the elements of the exposition online at http://miyarrkamedia.com/projects/christmas-birrimbirr-christmas-spirit/. For the Yolngu in general, see Ian S. McIntosh's *Aboriginal Reconciliation and the Dreaming* (Allyn and Bacon, 2000); W. H. Edward's *Traditional Aboriginal Society: A Reader* (Paul and Co., 1998; 2nd ed.); and Ian Keen's *Aboriginal Economy and Society* (Oxford University Press, 2004).

18

Action

The discussion in the previous chapter about human expression provides a bridge to this last chapter. One crucial kind of expression, after all, is action. Since anthropologists are people with their own backgrounds and interests, the kind of action they deem most useful is sometimes different from that for other people. For example, since anthropologists often work with people who are at the weaker end of the power spectrum, they tend to be particularly sensitive to power differentials and the damage they can do. The less powerful have options, but those options may be limited to little more than resistance—though that resistance may be both creative and determined. In many cases the power differential is so severe that people's lives are at risk. They may die as a result of the direct actions of the more powerful, or may die of disease and malnutrition as a result of being limited to less food or medical resources. In yet other cases the dangers may be less life threatening than identity destroying. The less powerful may survive but only by becoming a part of somebody else's world—rather than remaining at the center of their own. The lesson that many anthropologists draw from this is that there is a need for action to improve material conditions in the world and to foster enough reduction in power differentials so that people are free to pursue their own destiny. That destiny includes, as Franz Boas suggested long ago on Baffin Island, their search for truth and humanity. In that search they may have constraints, but they also have what anthropologists often call *agency*—the ability of people to act on their own behalf in crafting their lives.

This concluding chapter addresses action in three parts. The first is a review of ways in which the contemporary world provides both similar and different options and constraints for human action. It is, after all, both a new world and very much the same old world. The second part is a consideration of one major way in which life is now different, and that is with a shifting alignment among biology, culture, and environment. Given the ways human beings can now control the environment and their own biology, "adaptation" now often refers more to adapting biology and environment to human purposes than humans adapting to biology and environment. The third part considers what an anthropology of the twenty-first century might be. The link between understanding and practical action noted in Edward Tylor's anthropology text of 1881 remains at the core of anthropology today. The first of the case examples at the end of the chapter concerns the crisis in which the Sakha, herders in Siberia, find themselves because of climate change. The second example draws from the refugee crisis that began in 2015, embroiled Europe, and elicited varied reactions in North America, with highly positive reactions in Canada but highly mixed and contentious ones in the United States.

A CHANGING WORLD

The early part of the twenty-first century displays a world that is in many ways similar to the one at the beginning of the twentieth century, when anthropology as we know it was in its infancy. It is still today a world with enormous inequalities within countries and between them. It is still a world where minority peoples are at risk both for their lives and for their ways of living. It is still a world where race is taken as an indicator of human value—despite a full century of anthropological effort to debunk the notion. It is still a world of hunger and epidemic disease, of war and natural disaster, of crime and terrorism. In other ways it is a different world. There is much good news in that. Colonialism is largely gone—though some fear that "globalization" is little more than a new and administratively simpler version of it. Democracy and prosperity have spread, if unevenly. Some of the many peoples and cultures anthropologists feared would disappear are alive and re-creating the lifeways anthropologists took such efforts to record.

In that consideration of change, one inevitable buzzword has been "globalization." In many ways the processes to which it refers are not new ones. Much of the world has been "global" for millennia. True, the trek along the Silk Road that linked the Mediterranean, South Asia, and East Asia was a slow and laborious passage. But it did not stop the flow of goods, and it did not stop the explosive spread of ideas and religious beliefs—especially Buddhism. In more recent times, what could be more "global" than colonialism, a process that brought virtually all parts of the world under the political and economic control of a small set of countries that had mastered new forms of commercial, industrial, military, and political control? For the twentieth century, what could be more global than two world wars or the subsequent forty-year clash of capitalism and communism that drew into battle even the smallest and most remote of countries?

Nevertheless, globalization in the contemporary world has some distinctive features that suggest it is indeed a different world in which we now live. Speed is one factor: the speed of travel, the speed of communication, the speed of production and changes in production. Both time and space are seemingly compressed. Some of that compression was achieved by the middle of the twentieth century: intercontinental jet travel, almost instantaneous world phone communication, the overnight sensations caused by Western products (Winston cigarettes, the Beatles), even space travel. Other aspects of that speed, such as movement of large amounts of data along physical wires (combined ultimately with wireless), are quite recent. But what is true of all these forms of speed is that they are far cheaper and thus far more available to more people. That brings the world and the world's peoples together in new ways. Humans are again on the move in all kinds of ways: as permanent migrants, business people, temporary laborers, spouses, students, travelers. Even when their bodies do not travel, their thoughts and feelings do through ever-expanding communication channels.

In this increasingly interconnected world, one crucial issue is who controls all these connections and all the tracks along which people and goods flow. Critics see not an expanding global economy that benefits everybody but a new kind of colonialism (sometimes explicitly labeled neocolonialism) that is sharpening social divisions between richer and poorer countries, and also sharpening social divisions within those countries. Those criticisms have increased as the "Great Recession" that began in 2008 and the collapse in commodity values (including oil) that began in 2015 have provided further evidence of the fragility of the global economic system. The United States is often seen at the core of this new system of control. As Arundhati Roy, eloquent writer and eloquent critic of the new US role in the world, once put it, the "New Imperialism is upon us. For the first time in history, a single empire with an arsenal of weapons that could obliterate the world in an afternoon has complete, unipolar, economic, and military hegemony."[1] All countries in the world, she points out, are "caught in the cross-hairs of the American cruise missile and the IMF checkbook." Those in the United States, by contrast, hardly feel they are in control of this newly complex world, and the presidential campaigns of 2016,

---

1   *Nation*, February 9, 2004, 11. The article was adapted from Roy's comments at the World Social Forum in Mumbai in January 2004.

especially the Republican side, showed massive concern about the uncertainties of the global world, especially its seemingly uncontrolled flows of goods (especially issues of free trade) and people (especially undocumented migrants and refugees).[2]

One troublesome aspect to the modern world is the degree of destruction and damage. Much of that damage is to people, and much is directly carried out by people. Genocide has occurred in several parts of the world. The sheer efficiency of the genocide in Rwanda was particularly stunning: roughly 800,000 people killed in three months in 1994. Yet the ensuing political and social breakdown in the neighboring Congo, which was to a great degree an aftereffect of the genocide, actually led to far more death, perhaps 2.5 million lives lost. These included a number of massacres, mostly along ethnic lines. But the destruction of people is not only in war. HIV/AIDS continues to ravage much of southern Africa; starvation appears periodically in various parts of the world (Ethiopia, North Korea); old, new, and terrifying viruses appear (Ebola, Zika); and the hazards of industrialism take their toll on people's health (chemical exposure) and their lives (industrial accidents).

There has also been severe damage to other living creatures and to the environment. Again, much of this is by people. Consider Asia as an example. The destruction of forestlands in highland areas of Vietnam contributes to flooding, as bare soil cannot hold the water from rains. This reflects development of those areas that included cutting of forests. As a result, the country has seen record-breaking floods in virtually every year since the late 1990s. Yet 2016 also witnessed devastating drought in Vietnam's southern delta that withered crops and allowed tidal salt to invade fields, damaging them for years to come. Farther north, dust storms originating in Mongolia can now shut down airports in Korea and deposit soil tainted by pollutants in Japan. Farther south, the clearing of forests for commercial use leads to long-burning peat fires in Indonesia whose smoke crosses the straits into Singapore and Malaysia. Throughout the region, the pollution that afflicted European cities during their early industrialization (read descriptions of London's "fog" in the nineteenth century) is now being reproduced in far more numerous and far larger cities. Even when there is continuity in the kinds of change occurring, as with basic industrialization, the scale of the change is new, with far broader impact on the world as a whole.

2　The irony is that the flows of both goods and people are, in many ways, more controlled now than in the past. Extensive movement across the Mexico-US border, for example, has been common since the early days of European settlement in North America. It was often completely unregulated—as was most of American immigration up until the 1920s.

A NEW ALIGNMENT OF BIOLOGY, CULTURE, AND ENVIRONMENT

At the beginning of this text, a general model was proposed of culture as a kind of buffer between humans as biological entities and the environments in which they live. But, over time, humans have tended to expand their control over both their bodies and their environments. In terms of the environment, they have moved from adapting to the environment to adapting the environment to them. The effects on environments can be seen in the sequence from adaptations more accepting of the natural environment (like foraging and pastoralism) to agricultural systems that radically change the land, and to urban, industrial systems that utterly transform landscapes. Humans, of course, must then adapt to the new manufactured environments that they have created. As the examples of pollution suggest, those new landscapes are often hazardous to human life, whether the clogged air, the poisoned soil, or the buildings themselves. Such common building materials as asbestos and lead have turned on their makers.

The human interaction with the environment has yielded increasing human control and interference in a variety of ways. Consider waterways. As dams are built to extract power, or levies built to protect cities, there is the possibility of error: of things poorly produced or poorly maintained. So-called natural disasters turn out to be combined natural/human disasters. During Hurricane Katrina, which hit New Orleans and the Gulf Coast in 2005, for example, much of the damage was not from the storm itself but from the failure of the human-built levies in the city. In Japan's 2011 tsunami, natural forces caused enormous damage, but the lasting damage from radiation was clearly the result of poorly maintained nuclear reactors. Such disasters are reminders of two rather different kinds of human limitation: inadequacy in the face of raw natural power (such as storms and volcanoes) and inadequacy in the construction or maintenance of the human-built environment. These limitations underline how governmental systems must have the abilities to respond to disasters as they occur and to limit the extent to which they (and their people) themselves create risk.

This mixed nature of disasters is, in one regard, a long-existing problem. Any building is at risk from any number of actions. Wood buildings burn; concrete buildings crack. The causes may lie more on the natural side ("nothing could withstand the tornado") or on the human side ("the building was structurally unsound"). That human side seems to be growing. For example, Oklahoma, a geologically stable area, had more earthquakes in 2015 than did California, a geologically unstable area. The cause was nothing natural; it was the result of pressured fluids being pumped below the surface in the process of oil and gas extraction (so-called fracking). The causes were thus public knowledge. The state government has tracked those earthquakes, assessed their dangers, and forced some changes in the industry. As it turns out, the risk of *severe* earthquakes remains low. For the moment, it seems fracking does not create massive earthquakes. So the industry changed some of its practices, and by 2016 the number of earthquakes was lower. This does not mean that there has not been damage from all these minor earthquakes, but the situation appears, for the moment anyway, to be manageable.[3]

The Oklahoma case is thus cautionary but not without hope: sometimes problems can be recognized and addressed before they become extreme. Climate change is a broader problem, and 2017 brought even more troubling news about the fragility of the Antarctic ice sheets. This problem is not easily isolated and not easily addressed within a single country or one of its subdivisions. Humans have already changed the environment in ways that cannot be undone. The effects are uneven, but we do know that ocean water levels are rising as ice caps melt. That part is predictable. The size of the changes and their effects in particular places are less predictable. Indeed, one crucial prediction of global warming is that weather will be increasingly unpredictable. Thus more collective effort will be required for an issue that demands rational action but whose very unpredictability may defeat efforts to resolve or ameliorate it.

The human relationship with the environment is thus changing. Humans are increasingly the masters and stewards of the environment, whether they want to be or not, whether they think they should be or not, whether they think they are capable or not. At the same time, the human relationship with our own biological nature is also changing. Even a simple medical development such as the sonogram can have sharp social effects. In countries where sons are valued, for example, the ability to "choose" male children (through abortion of female fetuses) has shifted sex ratios at birth toward males in some places. When those males grow up, they face a shortage of marriage partners. Barring polyandry (which exists but is relatively rare), the men must then either remain bachelors or find women from somewhere else. Some of the current trafficking in women is not into prostitution or other forced labor, but into marriage with these men. This is exactly the case in China today as discussed in a previous chapter: a nation of bachelors as numerous as the population of Colombia, Kenya, or Spain.

People now have increasing control over their own bodies. Some of that is lifestyle, including diet and exercise. The human body can be improved. But modification of the body through a highly medicalized plastic surgery industry has also exploded in volume in recent decades. If you can afford it, you can choose what you will look like. Gender reassignment surgery is also increasingly common, allowing a complex biological and social change in identity. Perhaps the truly huge changes,

---

3   There were, however, other kinds of negative effects. The insurance industry decided that these earthquakes were risky at some level, and policyholders in Oklahoma saw sharp rises in their premiums in 2016, and some insurers stopped offering earthquake insurance entirely.

however, are the ability to work at the genetic level. By 2016, for example, clus-tered regularly interspaced short palindromic repeats (CRISPR) editing of genetic sequences was reaching operational levels with success rates of over 50 percent. In the gene-editing case, it will be extremely difficult to resist using the technology for medical purposes, and, indeed, use of gene editing for cancer treatment in humans was well underway by 2017.[4]

There is now, then, a new and evolving relationship between people and their bio-logical nature. There will certainly be beneficial effects for some individuals, but the societal implications are less clear. Even when the ability to control our own biology can be used for good purposes, those "good purposes" are likely to be more acces-sible to the rich and influential. Those with more power and money will not only be able to buy better health care and surgical enhancements to their bodies, but they will be able to buy better-engineered bodies. Even if they choose not to do so for themselves, it will be hard for them to resist doing so for their children. Ironically, after all these many years of arguing about racial differences and whether they even exist, human beings could indeed come to be divided in genetic terms with two clear races: a rich one and a poor one.

AN ANTHROPOLOGY FOR THE TWENTY-FIRST CENTURY

The twenty-first century provides many continuities with the past and with the early anthropological understanding of human life. However a new constellation of the density of human life, the complexity of global society, and the vastly increased control over human biology and the environment suggest that a more coherent, inclusive, and rational way of dealing with the world is needed. This includes, like it or not, a new kind of stewardship. It is no longer simply that humans "should" be stewards of the world, but that they have no choice but to manage the opportunities and risks that they have themselves created.

This overall obligation to the world has recently received increasing attention in anthropology under labels such as public anthropology, engaged anthropology, and the anthropology of policy, and has long been the focus of applied and practicing anthropologists generally. But the roots of the anthropological commitment to the "real" world go back to the origins of the discipline. In what is usually credited as the first anthropology textbook, Edward Tylor in 1881 extolled anthropology for the way it brought together in one framework the entirety of the human experience. Anthropology, he pointed out, "connects into a manageable whole the scattered

---

4   There is also the potential for human cloning. It will be extremely difficult to keep at least some people in the world from trying it. There are already claims by Chinese scientists that say they have the ability to fully replicate human beings, and the cloning of animals like dogs and cows has become a near-routine process.

subjects of an ordinary education" (Tylor 1881, v). Anthropology is a way of understanding the world that, as anthropologists would argue anyway, is a uniquely complete and inclusive way of understanding. But Tylor went further. For him this inclusive and unified anthropological framework "at once passes into the practical business of life . . . [and] may guide us in our duty of leaving the world better than we found it."[5] Tylor thus married together at the beginning anthropology's holism (all aspects of all peoples' lives) and its connection to practical affairs.

That dual commitment to understanding and action has seen its ups and downs in the many years since. In early American anthropology, for example, Franz Boas was extremely active in the examination of immigrant life in America and noting how truly adaptable immigrants could be. He was also a staunch defender of indigenous people and constantly debunked popularized views of different racial capabilities. Later on, during the Second World War, many prominent North American anthropologists were directly involved in the war effort, recognizing that this "practical business of life" required their contribution even if specific government policies were anathema to them (for example, the internment of Japanese Americans in camps in both Canada and the United States). As the public became disenchanted with much of government policy in succeeding decades, perhaps especially with the Vietnam War, North American anthropologists also tended to drift away from involvement in the newly distasteful affairs of state, instead taking an external critical role toward government.

If the comment about a new stewardship is on target, however, we may once again be at a point in time that direct anthropological involvement is needed in the dismal science of economic policy, the often distasteful world of politics, and the convoluted skeins of public policy development and implementation. To that reimmersion in the "practical business of life," anthropology brings its inclusiveness (all people belong) and its sense of human equality (they all belong equally). Anthropologists can also bring to the task an acute sense of the biological, cultural, and environmental aspects of being human and of how the balance among the three is under increasing pressure. That reimmersion may also help re-create a unified anthropology of understanding and action, bringing back together the too-often separated worlds of academic, applied, and practitioner anthropologists.

CASE EXAMPLE—A PEOPLE IN CRISIS: AN UNPREDICTABLE ENVIRONMENT FOR THE SAKHA

The scientific evidence and forecasts of global warming are constantly evolving. But there has clearly been human-caused climate change. How does this change affect

---

5   E. B. Tylor, *Anthropology* (MacMillan and Co., 1881), 439–40.

The ice of Antarctica will determine much of human destiny in this century. (Credit: John Carnemolla/iStock)

people on the ground in specific locations? Susan Crate provides one example from her long-term research with the Sakha of Siberia. Her original fieldwork describes a traditionally oriented people whose key values lay with kin and cows. Their localized economy required detailed understanding of the land and what it could produce to support the cows. In a frigid climate, this was far from easy. The task became harder as the Sakha were absorbed into the Soviet system with its emphasis on central economic planning, a more industrialized version of agriculture, and a commitment to mining. With the demise of the Soviet Union, the Sakha began returning to a more independent and self-reliant system.

However, the environment had changed. There was now standing water in places where the Sakha had traditionally grown hay for the cows. They knew they needed to harvest approximately two tons of hay during the summer to have enough to last the cows over the roughly nine months of winter. With higher standing water, this became increasingly difficult. Furthermore, there was now constant rain that was often ruinous to the crops that they could grow. One elder commented to Crate that "we have rain, rain, rain all the time . . . the hay does not dry and . . . the quality

Syrian refugees caught on the border between Greece and Macedonia. (Credit: verve231/ iStock)

is bad." Another noted "the land is going under water and the hay lands are smaller and smaller and . . . the hay itself has less nutrition." The problems of wet summers were, to the Sakha, related to the problem of warmer winters. A female elder explained that "we need strong cold here . . . The nature, people, animals, and plants here are supposed to have very cold winters and very hot dry summers. That is the best for all life here."[6]

The Sakha are astute observers of the environment. They recognize there is change. The problem for them, as for people in general in time of change, is that they have to think through what kind of change is involved and what to do about it. The Sakha elders, for example, know that there are cyclical changes in the environment. They also recognize the different factors that may be affecting their local environment. For example, a reservoir built in the area as part of mining operations might be partially at fault. But this current situation seemed different. Nature was "mixed up." It no longer rained when it was supposed to. The environment had become uncertain and unpredictable. As Crate notes, the experience of the Sakha suggests that climate change is not simply a new environment to which people can adapt practically, emotionally, and spiritually, but a different kind of environment that

---

6   The specific quotations are from Susan A. Crate and Mark Nuttall, eds., *Anthropology and Climate Change* (Walnut Creek, CA: Left Coast Press, 2009), 140–42.

follows neither the objective experience that people have nor their understanding of the way the world is supposed to be in its more spiritual guise. Here the relationship between people and their physical environment is at risk. Climate change is thus a full-scale assault on the human experience. It changes the rules.

As those rules change, so too does the nature of anthropological action. In this Sakha case, Crate soon found herself involved not only in understanding climate change and the Sakha's understanding of it but also in collaboratively working with the Sakha on how to address the local consequences. But, of course, there was also the larger issue of climate change and the way in which the United States has been particularly slow to accept its existence. Crate thus found herself in Washington lobbying for science as a way to recognize and address major global issues. She might well have chosen to advocate for those affected by climate change—that would be the traditional anthropological approach. Instead the main focus of that lobbying was the broader, more policy-oriented one of how to develop a zone of reliable information on which governments can draw to make informed public policy, rather than devolving into political arguments.

CASE EXAMPLE—A CRISIS OF PEOPLE: SYRIANS IN SEARCH OF REFUGE

By 2017, the number of displaced people in the world had surged to 66 million, the highest number since the years immediately following the Second World War. A wide range of governments, international agencies, and nonprofit organizations have attempted to address the plight of these forcibly displaced people, while at the same time trying to address the even greater numbers of other, more voluntary migrants of varying legal statuses. For refugees the result is sometimes temporary camps to provide security, shelter, and food; sometimes intervention in the origin countries to address the "root causes" of flight; sometimes returning people to their home countries after conditions have stabilized; sometimes sending them on to other countries for resettlement there. North America has been a major destination for those refugees who are sent on for resettlement in a new country. Both Canada and the United States have long been immigrant-oriented countries, and both have welcomed large numbers of refugees: the United States the greater overall number; Canada the higher per capita numbers. Mexico also accepts refugees, but in far smaller numbers.[7]

---

7   The situation of refugees when resettled in North America has been of interest to many anthropologists. In moral terms, refugees represent the dispossessed, and anthropology has a long history of trying to assist the dispossessed. In practical terms, the situation of refugees requires exactly the skills that anthropologists tend to have in balancing the interests and needs of people from different backgrounds and languages. Indeed, the range of backgrounds of refugees has been enticing to anthropologists. The

Perhaps the most dramatic element of this surge in refugees was the Syrian refugee crisis that escalated in 2015. In Europe the crisis was acute and the reactions extremely varied among different countries. Ultimately the European Union's borders were closed, but not before a large number of refugees and other migrants had entered Europe, with a generally preferred destination of Germany. The arrival of roughly 1 million refugees and migrants in Germany that year was a massive challenge. But what was the response of Canada and the United States, situated well away from the crisis zone but both with major, long-standing commitments to refugee resettlement?

In the heart of the crisis in late 2015, US president Barack Obama announced an initiative to take 10,000 Syrian refugees over the succeeding year. In doing so, he invoked deep American traditions in his Thanksgiving address that year: "Nearly four centuries after the Mayflower set sail, the world is still full of pilgrims—men and women who want nothing more than the chance for a safer, better future for themselves and their families. What makes America America is that we offer that chance."[8]

At roughly the same time, the new Canadian prime minister, Justin Trudeau, also announced a plan to take in Syrian refugees. His rationale, as given in a Christmas address that year, was distinctly Canadian but not far in tone from the US President's comments: "This year, Canadians are welcoming thousands of Syrian refugees to our country—people who have been forced to flee their homeland due to war and conflict. I encourage all Canadians to show them a warm holiday welcome in keeping with our values of compassion, kindness, and generosity . . . After all, we share values of love, hope and compassion—it's what we do, and it's who we are."[9]

So far, one might see a similar response from these two established immigrant and refugee-receiving countries. Furthermore, there were clear indications that many people at the local level in both countries were indeed quite anxious to help; this was not simply some governmental initiative. But there were two differences in what happened. One difference was that the proposed Canadian number was much higher: a Canadian 25,000 versus a US 10,000. Given the relative population size of the two countries, the Canadian target was roughly twenty-five

---

involvement of anthropologists in refugee relief and resettlement has been wide-ranging: some have worked in research and advocacy, others in the nonprofit sector, and yet others in governmental program management and policy development, whether at the federal, regional, or local levels. Providing the bridge between new arrivals unprepared for life in North America and receiving communities that often know little about the arrivals is a traditional and generally satisfying endeavor.

8   Barack Obama, "Weekly Address: This Thanksgiving Recognizing the Greatness of American Generosity," The White House (November 25, 2015).

9   Justin Trudeau, "Statement by the Prime Minister of Canada on Christmas," Ottawa, Canada (December 23, 2015).

times as high as the US figure. The second difference was that the Canadians actually met their goal. By the time they had resettled 25,000 refugees in early 2016, the United States had barely resettled 1,000, although the US goal was finally met by the end of the fiscal year.

That is a huge difference in public policy response, and it raises broad questions about the nature of human mobility in the modern world, the way international borders work, the way people in countries receiving immigrants respond, and the way governments do or do not manage these complex issues. How can there be such sharp differences in seemingly similar countries? Part of the answer is political: an extremely contentious presidential election cycle in the United States in 2016 saw virtually all Republican candidates lashing out against Syrian refugee admissions and, at least in Donald Trump's case, against all Muslim entry to the United States. Part of the answer is the structure of governmental policy: Canada has a dual resettlement scheme that allows people who support refugees to more directly sponsor them than occurs in the United States. In the United States, people desiring to sponsor Syrian refugees had to fight their way through a political system that included many Republican governors trying to refuse any Syrian refugee resettlement in their states. Finally, part of the answer is administrative: the Canadian system simply worked better and faster in the many different tasks needed to resettle the refugees, from security checks to transportation to housing to healthcare.

This is an interesting case in comparative analysis of public attitudes and public policies. But the analysis of why differences such as this exist provides little solace in a world that increasingly demands rational assessment of options, opportunities, and risks among multiple countries, and in which the movement of people as migrants and refugees is more likely to increase than decrease. Therein lies one fundamental dilemma that an anthropology of the twenty-first century must address: how to extract from a competitive political world the actual issues with which we need to engage and the actual policy options through which we can do so. That will be a new kind of holism for anthropology in this twenty-first century.

SOURCES

This chapter somewhat obliquely raises the frameworks of applied and practicing anthropology, though I have chosen to phrase the discussion as a general anthropological one (which I think it is). For more conventional discussion, see such general texts as Erve Chambers's *Applied Anthropology: A Practical Guide* (Waveland, 1989); Alexander M. Ervin's *Applied Anthropology: Tools and Perspectives for Contemporary Practice* (Pearson, 2004; 2nd ed.); John van Willigen's *Applied Anthropology: An Introduction* (Praeger, 2002; 3rd ed.); and Riall Nolan (ed.), *A Handbook of Practicing Anthropology* (Wiley-Blackwell, 2013). The journals *Human Organization* (somewhat on the academic side) and *Practicing Anthropology* (more on the practitioner side) are also helpful. (Both are published by the Society for Applied Anthropology.) For discussions of public anthropology and the anthropology of policy, two useful websites are the Center for a Public Anthropology at http://www.publicanthropology.org/ and the Association for the Anthropology of Policy at http://anthofpolicy.org/. There are also entries for both in the forthcoming *International Encyclopedia of Anthropology* (Wiley-Blackwell), as well as entries for applied anthropology and practicing anthropology that may help clarify the differences and overlap among these approaches.

For the Sakha case, see Susan Crate's *Cows, Kin, and Globalization: An Ethnography of Sustainability* (AltaMira, 2006) for basic material and her two edited volumes with Mark Nuttall for broader discussion of climate change issues: *Anthropology and Climate Change: From Encounters to Actions* (Left Coast Press, 2009) and *Anthropology and Climate Change: From Actions to Transformations* (Routledge, 2016). Most of the specific discussion here is from her article in the first of those two volumes ("Gone the Bull of Winter?"), updated with her comments on lobbying from "Lobbying for Science," *Anthropology News*, August 2015. A documentary on her work was released in 2015 (*The Anthropologist*). For refugees, basic data are readily available online. The Migration Policy Institute (http://www.migrationpolicy.org/) has produced policy briefs on refugees that are relatively centrist. For a sampling of the invective against refugees in the United States (and migrants generally), consult the Center for Immigration Studies (http://cis.org/) a very restrictionist organization. The US response in the Syrian case has amazed many of us who have been involved with the US refugee program because, until recently, the program has had considerable bipartisan support. My own thoughts on the issue are in a 2015 Thanksgiving essay for the American Immigration Council at https://www.americanimmigrationcouncil.org/research/refugee-experience-united-states.

Glossary

ADJUDICATION. Dispute resolution mechanism based on determinations by a formal authority (that has the power to impose a decision).

AFFINES. In kinship, refers to people who are related through ties of marriage.

AGE. With sex, the most important biological variation in human society. Also, as with sex, its significance and cultural elaboration vary greatly from society to society.

AGENCY. Word frequently used in anthropology to indicate people's autonomy and ability to control as least some parts of their lives.

AGRICULTURE. Environmental adaptation in which humans cultivate plants based on specialization in one or a few crops and usually the use of fertilizer, irrigation, and a plow.

ANIMATISM. Belief in a pervasive spiritual force that permeates the natural world.

ANIMISM. Belief in spirits.

ARBITRARINESS. In this text, refers to the flexibility in constructing human language.

ASCENDING GENERATION. One generation "up"; thus for you: your parents, aunts, and uncles.

AUTHORITY. As contrasted with *power*, refers to the capacity of people or organizations to tell people what to do based on their inherent right to do so—and perhaps their perceived wisdom as well.

AVUNCULOCAL. Type of postmarital residence in which the couple resides together with an uncle, usually the husband's mother's brother from whom the husband would inherit in a matrilineal society.

AXON. A single, often quite long, tentacle by which a neuron sends messages to other cells.

BALANCED RECIPROCITY. Exchange of goods between individuals that follows a pattern of gift, return gift, gift in response to the return gift, and so on.

BALANDA. Australian aboriginal term for nonaborigines (see discussions of Yolngu in chapters 3 and 17).

BANDS. Type of political organization based on small, loosely organized groups with informal leadership.

BARBARISM. Term used by early evolutionists to designate societies with relatively advanced technology but lacking the refinements (for example, a writing system) of fully "civilized" people.

BERDACHE. Term usually used for men in Native American tribes who lived as women (*transgendered* in current terminology). The word itself is European in origin and arrived in North America with the French. Native American groups, however, prefer notions of "two-spirit" that capture both the sexual and spiritual aspects of those who act outside usual stereotypes.

BIOLOGY. As used in this text, refers to aspects of human beings and their behavior that hinge on their unmodified physical nature as opposed to environment or culture.

BLENDED FAMILIES. Contemporary term used to describe the merging of different family fragments, particularly those resulting from death and divorce.

BOUND MORPHEME. A morpheme that cannot stand on its own (for example, the "z" sound in English that indicates a plural).

BROADCASTING. System of agriculture in which seed is thrown out ("broadcast") on the soil rather than actually planted in the soil.

BYRES. Fences or similar structures used to hold animals.

CASTE. A rigidly imposed system of social differences, often based on occupation but with strong social and cultural implications. Castes are typically not allowed to intermarry and are rigidly stratified.

CATEGORIES. In contrast to *groups*, refers to sets of people who are designated as being the same, whether or not they actually interact with each other.

CENSORATE. Refers to the early Chinese system of having special officials who monitored the work of other government officials.

CHIEFDOMS. Type of political organization based on centralized entities with at least some defined political offices.

CHINAMPAS. Fields in which multiple kinds of fertilizer create very high yields without the use of a plow. Such fields can be traced to the Aztecs but still exist today.

CIRCULATION. In this text, refers to the way goods in a society are moved among people.

CIVILIZATION. Term used in many ways, often self-serving, but for early anthropologists designated societies that had certain "advanced" characteristics, such as a written language.

CIVIL SOCIETY. Refers to the concept of an organized, engaged citizenry that provides a framework for governance that runs parallel to the formal government. The phrase is usually used in a positive sense, but recent experience with highly militant "civil" organizations (including militias) provides an alternate, less positive view.

CLAN. A set of kin who belong together because they are believed to descend from a common ancestor.

CLASS. Refers largely to economic distinctions within a society, though with pervasive social and political implications. Class membership can be rigidly imposed and inherited; it can also be loosely imposed and subject to change.

CLASS MOBILITY. Refers to the ability to change one's class status. That ability ranges from none (you are what you were born to be), to some (maybe not you but your children can move ahead), to a great deal (you can indeed rise to a higher status).

CLASSIFIER. A kind of particle used in many languages to indicate what kind of object is being discussed (for example, an animal, something flat and thin, something round).

COGNATES. In kinship, refers to people who are related through blood ties.

COGNATIC DESCENT. System of reckoning descent that puts together all people descended from the same ancestor.

COLONIALISM. Economic and political system in which some countries or peoples utterly dominate others. To distinguish more recent variants from the classic European and Japanese empires of the nineteenth and early twentieth centuries, hybrid phrases are often used: thus *neocolonialism* for recent situations of dominance among nations, and *internal colonialism* for domination of a set of people (especially indigenous minorities) within a country.

COMPENSATION. As contrasted with "punishment," refers to a resolution of disputes that brings things back into balance among the parties. Usually involves payments of some kind.

COMPLEXITY. One of four themes in human adaptation. Refers to the overall complexity of social arrangements. Usually (but not always), it increases with control over nature and density of settlement.

CONCEPTION. In contrast to "perception," involves the more abstract aspects of human thinking.

CONSUMPTION. In this text, refers to the way goods in a society are actually used by people, both as individuals and as groups.

CONTROL. One of four themes in human adaptation. Refers to the degree of control over the environment. However, that increased environmental control usually also requires increased social control.

CORRUPTION. In this text, refers to the problem of people in government acting in their own interest rather than in the government's and society's interest. This is a recurring problem in most political systems.

CREOLE. A fully formed language that typically develops from a more limited pidgin (trade language).

CULTURAL GENOCIDE. An attempt to exterminate an entire people by obliterating their culture rather than by physically killing them.

CULTURAL RELATIVISM. A view that cultures need to be understood on their own terms, rather than on those of the people studying them. This is an issue of understanding but not necessarily of agreement.

CULTURE. As used in this text, refers to the full range of acquired human characteristics and behavior versus those that are biologically or environmentally derived.

CURRENCY. Any object that can be used as a mechanism of exchange. A currency can range from something such as sweet potatoes in a horticultural society, to gold currency in an advanced agricultural society, to bitcoins in the contemporary world.

CUSTOM. As contrasted with "law," refers to informal, traditional understandings of the way things should be, including how disputes should be resolved.

DAUGHTER PREFERENCE. Parental preference for having daughters.

DENDRITE. One of a small set of tentacles by which a neuron receives information from another cell.

DENSITY. One of four themes in human adaptation. Increased density of people usually has serious social implications but may also increase the burden on the environment.

DESCENDING GENERATION. One generation "down"; thus for you: your children, nephews, and nieces.

DESCENT. A crucial part of kinship as people organize themselves in terms of their ancestry, with many societies having complicated systems that cover the connections across many generations.

DIALECT. A version of a language that is still comprehensible to other people speaking the same language.

DIBBLE STICK. Small stick used to poke holes into the ground, into which seeds are then placed. This is a common tool in horticultural societies.

DISCOURSE ANALYSIS. Widely used term both in and outside anthropology. It is a kind of sociolinguistic analysis that tends to emphasize how language is used in structures of power.

DISPLACEMENT. In this text, refers to the ability of language to deal with objects that are somewhere else.

DIVERGENCE. A frequent characteristic of languages as dialects drift so far apart that they become truly different languages.

DIVERSITY. Literal meaning is that people vary, but use of the term is now conventional for describing situations in which human difference is believed to be good. Often used in conjunction with "multiculturalism."

DIVISION OF LABOR. Refers to the way in which different tasks are assigned to different members of a society, whether on the basis of age, gender, education, skill, or other factors.

DIVORCE. General term for any revocation of a marriage arrangement. Individual societies vary in how they define divorce and whether divorce is one thing or many (for example, annulment versus divorce proper in North America).

DIYI. Spirits or powers. (See the discussion of the Cibecue Apache in chapter 13.)

DOMESTICATION. For anthropologists, generally refers to human control over plants and animals (for example, corn in fields, pigs in pens).

DOV. Dried on the vine. A technologically advanced system for automated harvesting of raisin grapes. (See discussion in chapter 11).

THE DREAMING. Term used to refer to the Australian aboriginal understanding of the past (see discussion of the Yolngu in chapters 3 and 17).

ECOLOGY. In this text, refers to a general framework that emphasizes the interaction of human beings and their environments.

ECUMENICAL. Mutually accepting views among different groups, especially different religions.

ENDOGAMY. General term that refers to marrying within some group such as a clan, village, or caste.

ENVIRONMENT. As used in this text, refers to the external features that condition human behavior, as opposed to biological or cultural factors.

ESKIMO KINSHIP TERMINOLOGY. Terminological system based on gender, generation, and core (that is, whether relatives are within the immediate nuclear family).

ETHNICITY. Common system for categorizing diversity. Ethnic labels can be positive or negative, volitional or imposed. They are usually strongest when historical origins, language, and culture are clearly distinctive to a group.

ETHNOGRAPHY. The study of people and their lives based on detailed fieldwork. Also used to describe an extended, usually book-length, description of the results of such research.

EVOLUTION. A view that, over time, human and other species change based on the differential advantages of new characteristics or behavior.

EVOLUTIONISM. General theoretical perspective that emphasizes the importance of evolution in human society. Early evolutionism is closely associated with Edward Tylor. (See discussion in chapter 1.)

EXCHANGE. System of circulation of goods based on their economic value. Usually called "market exchange" even though physical markets are not always present.

EXOGAMY. General term that refers to marrying outside a group, such as a clan, village, or caste.

EXTERNAL RELATIONS. One of three key responsibilities of any political system: managing the areas and people beyond the limits of the immediate political system.

FAMILY. Somewhat ambiguous term that often refers to the most immediate kin, but can also refer to the full range of kin, and sometimes to those people considered closest to you whether they are actually related by blood or not. Anthropologists generally use the word "kin" instead.

FORAGING. Environmental adaptation in which plant and animal food is gathered rather than cultivated or herded. Often also called "hunting and gathering."

FOREBRAIN. From the front, the first of the three main parts of the mammalian (and human) brain. Used especially for abstract reasoning.

FRATERNAL POLYANDRY. System of marriage in which a woman marries two or more brothers.

GARIMPEIROS. Independent, invading gold miners in the Amazon river basin. (See discussion of the Yanomami in chapter 12.)

GENDER. Technically refers to the social construction of sex but is also now widely used to refer to the combination of the biological and cultural aspects of being male, female, or some other construct (for example, third and fourth genders among many native American tribes).

GENERALIZED RECIPROCITY. Reciprocity in which the exchange is channeled through individuals but largely for group purposes. Compare a wedding (generalized reciprocity) with the exchange of wedding anniversary presents between a couple (balanced reciprocity).

GENOCIDE. The attempted extermination of an entire people.

GIFT GIVING. Crucial anthropological focus is on how a gift requires a countergift ad infinitum. Thus studying the exchange of gifts provides a visible map of social relations. (See "reciprocity.")

GLIAL TRAIL. "Trail" marked out in the developing brain by glial cells. Used by neurons as they "migrate" to their final positions.

GLOBALIZATION. Refers to expanding and intensifying economic, political, and cultural interactions in the contemporary world. The word is used both positively (globalization is good for everybody) and negatively (especially that it is a new, even more pernicious kind of colonialism).

GOSSIP. A useful social sanction widely used in human societies. Especially in close-knit societies, it works well to control people's behavior.

GOVERNANCE. As contrasted with "politics," refers to the ways the work of government is actually carried out.

GOWA AND GOTA. Apache terms, respectively for clan and household. (See discussion of Cibecue Apache in chapter 9).

GROUPS. As contrasted with "categories," refers to sets of people who actually interact with each other.

HAWAIIAN KINSHIP TERMINOLOGY. Terminological system based solely on gender and generation.

"HEADLESS" GOVERNMENT. Refers to a kin-based political system without formal leadership roles. (See discussion of Nuer in chapter 12.)

HETERODOXY. Literally, "other" beliefs, but the term usually conveys a notion of power and of the "other" beliefs being incorrect, dangerous, and perhaps subject to persecution.

HETEROPRAXY. Literally, "other" practices or actions, but the term usually conveys a notion of power and that the "other" practices are incorrect and dangerous.

HINDBRAIN. The third of the three main parts of the mammalian brain. Tied to basic biological functioning.

HISTORICAL-PARTICULARISM. General theoretical framework that emphasizes the uniqueness of people's histories and the importance of the details (particulars) of their lives. Associated especially with Franz Boas.

HOLISM. A view that all aspects of a situation, or of a people's culture, must be understood together as a whole, rather than as separate pieces.

HORTICULTURE. Environmental adaptation in which plants are brought together in gardens, usually also with some animals (such as pigs).

HOUSEHOLD. Refers to the core set of people living together, usually on a daily basis in a shared dwelling. Households may include kin and nonkin.

HUNTING AND GATHERING. Environmental adaptation in which animal and plant food is gathered from the environment. In this text, referred to as "foraging."

HYPERGAMY. System of marriage in which the woman marries "up" into a higher-status household.

HYPOGAMY. System of marriage in which the woman marries "down" into a lower-status household.

INCARCERATION. Putting people in jails, prisons, or the like. As a sanction, it requires a notably high level of costs as compared with ostracism, gossip, or even direct revenge.

INDIGENOUS PEOPLES. Refers to those people originally in a particular area who have been displaced, subjugated, or sometimes just destroyed by new arrivals.

INDIVIDUAL. In contrast to "person," highlights a human being as freestanding, autonomous, and separate from other human beings.

INDUSTRIALISM. Environmental adaptation based on extraction of a broad range of resources and the sharp expansion of productive capabilities.

INFIX. A bound morpheme that appears in the middle of a word. (Infixes are common in some languages though not in English.)

INFRASTRUCTURE. In this text, refers to the economic, transportation, and communication systems within a political entity.

INHERITANCE. Transfer of property, status, or rights, usually after someone dies.

INSTITUTION. Refers either to an established activity or relationship (for example, the institution of marriage) or to a formally incorporated organization (for example, a governmental institution).

INTERNAL ORDER. One of three key responsibilities of any political system: ensuring that there is relative peace within the area governed.

IROQUOIS KINSHIP TERMINOLOGY. Terminological system based on gender, generation, and line (that is, whether kin are on the mother's or father's side).

KARMA. Hindu and Buddhist notion that the relative accumulation of merit affects not only this life but future ones as well.

KINDRED. Kin group that is based on relationships to the individual, thus "ego-oriented." Only siblings can have the same kindred.

KINESICS. "Body language": the gestures and movements that, together with formal language, create the situational meaning of in-person communication.

KINSHIP. The ways in which people are attached to each other by blood and marriage, including both real and "fictive" ties.

KINSHIP TERMINOLOGY. Set of words used to designate different kinds of kin. The individual terms and their relationships vary widely in different cultures.

KULA. Ceremonial exchange of necklaces (*soulava*) and armbands (*mwali*) in the Trobriand Islands.

LAW. As contrasted with "custom," refers to formal, usually written guidelines about how things should be, including how disputes should be resolved.

LEVIRATE. System of marriage in which a dead husband is "replaced" by his brother.

LEXICON. The words used in a language.

LINEAGE. A group of kin who share the same known descent through an ancestral line, usually of men (patrilineage) or of women (matrilineage).

MANA. Polynesian notion of a pervasive force emanating through the day-to-day world.

MANIFESTED AND MANIFESTING. Benjamin Whorf's words for the two-part Hopi sense of time that he contrasted to the three-part Euro-American sense of time (that is, past, present, and future).

MARKET. A place where goods can be exchanged. In nonindustrial societies markets are often periodic (monthly, weekly).

MARKET EXCHANGE. System of circulation of goods based on their economic value. Note that "market exchange" is used to describe economic exchanges even when physical markets may no longer be present.

MARRIAGE. General term for any formal linking of nonrelated people into a permanent sexual (and usually procreative) relationship. Individual societies vary greatly in how they define marriage.

MATRIARCHY. System in which women (technically mothers) are in charge. Often used incorrectly to refer to matrilineality.

MATRICLAN. Set of kin who believe they are descended from a common ancestor through a line of women.

MATRILINEAGE. Group of kin who share the same, known ancestry through a line of women.

MATRILINEALITY. Kinship system in which the kin relationships between people are traced through women.

MATRILOCAL. Type of postmarital residence in which the couple reside together with the wife's family. (Technically this is "uxorimatrilocal.")

MEDIATION. Dispute resolution mechanism using intermediaries between the parties. The parties must still agree on any resolution the intermediaries propose.

MIDBRAIN. The second of the three main divisions of the mammalian brain. Used for routine functioning.

MOBILITY. One of four key themes in human adaptation. Unlike control, density, and complexity, mobility does not always change in a linear way: thus industrialists and foragers share much in the way of mobility, but not very much in terms of control, density, and complexity.

MOIETY SYSTEM. A system in which all members of a society belong to one of two marriage groups (moieties).

MOLIMO. Trumpet-like musical instrument used by the Mbuti (see discussion of the Mbuti in chapter 3).

MONOGAMY. System of marriage in which there is only one spouse at a time.

MONOGRAPH. A specialized, usually book-length, analysis of a particular subject or topic. Tends to be more narrowly focused than an ethnography.

MONOTHEISM. Technically, refers to a belief in a single god. Tylor's early notion of a Supreme Being is perhaps more accurate since many so-called monotheistic religions also acknowledge other spiritual entities.

MORPHEME. The smallest unit of meaning in a language (for example, "dog" or the "z" sound that makes plurals in English).

MORPHOLOGY. The structure of words in a language.

MULTIPLICITY OF PATTERNING. In this text, refers to the way different components of a language can be structured in different ways.

MWALI. The armbands used in the famed *kula* exchanges in the Trobriand Islands.

NATION. Originally meant "a people" and in older documents is used much as the word "ethnic" is used today. In contemporary usage, however, "nation" is often associated with "state" for nation-state. That combined nation-state is a powerful concept: a common people in a shared political system.

NEGOTIATION. Dispute resolution mechanism involving direct discussion among the parties involved.

NEOLOCAL. Type of postmarital residence in which the couple reside together at a new location.

NEURAL TUBE. Earliest development of the brain and spinal cord in the fetus.

NUCLEAR FAMILY. A family that includes two genders and two generations, thus mother, father, and child(ren).

ONE-CHILD POLICY. Formal policy that parents can have only one child. Implemented in China with considerable success in reining in population growth, but discontinued in 2015.

OPENNESS. One of the crucial aspects of human language and of human thought.

ORTHODOXY. Literally "straight" beliefs, but the term usually conveys the forced nature of those "straight" beliefs.

ORTHOPRAXY. Literally "straight" practices or actions. As with orthodoxy, the term conveys the notion of control, of some person or group deciding and enforcing those "straight" practices.

OSTRACISM. Expelling a person from his or her family, community, or society. It is a highly effective sanction in small-scale societies where people depend on each other for practical and emotional support.

OWNERSHIP. A particular concept about the relationship between people and resources that assumes the relationship is singular and total. Thus if you own something, you own all parts of it forever until you die or sell it. Compare that to a more flexible notion of "rights of use," where many different people might be using the same resource at different times and for different purposes.

PARALANGUAGE. Vocal parts of communication (yelling, whispering, speed of speech) that, though not technically formal language, nevertheless convey meaning.

PASTORALISM. Environmental adaptation in which people specialize in one or a few animals (though they also often grow some crops).

PATRIARCHY. System in which men (technically, fathers) are in charge. Often used incorrectly for patrilineality.

PATRICLAN. Set of kin who believe they are descended from a common ancestor through a male line.

PATRILINEAGE. Group of kin who share a known descent through a line of men.

PATRILINEALITY. System in which the kin relations among people are traced through men.

PATRILOCAL. Type of postmarital residence in which the couple resides together with the husband's family. (Technically this is "viripatrilocal.")

PATRINOMIAL. System in which children use (inherit) the names of their fathers.

PERCEPTION. In contrast to "conception," involves the direct physical sensing of the environment.

PERSON. As contrasted to "individual," suggests a human being as enmeshed in a social web and therefore not fully autonomous and separable.

PHONEME. The smallest unit of distinguishable sound in a language (for example, the "d" or "oh" sounds in English).

PHONOLOGY. The sound system of a language.

PHRATRY/PHRATRIES. A group of related clans.

PIDGIN. A simplified trade language with a rudimentary grammar that develops in multilingual situations. Most (but not all) aspects of the pidgin derive from the economically or politically dominant language.

PRIMUS INTER PARES. "First among equals." Refers to situations in which leaders do not have formal authority over other people.

POLITICS. As contrasted with "governance," refers to the processes by which general goals and policies are chosen.

POLYANDRY. System of marriage in which there can be multiple *husbands* at the same time.

POLYGAMY. System of marriage in which there can be multiple spouses at the same time. Thus polyandry and polygyny are kinds of polygamy.

POLYGYNY. System of marriage in which there can be multiple *wives* at the same time.

POLYTHEISM. Belief in multiple gods.

POSITIONALITY. In this text, refers to the ability of language to "view" an object from any desired position.

POSTINDUSTRIAL. Term used to suggest that the basic characteristics of contemporary life are so different from classic or early industrialism that a separate designation is needed.

POSTMARITAL RESIDENCE. Refers to the place in which a couple lives after marriage. Decisions about postmarital residence are crucial for the future composition of the household and the nature of the kinship system overall.

POWER. As contrasted with "authority," refers to the ability to force people to do something against their will, or at least regardless of their own views.

PREFIX. A bound morpheme that appears at the beginning of a word (for example, the "re" in *revisit* in English).

PREVARICATION. A fancy, somewhat more neutral term for lying.

PRIEST. A usually full-time religious practitioner whose vision, competence, and authority derive from a formal religious organization. Contrasts with "shaman."

PRODUCTION. In this text, refers to the ways in which goods in a society are actually created.

PROPERTY. General term used to refer to any kind of object or place that can be owned. Property can be movable (horse, furniture) or immovable (land).

PUKTUNWALI. Pashtun code of hospitality and revenge. (See discussion in chapter 14.)

PUNISHMENT. As contrasted with "compensation," refers to a system of extracting pain and property from the "guilty" rather than trying to repair the social relationships between the person who committed the "crime" and the person who lost something by it.

RACE. A term that usually implies, without much scientific basis, clear biological distinctions between different, defined sets of people.

RECIPROCITY. System of exchange of goods based on personal connections and mutual trust.

RECONCILIATION. Contemporary term used to refer to efforts to bring together societies that have been fractured by genocide, apartheid, civil war, or other sharp cleavages.

RECRUITMENT. In this text, refers to the need of complex political systems to gain competent, reliable people for government work.

REDISTRIBUTION. System of exchange of goods based on the authority of the person or organization managing the exchange.

REFUGEE. In general terms, any person fleeing anything. In formal international law, a person moving across a state border for fear of persecution on the basis of nationality, religion, race, political opinion, or membership in a particular social group.

RIDICULE. Like gossip, a useful social sanction in most societies, but particularly in relatively small-scale ones.

RIGHTS OF USE. Contrasts with conventional Euro-American notion of ownership. Instead of a single "owner" with all the rights, different people may have different rights of use or rights of use for a limited duration.

RITUAL. An ordered, repetitive event (or set of events) that is used in establishing and reestablishing spiritual and social connections.

ROUTINE. A habitualized way of doing something that usually requires little conscious thought, freeing up the mind for other issues that do require more conscious thought.

SANCTIONS. Actions taken against people either to change their behavior or simply to punish them for having done something wrong.

SAPIR-WHORF HYPOTHESIS. Notion that a language influences, and possibly determines, the nature of thought for people using that language.

SAVAGERY. A term used by early evolutionists for societies with relatively simple technology.

SEDENTARY. Refers to a lifestyle that does not involve frequent movement beyond the immediate areas of home and fields.

SEMANTICITY. In this text, refers to the ability of language to convey abstract meaning.

SENIORITY. Used to differentiate based on many possible characteristics, but in anthropology seniority usually refers to seniority by age. Such seniority is crucial in kinship systems.

SENSE MAKING. Refers to the full range of conscious and unconscious thinking by which people make practical sense of their environments.

SEX. Refers to the biological differences between males and females. Gender (which refers to the social construction of biological sex) is often now used to refer to biological sex as well as the social constructions of gender.

SEXUAL ORIENTATION. Culturally conditioned notion of how people are drawn to potential sex partners. Current North American convention involves a list of heterosexual, gay, lesbian, transgendered, bisexual, and questioning, but cross-cultural data suggest sexual orientations are often rather more overlapping and situational.

SHAMAN. A usually part-time religious practitioner whose vision and expertise comes from his or her own personal experiences. Contrasts with "priest."

SIGN. In this text, refers to a relatively simple symbol that has clear practical implications. (But note that the word is also sometimes used in a much broader sense.)

SIGNAL. In this text, refers to the most elementary of symbols, to something for which the required action is very clear, such as a traffic signal.

SKILL. As used in this text, refers to varying abilities of any kind. Some skills may be biologically based; many others are environmentally conditioned, and especially in agricultural and industrial societies, many require formal education and training.

SOCIOLINGUISTICS. Refers to a broad range of topics associated with the interaction of language and social relations.

SOLIDARITY. Refers to the ways in which, and degree to which, people are united with each other. They can be united because they are the same or because they are different but complementary.

SON PREFERENCE. Parental preference for sons rather than daughters. This is a crucial demographic force in strongly patrilineal societies.

SORCERY. The ability to control events through means that are at least partly spiritual or supernatural. The emphasis is usually on the sorcerer's control.

SORORAL POLYGYNY. System of marriage in which a man marries two or more sisters.

SORORATE. System of marriage in which a dead wife is "replaced" by her sister.

SOULAVA. The necklaces of the famed *kula* exchanges in the Trobriand Islands.

SPECIALIZATION OF LABOR. Refers to any situation in which some people have or develop the ability to do work that others cannot or will not do.

STATES. Type of political organization based on complex, centralized political entities with defined borders and numerous full-time officials.

STRATIFICATION. Social system in which differences are organized into vertical layers ("strata"). Those strata may be fairly loosely organized or very rigidly enforced (for example, caste).

STRUCTURAL-FUNCTIONALISM. General theoretical framework that emphasizes the way societies are structured systems, with different aspects of the culture having important functions for the whole. Especially associated with A. R. Radcliffe-Brown and Bronislaw Malinowski.

SUDANESE KINSHIP TERMINOLOGY. Terminological system based on the full range of possible kin characteristics, thus often called "descriptive kinship terminology."

SUFFIX. A bound morpheme that appears at the end of a word (for example, the "z" sound that indicates plurals in English).

SURPLUS. In this text, used to refer to anything produced beyond what is immediately consumed.

SWIDDEN. Technical term for a system of slash-and-burn horticulture.

SYMBOL. Something that stands for something else. In this text, the term covers the full range of possibilities, from a direct signal (for example, a traffic light) to a broad cultural and emotional representation (for example, a national flag).

SYNTAX. The way that phrases and sentences are constructed in a language.

TERRITORIALITY. Refers to how people are attached to territory, which is a combination of how they are linked to territory and the strength of that link.

TRANSGENDERED. Changed in gender. Actual surgical change would be transsexual.

TRANSPLANTING. System of agriculture in which seedlings are first grown in one set of fields and then replanted later in the main fields.

TRIBES. Type of political organization based on well-defined groups related through kinship.

UNBOUND MORPHEME. A morpheme that can stand on its own (like "dog" in English).

UNILINEAL DESCENT. System of reckoning descent that groups together people who can trace their descent through a single line.

UXORILOCAL. Type of postmarital residence in which the couple resides together at the wife's residence.

UXORIMATRILOCAL. Type of postmarital residence in which the couple resides together with the wife's family. Usually just termed "matrilocal."

VIRILOCAL. Type of postmarital residence in which the couple reside together at the husband's residence.

VIRIPATRILOCAL. Type of postmarital residence in which the couple reside together with the husband's family. Usually just termed "patrilocal."

WITCHCRAFT. Involvement in activities that are at least partially "supernatural." In anthropological terms, witches are often contrasted with sorcerers. Sorcerers are people controlling the spirit world for quite human goals, whereas witches are part of the spiritual world and may not even be able to control their activities. (North American popular usage of the term *witch* is very different, something of a mix of what anthropologists would distinguish as sorcerers, witches, shamans, and priests.)

Index

Page numbers in italics indicate illustrations.